BREAK DOWN THE WALLS

EXPERIENCING BIBLICAL RECONCILIATION AND UNITY IN THE BODY OF CHRIST

RALEIGH WASHINGTON & GLEN KEHREIN
AND CLAUDE V. KING

MOODY PRESS
CHICAGO

Photo Credits—Wayne Armstrong: pp. 5, 28, 49, 70, 76, 84, 116, 149, 168; Louis Deluca: p. 172; John D. Evans: p. 32; Brian Gadbery: p. 20; Leonard Ortiz: pp. 54, 59, 104, 158, 171; Unknown: pp. 34, 90.

Published by Moody Press, Chicago, Illinois 60610

Moody Press, a ministry of the Moody Bible Institute, is designed for education, evangelization, and edification. If we may assist you in knowing more about Christ and the Christian life, please write us without obligation: Moody Press, c/o MLM, Chicago, Illinois 60610.

Published in association with the literary agency of Alive Communications, Inc., 1465 Kelly Johnson Blvd., Suite 320, Colorado Springs, Colorado 80920.

Additional copies of this book are available from your local Christian bookstore. If you should have difficulty finding them in a bookstore, you may order by calling 1-800-456-7594.

1 2 3 4 5 6 7 8 9 10 Printing/Year 00 99 98 97

ISBN: 0-8024-2618-2

Printed in the United States of America

CONTENTS

About the Authors 4
Foreword by Bill McCartney 5
Preface 6
"The Reconciliation Song" 7
Before You Begin This Course 8

UNIT 1: UNITY IN CHRIST 15
Lesson 1: Seeing from God's Viewpoint
Lesson 2: Overviewing *Break Down the Walls*
Lesson 3: Jesus Prayed for Unity
Lesson 4: The Basis of Our Unity
Lesson 5: Barriers to Unity

UNIT 2: A HEALTHY BODY OF CHRIST 33
Lesson 1: Jesus Provided for Unity
Lesson 2: Three Illustrations of Unity
Lesson 3: The Body of Christ
Lesson 4: No Divisions Among You
Lesson 5: Becoming Christlike in the Body

UNIT 3: CALLED TO RECONCILIATION 50
Lesson 1: Reconciled to God
Lesson 2: The Ministry of Reconciliation
Lesson 3: The Principle of Call
Lesson 4: Reconciled to My Brothers
Lesson 5: Special Assignments from God

UNIT 4: COMMITMENT TO RELATIONSHIP 71
Lesson 1: The Principle of Commitment to
　　　　Relationship
Lesson 2: Committed Relationships
Lesson 3: God's Model for Relationships
Lesson 4: Accepting One Another for
　　　　Relationships
Lesson 5: Love Relationships

UNIT 5: INTENTIONALITY 89
Lesson 1: Making Every Effort to Maintain Unity
Lesson 2: God-Centered Intentionality
Lesson 3: The Principle of Intentionality
Lesson 4: Breaking Down Walls Intentionally
Lesson 5: Becoming Intentional

UNIT 6: SINCERITY AND SENSITIVITY 101
Lesson 1: The Need for Sincerity
Lesson 2: The Principle of Sincerity
Lesson 3: Developing Your Sincerity
Lesson 4: The Need for Sensitivity
Lesson 5: The Principle of Sensitivity

UNIT 7: DEVELOPING SENSITIVITY 115
Lesson 1: Developing Ethnic Sensitivity
Lesson 2: Help Me Understand
Lesson 3: Sensitivity Building
Lesson 4: Developing Denominational Sensitivity
Lesson 5: Treating Brothers as Brothers

UNIT 8: SACRIFICE 130
Lesson 1: Jesus and Sacrifice
Lesson 2: The Principle of Sacrifice
Lesson 3: Learning Sacrifice
Lesson 4: Jesus Calls for Servanthood
Lesson 5: Instructions for Sacrificial Service

UNIT 9: EMPOWERMENT 143
Lesson 1: The Principle of Empowerment I
Lesson 2: The Principle of Empowerment II
Lesson 3: Confession
Lesson 4: Repentance and Restoration
Lesson 5: Godlike Forgiveness

UNIT 10: INTERDEPENDENCE 159
Lesson 1: Interdependence in the Body
Lesson 2: The Principle of Interdependence
Lesson 3: Caring for All Members of the Body
Lesson 4: Final Course Review
Lesson 5: Seeking God's Assignment

APPENDIXES
How to Be Reconciled to God 170
Key Statements of Promise Keepers 172
Sensitivity Builders 178
Intentionality Project Ideas 187
Resources for Further Study 189
Small-Group Leader's Guide 190
Memory Cards 209

ABOUT THE AUTHORS

Raleigh Washington & Glen Kehrein

Raleigh Washington and Glen Kehrein have been working together since 1983 in the inner city Chicago neighborhood of Austin. Raleigh is currently the Vice President of Reconciliation for Promise Keepers and he continues to serve on the pastoral staff at Rock of Our Salvation Church. Glen is Executive Director of Circle Urban Ministries. The eight principles of reconciliation you will be studying in this course were forged in the context of this ministry partnership. They relate their ministry experiences and discuss application of the principles in the Moody Press book *Breaking Down Walls: A Model for Reconciliation in an Age of Racial Strife* which received the Gold Medalion Award. Acknowledging their contribution to the cause of racial reconciliation, Westminster

College conferred upon Glen and Raleigh the degree of Doctor of Peacemaking in April of 1997.

Before forming their ministry partnership, Raleigh spent 20 years in the United States army and reached the rank of Lt. Colonel. He is a graduate of Florida A&M and Trinity Evangelical Divinity School. Today Raleigh serves as Vice President of Reconciliation for Promise Keepers. Raleigh and His wife, Paulette, have six children.

Glen founded Circle Urban Ministries on Chicago's west side in 1973 where he and his wife Lonni have lived and reared three children. Glen is a graduate of Moody Bible Institute and Wheaton College.

Claude V. King

Claude serves as a Mission Service Corps consultant and writer for the Office of Prayer and Spiritual Awakening, Southern Baptist Convention. Claude is a graduate of Belmont College and holds Master of Divinity and Master of Religious Education degrees from New Orleans Baptist Theological Seminary. He has coauthored several books and courses, including *Experiencing God* and *Fresh Encounter* resources with Henry Blackaby, *The Mind of Christ* and *In God's Presence* with T. W. Hunt, and *WiseCounsel: Skills for Lay Counseling* with John Drakeford. Claude and his wife, Reta, have two daughters: Julie and Jenny.

FOREWORD

by Bill McCartney

When God brought Promise Keepers into being, we had little idea what He had in mind. Each of the seven core promises came straight out of God's heart, and men started to respond like never before. As Folsum Stadium filled for the first time, we began to pray to see a million men fill stadiums across this country by the year 2000. God's timetable was faster, and that dream was realized in 1996. Each man was hungry to learn what God had for him, and many became sincere promise keepers. But the sixth promise was the tough one: "A Promise Keeper is committed to reach beyond any racial and denominational barriers to demonstrate the power of biblical unity."

God has especially laid this promise on my heart. Many of you have heard the personal stories I've told of how God has broken my heart as I've come in touch with the pain felt by men of color. But the greatest pain I feel comes from the way the church of Jesus Christ has been fractured and divided by the walls of racial strife and sectarianism. Not only has Satan infected the world, but he has also smitten the church with this evil. With well-intended motives, we have separated ourselves by denominations to preserve our doctrine, building barriers to Christian fellowship in the process. We've allowed the lies of racism into the hearts of followers of Jesus Christ. The condition we face is the same one Paul wrote about in Ephesians 6:12, *"For our struggle is not against flesh and blood, but against the rulers, against the authorities, against the powers of this dark world and against the spiritual forces of evil in the heavenly realms."*

Men, we are at war! Satan has used race and sectarianism to divide and alienate us to keep us from being the bride of Christ *"without spot or blemish."*

But there's a stirring among God's people. God is doing a new thing. Men are awakening to face the enemy and do battle. Promise Keepers is part of that army. I pray that you, too, have enlisted.

A number of years ago, Promise Keepers began to articulate God's heart for reconciliation. In the stadiums, men responded with broken hearts. But we soon learned there was a problem as they began to ask, "What should I do when I go home?" Committing to become an active agent of reconciliation requires training. This workbook and its accompanying video series is our response to that question. It has been written by two men, Glen Kehrein and Raleigh Washington, who have "walked the walk" together for more than fifteen years. The eight biblical principles of reconciliation they present, which form the foundation of the workbook, are time tested in the crucible of everyday life. Claude King has joined with Glen and Raleigh to add his unique interactive style.

This is a workbook of substance! Don't even begin this process if you aren't ready for God to change your life! But if you are, and if you enter into this study with a group of men who are committed to becoming agents of reconciliation, you will never be the same. You'll get your questions answered; you'll discover what God wants you to do. Study this workbook and then apply it. Be a part of the generation of reconciliation and peace!

PREFACE

Welcome to *Break Down the Walls*. You are about to begin a process that could have significant historical, social, spiritual, and eternal consequences. On the night before His crucifixion, Jesus prayed for complete unity among those who would believe in Him (see John 17:20–23).

> That is Jesus' desire for His people today: "complete unity."

That is Jesus' desire for His people today: "complete unity." Jesus said the world would come to know He was God's Son by the unity displayed by His disciples. Could that be one reason our world is rejecting the message of His gospel? Do they reject our message because the Christians they see can't get along with each other? Biblical unity such as Jesus prayed for may be the best way we could reveal Christ to a watching world.

Two Giants

Two big "giants" have been mocking Christians the way Goliath mocked Israel in King David's day. Racial hatred and bigotry, along with a factional spirit that judges and condemns other denominations or Christian traditions, have mocked Christian unity as an impossibility. God has called us to step forward like David, with his sling and five smooth stones, to confront these sins in the Christian community. And just as David depended on God for success, so we know that bringing down these two giants also depends upon God's power and guidance.

Some people—like David's brothers—may accuse us of arrogance in thinking we could do something that seems so impossible. Some may ridicule and discount our efforts as hopeless or meaningless. We know that, in comparison to these giants, we are indeed weak. We realize our efforts will be fruitless unless *God* does something. We come against these two giants remembering David's response to Goliath:

> *"You come against me with sword and spear and javelin, but I come against you in the name of the LORD Almighty, the God of the armies of Israel, whom you have defied. This day the LORD will hand you over to me, and . . . the whole world will know that there is a God in Israel. All those gathered here will know that it is not by sword or spear that the LORD saves; for the battle is the LORD's, and he will give all of you into our hands"* (1 Samuel 17:45–47).

Ephesians 2:14–18
"For he himself is our peace, who has made the two one and has destroyed the barrier, the dividing wall of hostility, by abolishing in his flesh the law with its commandments and regulations. His purpose was to create in himself one new man out of the two, thus making peace, and in this one body to reconcile both of them to God through the cross, by which he put to death their hostility. He came and preached peace to you who were far away and peace to those who were near. For through him we both have access to the Father by one Spirit."

We know this course is just one stone's throw (not even the first) in a battle that will take time and the involvement of many others. But we believe God has an answer for His people that will allow us to experience biblical reconciliation and unity. We believe God *is* going to bring down these giants of racism and sectarianism in the body of Christ.

We're convinced God is working to answer the prayer of Jesus in John 17. He's tearing down barriers between believers. In Christ, God has already provided all we need to experience biblical unity (see Ephesians 2:14–18). And He may use this course to help you and others experience fresh dimensions of that unity in the body of Christ.

This will not be just a mental exercise. It will be a relational experience you share with other brothers in Christ. Together, you will experience God's presence and power in what it means to love one another. People will recognize you as disciples of Christ because of the demonstration of that love. As God establishes that spirit of unity across racial and denom-

As God establishes that spirit of unity across racial and denominational lines, we believe many lost people will recognize that Jesus is God's Son and will come to salvation in Christ.

inational lines, we believe many lost people will recognize that Jesus is God's Son and will come to salvation in Him.

We know this battle is the Lord's. We invite you to join us as we seek and obey God's directions. Let the following song be our theme as we study together and seek to "be the generation of reconciliation and peace."

THE RECONCILIATION SONG[1]

By Morris Chapman, Buddy Owens, and Claire Cloninger

O let us be the generation
Of reconciliation and peace
And let us be a holy nation
Where pride and prejudice shall cease
Let us speak the truth in love
To the lost and least of these
And serve the Lord in unity
So others will believe
Let us be the generation
Of reconciliation and peace

O let us be the generation
Of reconciliation and peace
And let us build on one foundation
Till He comes and the wars of men shall cease
Let us share the love of Jesus
Without hypocrisy
Let mercy and forgiveness
Begin with you and me
Let us be the generation
Of reconciliation and peace

Have we not one Father
Have we not one faith
Have we not one calling
To become one holy race

O let us be the generation
Of reconciliation and peace
And let us pray for restoration
And seek the Lord together on our knees
Let us keep our hearts from evil
And cling to what is good
Let us honor one another
And love the brotherhood
Let us be the generation
Of reconciliation and peace

[1] © Maranatha! Music and Word Music (a div. of Word, Inc.) and Juniper Landing Music. Admin. by Word Music. All rights reserved. International copyright secured. Used by Permission.

Recorded on "Break Down the Walls — Conference Edition" cassette tape or compact disc by Maranatha Music.

BEFORE YOU BEGIN THIS COURSE

Break Down the Walls is a small-group course designed for Christian men to study together. It's prepared especially for men who are different racially, socioeconomically, or in their denominational affiliation. Before you jump in, we want you to prepare for this course. It will be a little different from what you may be used to. Take time to read through this section first. Carry out the actions necessary to get ready. Then go for it! Below we have answered most of the questions we think you would ask. If we've missed one of your questions, be patient with us—we may answer it yet.

COURSE GOALS

1. Knowledge and Understanding
You will know what God has to say about reconciliation, unity, and right relationships in the body of Christ. You will understand how God guides and enables you to experience biblical reconciliation and unity with other believers.

2. Application to Life
You will demonstrate your love for God and for other believers by seeking reconciliation and unity with them in a Christlike manner.

Where Are We Going?
If you've already read the foreword and preface, you know this course is about biblical reconciliation and unity. If you haven't read them (pp. 5-7), do that right now.

This course is targeted at two giants within the body of Christ that seem to mock Christianity:
1. Racism and isolation among Christians who belong to the same family of God; and
2. Sectarianism, or a judgmental spirit, competition, and fighting between Christians from different denominations or traditions.

God wants to eradicate these giants for the sake of His kingdom. It can begin as one man experiences biblical reconciliation and unity with another man or a few other men. It will continue as one church experiences this with one church or a few other churches. It will grow as Christians in a whole community begin to experience it. As individuals, churches, and cities across the nation and around the world experience biblical reconciliation and unity, God will receive glory. Our specific goals for this course are in the margin.

Why Are We Going There?
Our primary reason for seeking biblical reconciliation and unity is that God wants them. They please and honor Him. The following are some of the reasons you personally may want to experience these realities in the body of Christ:

Your Purpose
- To bring glory and honor to God and His Son, Jesus Christ.
- To reveal to the world that Jesus is the divine Son of God.
- To demonstrate to a watching world what Christian love looks like.
- To experience reconciliation with God and your brothers and sisters in Christ.
- To be forgiven and cleansed of sins and unresolved guilt that have been barriers to unity.
- To experience healing of the wounds that have come from division.
- To become sensitive to the feelings, beliefs, and experiences of Christians who are not like you.
- To experience the joy and power of biblical unity without losing your uniqueness or our diversity.
- To become more like Christ in your relationships with others.
- To join God in restoring wholeness to a broken world.

Your Pastor
How Should My Pastor Be Involved?
We have developed this course to help your local church in its ministry to men. We know we are dealing with two sensitive issues. Some churches

may need time to move in the direction God wants them to move. His leadership and timing will be critical for this course to be of greatest value. Our desire is to see this course *strengthen* your local church.

Our desire is to see this course strengthen your local church.

God has given your pastor an assignment to be an undershepherd of God's flock (your church). As you consider being part of this study, seek your pastor's counsel and involvement. As you talk and pray with him, trust that the Lord will guide him in a way that's right for your church. Below are some possible thoughts your pastor may have. Pray with him to discern what God's will and timing are for your church.

1. God has prepared me and our church to reach out across racial and/or denominational barriers. Let's begin praying about "who" and "when." I may even want to go through this study with some other pastors in the area while our men are also doing it.
2. I know God wants us to move in that direction. Let's consider taking some of our men through this study to understand what we're getting into. We can pray through the process and let God lead us to the next step.
3. Our church has internal divisions that need to be dealt with first. Let's begin praying and see how God might use this study in our own church first. As God brings reconciliation and unity here, we'll be better prepared to experience the broader dimensions with other groups.
4. Because of our church's history with racial and sectarian issues, we need to prayerfully seek God's direction for how to proceed. We don't want to divide our church over a unity message. Let's get the church staff and a few key leaders to go through this study ourselves. We can pray for God to guide us in a way that will accomplish His purposes without dividing His people.

Don't bypass your pastor. He is an important player on your team.

Don't bypass your pastor. We are called to honor his leadership. He's an important player on your team. You need his counsel and support. He may refer the matter to a staff member or another group. Or he may give you the go-ahead right away. At least give him the opportunity to be involved in the process.

Your Leader

Who Will Be Our Leader?
Like every other decision you need to make, this should be a matter of prayer. Ask the Lord to guide you in selecting the right leader. Your pastor may have some counsel here. Perhaps God has given you the burden for this study and this is an assignment He has for you. Here are some factors to consider:

- The leader doesn't have to be an expert teacher. This workbook will present the content to members as they study prior to each session. Specific suggestions for prayer, activities, and questions for discussion will be provided at the end of each unit. So the leader doesn't have to spend a great deal of time in preparation for a session.
- The leader is a player-coach or a lead learner. He learns, studies, and participates along with the rest of the group. He doesn't have to be trained or certified. Nor does he have to have completed the study himself before becoming the leader. He will, however, want to read the general suggestions for a leader beginning on page 190.
- The leader should be a godly man, one who walks with God, prays, and depends on the Lord for guidance.
- The leader needs to have some small-group study skills. He should be adept at guiding discussion and prayer. He should be sensitive to relationships within the group and know how to respond to any conflict that may arise.

- The leader needs to be a servant rather than a ruler. Humility will mark his lifestyle and relationships. He should seek to meet the needs of the individual members and the group. He should not be demanding, harsh, threatening, manipulating, or controlling.
- Some groups may want to rotate leadership among willing members. Other groups may prefer to have two coleaders from different backgrounds. That's okay, but we suggest that one person should coordinate the overall group process.

Your Group

Who Will Go with Me?

God is actively involved in your life. Most importantly, He will be with you; and He has a plan! First you will want to pray and ask the Lord what He is doing in and around your life. Ask Him to guide you to just the right group for this study. Again, your pastor may have some valuable counsel for you.

We recommend a group of four to six.

Groups can vary in size. You could go one on one, but we recommend a group of four to six. Eight would probably be an outside maximum. If you have more than eight men who want to participate, start more small groups. Keep the following factors in mind as you form your group:

Christian Men Only

- **Christian Men.** This study is written with Christian men—men who trust in Jesus alone for their salvation—primarily in mind. Men from non-Christian groups will sidetrack the process. The presence of Christ in the lives of your brothers is a key factor in the kind of experience you will have. People without a personal relationship with the Lord may become a hindrance to what you're trying to accomplish. Be careful, however, to reserve judgment about the salvation of men from other Christian denominations or traditions. When Christ dwells in another person, you will recognize Him in that person.

- **What About Your Wife or Other Women?** This course deals with a subject that applies to all Christians; women would certainly understand and benefit from it. But they'll have to "wade" through our men-focused wording. If you realize you need reconciliation in your marriage or your church, you may want to go through this study with your wife or with your larger church family. Keep in mind, however, that God may work through the men in your church to lead the way toward reconciliation.

. . . with brothers who are different—racially, socio-economically, or denominationally

- **Affinity or Diversity?** The ultimate goal of this study is for you to go through it with brothers who are different—racially, socioeconomically, and/or denominationally. This is where you will experience reconciliation and unity in deeply meaningful ways. However, you may decide to go through the study the first time with men who are more like you. That's okay; you may join with men from your church or another church of your same denomination. *But don't stop there.* Perhaps by the second time through, you'll be ready to experience the course with brothers who are different. Ask the Lord to guide you in this choice.

You should not add members after session 2.

- **Closed or Open Group?** The nature of this study will require men to work through it together. New members can't be added later without hurting the learning and discussion process. You can add members after the introductory session, but someone will need to help them get the same orientation one on one. After the first session (unit 1), a person would have a great deal of catch-up work to do. This could be done if someone were willing to help him. You should not add members after session 2. If others want to join the study, put together a waiting list, and start a new group as soon as you have enough men interested.

Ask the Lord to guide you to the men with whom He wants you to study. He may identify specific individuals for you to approach with an invitation. Pay attention to what God is already doing in your life.

❑ Has He given you a concern for reconciliation and unity in your church? Then you may need to start with a group of men in your church.

❑ Has He given you a burden for reconciliation and unity with other races? Then look around you for people of other races for your group.

❑ Do you long to experience unity with men from other denominations? God may have you start your group with men from other churches.

❑ Have you met other Christian men from your community through a Promise Keepers conference or other Christian event? That may be a group to pray with about starting the study.

❑ Do you already have a men's group that needs a focus? This may be the right tool to use in that setting. Discuss it with them, and pray for the Lord's direction.

❑ Are there Christian men at your workplace who have discussed doing a Bible study together? This may be the right tool.

❑ When you begin to sense God's direction, discuss your interest in this study with other men, and see how they react. A positive response may indicate the lives in which God is working.

Be patient. If a group doesn't surface right away, keep praying. God has a right timing. Trust Him to bring it to pass according to His timetable.

When and Where Will We Meet?

When and Where?

The people interested in the group should help you decide on a right time and place. No matter what you choose, some adjustments and sacrifice will be required. If the group is from your church, you might meet as part of a Sunday evening discipleship group at church. People from different denominations may want to choose a neutral location like a restaurant, office, or community center. They might prefer, however, a central location at one of your churches. Groups could meet before or after work, and maybe even in your workplace. You could meet in a home of one member or even rotate the meeting between your homes or churches.

Almost any time and place are possible, depending on the needs of your group. The meeting place needs to provide a degree of privacy. You don't want your discussion and prayer times to be interrupted by people coming and going around you or by telephones that must be answered. Choose a place that's big enough to be comfortable but small enough to keep you close together.

How Long Will It Take?

ninety-minute to two-hour sessions

Each session should last ninety minutes to two hours. Because of the nature of the discussion, a ninety-minute session would be a minimum. To enable a clear focus, we recommend that you *not* combine this study with a meal. If you do, however, allow a minimum of ninety minutes for the session in addition to the meal. If you provide refreshments, keep them simple and light. Don't get caught up competing with each other over fancy or abundant refreshments. Keep them simple, if you have them at all.

Recommended: 12 weeks
1 introductory session
10 study sessions
1 mid-term get-together

This course is designed for twelve sessions—an introductory session, ten study sessions, and one mid-term get-together that will allow members to catch up on incomplete lessons. On this schedule, members would study five lessons (one unit) between sessions. You may want to vary that schedule to suit your group's needs. In some cases, you may want to take an additional week off from homework and continue your discussion and review. That will permit members to catch up on lessons they haven't completed. Some other possible options include:

- Weekly meeting studying a half unit (two or three lessons) per week—twenty-two weeks
- Biweekly meeting studying one unit per meeting—twenty-four weeks
- Monthly meeting studying one unit per meeting—twelve months

As you complete the course, you will be guided to decide what to do next. Some groups may continue meeting for discussion and prayer. Others may choose to work on a project together. Some may decide to go back through the study a second time with a new group of brothers who are different racially and/or denominationally.

The goal for this study is not just to cover the content. Building relationships is also a primary part of the purpose.

The goal of this study is not just to cover the content. Building relationships is also a primary part of the purpose. Experiencing reconciliation and unity will take time. Some factors to consider in choosing a schedule should include:

- The more your members are alike, the less time you'll need to build relationships. This is also true if members already know each other.
- The more your members are different, the more time you'll need to build relationships.
- If your group includes people with slower reading and learning skills, slow the pace so they can keep up.
- Consider adding two or three "breaks" to the schedule where no additional lessons will be studied. This provides catch-up time for any who have fallen behind. It also increases the time for building relationships along the way. Monitor the group's needs, and slow down or speed up to best meet those needs. One such break is built into the recommended twelve-week plan.
- Consider holding some special events along the way. You might plan a social outing midway through the course or get together a couple of times for a cookout—with no study agenda, of course. You do have permission to *enjoy* this time together!

Your Ground Rules

What Are the Ground Rules?
This study needs to be meaningful and purposeful. Rules and commitments ought to be kept to a minimum—but there are some minimums. Important basics include:

1. Preparation. This is a self-paced interactive course. You'll need to complete a personal study of the lessons prior to each group session. *Self-paced* means you study as fast or as slowly as you choose. The content is interactive. We'll present Scripture or insights. Then you will encounter a learning activity that will call you to respond in some way. The activity will look like this:
➡ **Turn to page 18 and find the first numbered learning activity in lesson 1. Place a check here when you have done so.** ❏

Don't skip the learning activities.

Learning activities begin with an arrow and indented boldface instructions. Did you complete the activity above? If not, follow the instructions above and do it now. Don't skip the learning activities. They're designed to help you learn, and to apply what you learn. You not only want to know about and understand biblical reconciliation and unity, but you want to experience God working actively in your life as well. After each activity, we'll give you some feedback if there's a correct answer or response. That way, you can make sure you're staying on track and learning as you go.

Normally, you'll study five lessons between meetings (unless your group chooses a different schedule). The content in these lessons will NOT be presented during the session. If you don't do your homework, you won't be prepared to participate fully in the group session.

You should plan to study one lesson at a time (one per day). By spreading lessons over a period of days, you'll be able to spend time meditating on what God is saying to you. You'll also have time to begin applying the truths to your life. Each lesson should take about thirty minutes for study and prayer. This course is thoroughly based in the Scriptures and can guide your daily devotional time while you're going through it. You may choose to spend more time to go deeper or pray longer. Don't wait until the last minute, however, because catching up is difficult.

2. Attendance. The small-group sessions are probably the most important part of this study. You'll miss out on God's best if you're not present. Make a firm commitment to attend every session. Don't miss one unless you have no alternative. If your schedule will require you to miss several sessions, you should wait and go through the study at another time. Both you and the group need this regular time together. Irregular attendance will hurt the group process.

If, for some reason, you haven't been able to complete your homework, go to the group session anyway. You need the experience with your brothers. You don't need to fake the fact that you didn't finish. If you get "put on the spot," confess that you didn't complete the assignments. You may even want to describe the "crisis" that kept you from study this week so they can pray for you. Try to get caught up by the next session.

3. Participation. Group study may be a new experience for you. You may be shy or timid around unfamiliar men. That's okay. We're going to help you get acquainted so you'll begin to feel like real brothers by the time you finish the study. However, we encourage you to participate. Be ready to listen when others are speaking. Try to get to know them and understand their life experiences, what they think, and how they feel. Be willing to tell them about yourself also. We'll take it slow so you can feel comfortable. But be prepared to take some risks. Some of the participation may be uncomfortable or even painful. That will probably be a part of the healing and reconciling process, so don't miss it. Your brothers are going to be there to help. You'll find that they'll need your help, too. This is going to be a team effort, and you're an important part of the team. Don't sit on the sidelines; get into the game!

4. Confidentiality. In small-group sessions, you never know when someone will need to say something painful, personal, or even potentially damaging to his reputation. Members need to feel the safety and freedom to speak openly and honestly without the fear that others will hear about it later. Agree with each other from the start that matters revealed in the group session will stay in the group. Once you make that commitment, be faithful and don't discuss the group session with others—even as "prayer requests."

5. Prayer. Your brothers in the group need you to pray for them. You need their prayers, too. During the sessions, make notes about ways you can pray for specific members. Lift your requests in their behalf to the Lord

If you don't do your homework, you won't be prepared to participate fully in the group session.

Each lesson should take about thirty minutes or less for study and prayer.

The small-group sessions are probably the most important part of this study.

This is going to be a team effort, and you're an important part of the team. Don't sit on the sidelines; get into the game!

Agree with each other that matters discussed in the group session will stay in the group.

during the week. You may even want to pray for one specific member each day of the week. Carry an index card with you with the member's name and prayer requests on it. Take a few moments during slack times in your schedule to pray for that member listed on your card.

Resources Needed

What Resources Do We Need?
In addition to your Bibles, this study guide is the only other physical resource you need. However, every member in your group will need a copy. Buy enough so every man has one available at the introductory session. The leader's guide is included in this book. General information for leaders begins on page 190. Specific suggestions for the group sessions follow this general leader information. The general information will tell the leader how to use these session suggestions. Other resources for further study are described on page 189.

How Do We Get Started?

Introductory Session

Once you have selected a leader and identified potential group members, you're ready to get started. The leader will need to schedule an introductory session for all potential group members. Instructions for this session begin on page 198. During the session, members will receive their books and overview the material together. This will also be a get-acquainted session for group members. If you're the one who will be serving as coordinator for this study, turn to page 190 and read the suggestions for the leader.

UNIT 1 UNITY IN CHRIST

Scripture Memory Verse
"I in them and you in me. May they be brought to complete unity to let the world know that you sent me and have loved them even as you have loved me."
—John 17:23

Unit Learning Goal
You will understand the importance of unity and the basis for it that comes through Christ, and you will demonstrate your faith by beginning to pray for that unity to become a reality.

Overview of Unit 1
Lesson 1: Seeing from God's Viewpoint
Lesson 2: Overviewing *Break Down the Walls*
Lesson 3: Jesus Prayed for Unity
Lesson 4: The Basis of Our Unity
Lesson 5: Barriers to Unity

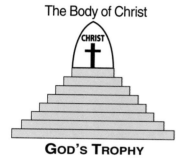

The Body of Christ

CHRIST

GOD'S TROPHY

EIGHT BIBLICAL PRINCIPLES FOR RECONCILIATION AND UNITY

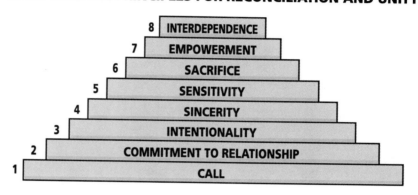

8 INTERDEPENDENCE
7 EMPOWERMENT
6 SACRIFICE
5 SENSITIVITY
4 SINCERITY
3 INTENTIONALITY
2 COMMITMENT TO RELATIONSHIP
1 CALL

Key Summary Statements from Unit 1
- Under the direction of its Head, Jesus Christ, the body of Christ joins God in the work of reconciliation. The members of the church carry the message of Christ to the lost world and call people to the Savior.
- The more opportunities we have to worship and serve with diverse groups of believers, the more we can experience what heaven will be like!
- A healthy body of Christ is a trophy for God to reveal His great wisdom to rulers and authorities in heavenly realms.
- Jesus wanted His people to be brought to complete unity to let the world know that the Father sent Christ and that the Father loves the disciples as He has loved Christ.
- Unity is critical to the redemptive work of the church.
- Our unity comes through a common relationship to God through Christ.
- The Holy Spirit of Christ who dwells in believers produces a unity that cannot be produced by any human effort.
- When Christians can't get along with each other, Jesus is grieved and brokenhearted.
- Pride is a wicked root sin that produces all kinds of fruit sins.
- Pride is a root sin of racism and sectarianism.

WALLS CAME DOWN IN MODESTO[1]

by G. Ron Darbee

Modesto, California, is a city of less than 200,000 that has grown around an agricultural base of almonds, grapes, and alfalfa. Though folks seem reluctant to put a name to it, something big is happening. "Names sometimes limit us," a Modesto church worker explained. "They give us the impression we have arrived at our goals. We don't want to make that mistake. This is a beginning. We want people to continue to strive rather than celebrate a premature victory."

Amidst the almond blossoms and walnut groves, surrounded by vineyards, orchards, and fields, a new crop is growing: Seeds of reconciliation, watered by faith and tended in unity, promise to bring forth a new harvest of Christian renewal.

In June 1996, 5,000 men from the Modesto area traveled seventy miles to attend the Promise Keepers conference in Oakland, California. Led by their pastors, these 5,000 men from myriad churches and a variety of ethnic backgrounds chose to lay aside their denominational identities and affiliate themselves with a greater body, a body that expresses the unity they are working to achieve. Most of their contingent came to Oakland sporting T-shirts that proclaimed the spirit of the movement now taking place. The off-white shirts carried a brightly colored logo that read "The Church of Modesto."

And what is "The Church of Modesto"? It's nothing more, and nothing less, than men and women breaking down the walls of race and crashing through denominational barriers to seek the face of God. It's people making conscious efforts to disregard economic standing and pray for and with one another. It's a group of believers standing together as a part of the unified body of the Lord Jesus Christ. Although they don't meet in a single building, they have agreed to meet with the single purpose of glorifying God.

What brought the community of Modesto to this place of renewal and promise? In January 1994, at the invitation of David Seifert, pastor of Big Valley Grace Community Church and president of the Greater Modesto Area Ministerial Association (GMMA), fifty-three pastors joined together to attend a prayer summit. At a coastal mountain retreat, these leaders spent four days fasting, praying, and seeking God's will.

"There was often a competitive spirit between pastors up until that point," says Pastor Wade Estes of First Baptist, Modesto. "I don't know about other communities, but I would guess we were pretty much the same. There was some ill will between members and former members of congregations. It wasn't necessarily that anyone was speaking badly about another. . . . It was more like, 'You do your thing, and I'll do mine.'"

Many pastors came to the prayer summit with their own individual agendas. But on the final day, the group broke up into smaller units to answer the question, *What does God want us to do?* Each returned with the same conclusion: Meet with Him regularly and pray.

To some, the idea seemed almost frightening. "With our busy schedules, who has time to meet apart from his own church every week to pray with a group of pastors?" Nevertheless, the group entered into a covenant, agreeing to meet each Wednesday at high noon for prayer and accountability. In the first year, the men met fifty of fifty-two weeks, taking time off only during the Christmas holidays. A second prayer summit the following year brought more than seventy pastors, and the group's numbers continued to climb.

Today, it's not at all unusual for 100 men of God to meet for the regular Wednesday prayer session. Visitors come from throughout the area, hoping to see something they can take back to their own communities, and members rarely miss a meeting. As Pastor Seifert put it, "If the men are in town, they know where they need to be."

What does a GMMA meeting look like? The pastors enter the meeting hall one, two, or three at a time, shaking hands and exchanging the normal pleasantries. At precisely 12:00, a worship leader's solo voice sings out in praise and is immediately joined by the entire assembly in a chorus of "There's Something About That Name."

Another pastor opens the session in prayer: "Lord, we relinquish all other thoughts right now. We put everything else aside for this moment. Though we've been working for You today, maybe we haven't really stopped to worship You. We focus in right now; nothing else is worthy of our attention. You are everything."

Clearly, it's the intent of the "Associate Pastors of the Church of Modesto" (as they call themselves) to seek the face of God. In the process, they put aside minor doctrinal differences and make concerted efforts to achieve an ethnic diversity that mirrors the city's demographics. They model a lifestyle of reconciliation for their flock.

But what of the congregations? Have the efforts of their

pastors filtered through to the men and women of the greater Modesto area?

Yes! In the spring of 1996, more than 1,500 men, women, and children met at the railroad tracks in Modesto as an outward sign of reconciliation. "The tracks," according to Wade Estes, "were long seen as dividing the city along ethnic and economic lines. They were viewed as a spiritual barrier the Christian community needed to overcome." A ribbon running some length of the tracks symbolized the division among both the churches and the people of Modesto. After the occasion was dedicated with prayer, the ribbon was cut, and Christians from both sides of town crossed over their own spiritual barriers to unite in fellowship. The believers then walked to a nearby church and held a community service.

Possibly the greatest evidence of God's work in the hearts of Modesto's people occurred during the heat of the summer. On July 7, more than 8,000 people braved the early evening heat to attend a rally targeted at chipping away racial and denominational walls. Backing up traffic for several miles, Christian families streamed to Johansen High School's football field to worship and hear Thomas Trask, general superintendent of the Assemblies of God, speak to the packed stadium.

Bearing a name borrowed from the 1996 Promise Keepers theme, "Break Down the Walls," the rally focused attention on diversity rather than division. Shepherds challenged their flocks to celebrate the common bond shared through faith in Jesus Christ. Pastors greeted the assembly in several languages, including English, Spanish, Cambodian, and Hindi.

Acknowledging the efforts of the congregations to see beyond home-church boundaries, leaders asked their people to look ahead and contemplate the existence of God's church in an even broader scope, beyond Modesto and San Joaquin County and outside the state of California.

That evening, the "Church of Modesto" also took an offering, not for their rally and not for the needs of the local community, but for two predominantly black churches among those burned in the recent arson fires plaguing the South. More than $25,000 came from the heart of this congregation to help rebuild facilities in Corinth and Kassuth, Mississippi.

If tentative plans are any indication, the future looks bright for the "Church of Modesto." While some worry that the path to diversity can go too far and fear trading a truthful presentation of the gospel for ecumenical harmony, that appears extremely unlikely to the GMMA members. "First and foremost, we profess salvation through faith in the resurrected Christ," declares Pastor Charlie Crane of Greater True Light Baptist Church. "That isn't negotiable."

Has revival come to Modesto, California? No one there makes that claim. This is by no means a completed work, they insist. But many pray for God to bring revival to their city, and they desire to lay a solid foundation for that day.

Still, in many ways, one might contend that revival is already stirring in this valley town. After all, when you get right down to it, it's not the stadium events or large rallies that indicate the heart of Christian Modesto. It's the smaller, more individual happenings—men seeking to glorify God through one-on-one relationships beyond racial and denominational lines, and families fulfilling their neighbors' needs out of love for their Savior. It's Pastor Krueger of Grace Lutheran Church noticing that another congregation's piano is out of tune and making a gift of having that piano tuned.

It's summed up by the banner adorning the front of Dry Creek Evangelical Free Church that reads, "The Church Within the Church of Modesto."

[1] Adapted from *New Man*, vol. 3, no. 8 (November/December 1996): 36-40. Used by permission.

LESSON 1   SEEING FROM GOD'S VIEWPOINT

Scripture for Meditation

"I in them and you in me. May they be brought to complete unity to let the world know that you sent me and have loved them even as you have loved me" (John 17:23).

A Beginning Prayer

Father, I am a disciple of Your Son, Jesus. I am starting this study because I want to get in on what You're doing. I believe You want to bring about reconciliation and unity in the body of Christ. I want to experience it. Guide me and begin teaching me how I can be involved in seeing reconciliation and unity come to pass in the body of Christ. Amen.

What we agree on is that there's a lack of unity and that God has the solution.

➥ **Read and think about the Scripture for Meditation in the left margin, and begin the lesson with prayer.**

❖ ❖ ❖

➥ **John 17:23 is your Scripture memory verse for this unit. Remove the perforated card for unit 1 from the back of your book, and begin memorizing it. Here are some tips to help you.**

Tips for Scripture Memorization
- Ask the Lord to help you commit His Word to memory.
- Read through the verse several times—out loud if possible. State the Bible reference with the verse each time.
- Think about the meaning of the verse.
- Practice reciting the verse one phrase at a time. Repeat a phrase until you can say it from memory. Then add another phrase. Continue until you can recite the entire verse.
- Carry your Scripture memory card with you during the week. Use spare moments to review it and pray about its application to your life.
- Continue reviewing the verse every week throughout the term of this course.
- Watch for opportunities to apply this verse to life or to share it with someone else.

Many Christian leaders today are writing about racial and denominational reconciliation. That's not just a fad but an indication that God is working to accomplish what Jesus prayed for in John 17. You'll find many different approaches to pursuing these two goals. You'll find many helpful insights in the writings of others. What we agree on is that there's a lack of unity and that God has the solution. He's the One who can bring reconciliation and unity to reality in our day. We pray that God will use this course, coupled with your experience in a small group, to accomplish His purposes.

This first lesson in your study of *Break Down the Walls* is designed to give you the "big picture" of what God is doing in our world. We want you to understand what God is doing in history to reconcile the world to Himself. We also want you to understand what God is doing to prepare His people for eternity. By looking at our world from His viewpoint, you'll be able to realize how you fit in with His plan.

➥ **1. Which of the following viewpoints will best help you to understand how God wants to work in His people to prepare them for eternity? Check one.**
   ❑ a. My viewpoint of the present is most important. God gave me a brain, and I can use it to decide what needs to be done to prepare God's people for eternity.
   ❑ b. God's viewpoint of all eternity is most important. He knows what His people will be in eternity, and He knows what needs to be done today to move us in that direction.

Did you check the second viewpoint? Our limited human viewpoint in the present can't come close to understanding God's plans and purposes for the present and the future. When we see from His viewpoint, we can better understand what He wants to do with us and through us today to prepare us for the future.

God Is Reconciling the World to Himself

God is working through Christ to reconcile the world to Himself. By faith in Christ and the forgiveness and cleansing He provides, a person is made right with God. God then places that person in the body of Christ (the church). Though made of many different members, the body is the means God uses to carry the message of Christ to a lost world. With Christ as its Head, the body has the assignment of being ambassadors of Christ and appealing to all: *"Be reconciled to God."* (See 2 Corinthians 5:19–20.)

2 Corinthians 5:19–20
"God was reconciling the world to himself in Christ, not counting men's sins against them. And he has committed to us the message of reconciliation. We are therefore Christ's ambassadors, as though God were making his appeal through us. We implore you on Christ's behalf: Be reconciled to God."

To summarize what God is doing in our world:

1. God reconciles people to Himself through Christ.
2. God places believers in the body of Christ with Christ as their Head, and He begins molding and shaping them—individually and as a group—into the image of His Son.
3. Under the direction of their Head, Jesus Christ, members of the body join God in the work of reconciliation. They carry the message of Christ to the lost world and call people to the Savior.
4. God continues to add to the body of Christ until, in eternity, they are a great multitude from every nation, tribe, people, and language. They will be a pure bride for their marriage to the Lamb of God—Jesus Christ.

This course focuses attention primarily on #2 above as preparation for #3. God has placed all believers in the body of Christ. Yet because of divisions, pride, judgmental spirits, racism, favoritism, and a multitude of other sins, the body is not demonstrating unity to the world as God intended. As you study *Break Down the Walls*, God will be working to help you become Christlike. Through the Scriptures, He will reveal the ways of Christ and confront you with sin that hinders your effectiveness in the body. As you grow in Christlikeness, He will work in and through you to establish Christlike relationships in the body.

➡ **2. God has chosen to work through the body of Christ to reconcile a lost world to Himself. Which kind of body will be most effective in joining God in this work? Check one.**

❏ a. an immoral and impure body that lives just like the world
❏ b. a divided, judgmental, and fractured body that's always fighting with itself
❏ c. a healthy, loving, caring body that acts just like Jesus toward its members and toward a sinful world
❏ d. a proud, apathetic, and satisfied body that doesn't care for its members or the rest of the world

Revelation 19:7–9
" 'Let us rejoice and be glad and give him glory! For the wedding of the Lamb has come, and his bride has made herself ready. Fine linen, bright and clean, was given her to wear.' (Fine linen stands for the righteous acts of the saints.)

"Then the angel said to me, 'Write: "Blessed are those who are invited to the wedding supper of the Lamb!" ' "

That's not a difficult choice to make, is it? God wants the body of Christ—both local churches and the larger Christian community—to be a healthy, loving, and caring body that acts just like Jesus toward its members and a sinful world. God wants to work in you, your church, your denomination, and the church universal to develop this kind of healthy body for His Son to be Head over.

A View from Eternity

Fortunately, we know the end of the church's story. By looking at what we'll be in eternity, we can understand what God will be doing today to mold us into that reality.

➡ **3. Read Revelation 19:7–9 and Revelation 7:9–10 in the left margin. Circle words that describe what God's people will be like in heaven.**

A Bride

As someone has said, Jesus is not coming back to get His harem (many women) but a bride. The Lamb is going to be married to *one* beautiful and pure bride (see Revelation 19:7–9). Did you notice that she will make *herself* ready? Now is the

Revelation 7:9–10
"After this I looked and there before me was a great multitude that no one could count, from every nation, tribe, people and language, standing before the throne and in front of the Lamb. They were wearing white robes and were holding palm branches in their hands. And they cried out in a loud voice: 'Salvation belongs to our God, who sits on the throne, and to the Lamb.' "

best time possible for us to begin the preparations!

A Multiethnic Multitude

When we stand before the throne with all believers, we'll worship the Lord together. This great multitude will include people *"from every nation, tribe, people and language"* (Revelation 7:9). No one will be excluded because of skin color, language, genetic heritage, or ethnic culture. So the more opportunities we have to worship and serve with diverse groups of believers, the more we can experience what heaven will be like! Why should we wait when we can begin to experience the reality of that oneness in Christ today?

➥ **4. In view of what we will be in eternity, what response are you willing to make to the Lord today? Check your response or write your own.**

   ❑ a. Lord, I want to begin experiencing the reality of eternity now. Show me the times and ways I can change to become more like that reality.

   ❑ b. Lord, I have many barriers in my mind and feelings that keep me from wanting to experience that reality just yet. I give You permission to begin breaking down those walls in my life.

   ❑ c. God, I can't call You Lord and not follow Your will. I'm not ready to move that direction yet. Please be patient with me and don't give up on me.

   ❑ d. Other: _____

➥ **What, if anything, do you sense God has said to you through today's lesson? Write *one* of the most meaningful things He has said below.**

_____

_____

➥ **Conclude today's lesson by praying. Tell the Lord what you're thinking and feeling. Invite Him to touch your mind, heart, and life during this study.**

> Now is the best time possible for us to begin the preparations!
>
> This great multitude will include people *"from every nation, tribe, people and language."*

Some of God's diverse people worshiping the Lord together at a Promise Keepers conference

LESSON 2 OVERVIEWING *BREAK DOWN THE WALLS*

Scripture for Meditation
"Study to shew thyself approved unto God, a workman that needeth not to be ashamed, rightly dividing the word of truth" (2 Timothy 2:15, KJV).

A Beginning Prayer
Father, as I begin this study, I look forward to what You're going to be teaching me and what You're going to do in my life. I pray that You will accomplish everything in me that You desire to do. Please encourage me to study in such a way that I will learn and apply Your truths to my life and relationships. Amen.

_____

_____

➡ **Read and think about the Scripture for Meditation in the left margin, and begin the lesson with prayer.**

❖ ❖ ❖

In the first lesson, we looked at God's plan for eternity. In this lesson, we'll help you understand how this course fits into God's plan. Let's overview the content of *Break Down the Walls* that you'll be studying during the next ten units. This lesson will take a quick look at the major topics. In lessons to come, we'll look in detail at the biblical foundations, examples, and applications of these truths to life situations. Then in your small-group sessions, you'll be guided to discuss, understand, and experience these truths with brothers in Christ.

A Quick Tour

➡ **1. Turn to the table of contents and read through the unit and lesson titles. Notice that the first two units focus more on the "big picture" of unity and reconciliation. The last eight units focus on principles of reconciliation and unity. Place a check mark beside any titles you are particularly interested in studying. Write the title of one of these units or lessons below.**

_____

➡ **2. Turn to the Appendix beginning on page 170 and flip through the pages just to see the topics and resources included there for your use. You don't need to read those sections today. Look for one resource that you think may be of interest or practical help to you. Write that resource or idea in the margin.**

➡ **3. If you haven't already done so, remove your Scripture memory card for unit 1. Review your memory verse for this week. Then see if you can fill in the missing words in the verse below.**

John 17:23— *"I in them and you in _____. May they be brought to complete _____ to let the _____ know that you sent me and have _____ them even as you have loved me."*

➡ **4. Read again the remaining lesson titles from the first two units, listed below. Of these eight titles, which one do you think you will be most interested in studying? Place a check mark beside it.**
❏ Jesus Prayed for Unity ❏ Three Illustrations of Unity
❏ The Basis of Our Unity ❏ The Body of Christ
❏ Barriers to Unity ❏ No Divisions Among You
❏ Jesus Provided for Unity ❏ Becoming Christlike in the Body

➡ **5. What's one question about reconciliation and unity (either racial or denominational) that you would like to have answered during this study?**

_____

_____

One of the things you will learn during our study is that Jesus has given us a model for right relationships with other people, and especially other believers. As the Lord has treated you, so you're to treat others.

➡ **6. Match the description in the left margin with the correct Scripture below. Write the letter of the Scripture beside each description.**

_____ 1. Accepted and now accepting

_____ 2. Forgiven and now forgiving

_____ 3. Loved and now loving

_____ 4. Served and now serving

_____ 5. Comforted and now comforting

A. *"A new command I give you: Love one another. As I have loved you, so you must love one another"* (John 13:34).

B. *"Whoever wants to become great among you must be your servant . . . just as the Son of Man did not come to be served, but to serve, and to give his life as a ransom for many"* (Matthew 20:26, 28).

C. *"Bear with each other and forgive whatever grievances you may have against one another. Forgive as the Lord forgave you"* (Colossians 3:13).

D. *"Accept one another, then, just as Christ accepted you, in order to bring praise to God"* (Romans 15:7).

E. *"Praise be to . . . the God of all comfort, who comforts us in all our troubles, so that we can comfort those in any trouble with the comfort we ourselves have received from God"* (2 Corinthians 1:3–4).

Did you realize God has modeled right relationships in such a clear way? In fact, if we would all apply the commands of those Scriptures in our relationships with others, there would be little need for a course like this. (Answers: 1-D; 2-C; 3-A; 4-B; 5-E.)

Eight Biblical Principles for Reconciliation and Unity
The major focus of the last eight units will be on eight principles that can help you experience reconciliation and unity in the body of Christ. These principles are like stairs: They build on one another and lead toward an interdependence we can experience as a healthy body. You'll learn that a healthy body of Christ is a trophy for God to reveal His great wisdom to rulers and authorities in heavenly realms. That's our goal.

➡ **7. Take a few moments to study the two diagrams below. They'll be like a "course map" for us. We will seek to study and apply the first principle and then move on to the second. Our prayer is that you'll begin to experience greater and greater degrees of unity in the body of Christ as we move through these eight principles.**

EIGHT BIBLICAL PRINCIPLES FOR RECONCILIATION AND UNITY

The Body of Christ

CHRIST

GOD'S TROPHY

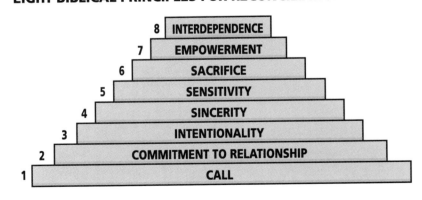

8 INTERDEPENDENCE
7 EMPOWERMENT
6 SACRIFICE
5 SENSITIVITY
4 SINCERITY
3 INTENTIONALITY
2 COMMITMENT TO RELATIONSHIP
1 CALL

➡ **8. Now read the eight principles on the following page. You won't be asked to memorize them, but we want you to become familiar with the key truth in each one. Circle one or two key words in each principle, and then write it (or them) on the corresponding line in the margin.**

Key Words from the Eight Principles*

1. _____

2. _____

3. _____

4. _____

5. _____

6. _____

7. _____

8. _____

_____

*The eight principles were originally described in *Breaking Down Walls,* by Raleigh Washington and Glen Kehrein. We have revised, refined, and updated them for this course.

1. CALL: We're all called to a ministry of reconciliation, and we're all commanded to be reconciled with our brothers across racial, cultural, and denominational barriers.

2. COMMITMENT TO RELATIONSHIP: Loved by God and adopted into His family, we're called to committed love relationships with our brothers.

3. INTENTIONALITY: Experiencing a committed relationship with our brothers requires purposeful, positive, and planned activities that facilitate reconciliation and right relationships.

4. SINCERITY: We must be willing to be vulnerable and express our feelings, attitudes, differences, and perceptions, with the goal of resolution and building trust.

5. SENSITIVITY: We must seek knowledge about our brothers in order to relate empathetically to people from different denominations, traditions, races, social standings, or cultures.

6. SACRIFICE: We must be willing to give up an established status or position and accept a lesser position in order to facilitate reconciling relationships.

7. EMPOWERMENT: Through prayer, personal brokenness, repentance, and forgiveness, we remove barriers and are freed to experience the power of the Holy Spirit in reconciling relationships.

8. INTERDEPENDENCE: As we recognize our differences, we also realize that God has placed us as members in the body of Christ where we need and depend on the contributions of each member.

➡ **What, if anything, do you sense God has said to you through today's lesson? Write *one* of the most meaningful things He has said below.**

_____

_____

➡ **Conclude today's lesson by praying for the coming weeks of this study:**
- Ask the Lord to reveal His will for unity in the body of Christ.
- Ask the Lord to conform you to the image of His Son, Jesus, so you will live like Him in relationships with other believers.
- Pray for your small group. Ask the Lord to allow you to experience genuine reconciliation and unity with other believers.
- Ask the Lord to reveal ways you can apply the principles of reconciliation and unity in a way that will bring glory to Him through a healthy body of Christ.

LESSON 3 JESUS PRAYED FOR UNITY

Scripture for Meditation
"How good and pleasant it is when brothers live together in unity!" (Psalm 133:1).

A Beginning Prayer
Father, if Jesus cared about and prayed for unity, I do, too. But I confess that I don't know what it would look like in my world. I don't know how it could ever come to pass. But I believe You alone have the answers. I ask You to begin today to show me how I can experience the unity Jesus prayed for. Amen.

➥ **Read and think about the Scripture for Meditation in the left margin, and begin the lesson with prayer.**

❖ ❖ ❖

On the night before going to the cross, Jesus ate a meal and spent time talking with His disciples. Just before going to the Garden of Gethsemane (where He would be arrested), He prayed for His disciples. He also prayed for us. This was a significant prayer.

➥ **1. Read the first part of Jesus' prayer in John 17:6–19. As you read, underline the things Jesus said He had done during His ministry with the disciples. We have underlined one for you.**

John 17:6–19

6 "*I have revealed you to those whom you gave me out of the world. They were yours; you gave them to me and they have obeyed your word. 7Now they know that everything you have given me comes from you. 8For I gave them the words you gave me and they accepted them. They knew with certainty that I came from you, and they believed that you sent me. 9I pray for them. I am not praying for the world, but for those you have given me, for they are yours. 10All I have is yours, and all you have is mine. And glory has come to me through them. 11I will remain in the world no longer, but they are still in the world, and I am coming to you. Holy Father, protect them by the power of your name—the name you gave me—so that they may be one as we are one. 12While I was with them, I protected them and kept them safe by that name you gave me. None has been lost except the one doomed to destruction so that Scripture would be fulfilled.*

13 "*I am coming to you now, but I say these things while I am still in the world, so that they may have the full measure of my joy within them. 14I have given them your word and the world has hated them, for they are not of the world any more than I am of the world. 15My prayer is not that you take them out of the world but that you protect them from the evil one. 16They are not of the world, even as I am not of it. 17Sanctify them by the truth; your word is truth. 18As you sent me into the world, I have sent them into the world. 19For them I sanctify myself, that they too may be truly sanctified.*"

➥ **Now answer the following questions based on the passage above.**

➥ **2. How did the disciples respond to:**

• God's Word? (v. 6) _____

• Christ's words? (v. 8) _____

➥ **3. Through whom did Jesus receive glory?** (v. 10) _____

➥ **4. What three things did Jesus ask the Father to do for the disciples?**

(v. 11) _____

(v. 15) _____

(v. 17) _____

Did you underline the things Jesus did? If so, you found that:
- Jesus revealed the Father to them (v. 6).
- Jesus gave them the words the Father gave Him (vv. 8, 14).
- Jesus protected the disciples and kept them safe (v. 12).
- Jesus sent the disciples into the world (v. 18).
- Jesus sanctified (separated from evil things and evil ways) Himself so the disciples might be truly sanctified (v. 19).

In His prayer, Jesus also described some of the disciples' responses:
- They obeyed God's word (v. 6).
- They accepted Christ's words (v. 8).
- They knew with certainty that Jesus came from the Father, and they believed God sent Him (v. 8).
- They brought glory to Jesus (v. 10).

Jesus asked the Father to do three things for the disciples:
1. Protect them—so they might be one as Jesus and the Father are one (v. 11).
2. Protect them from the evil one (v. 15).
3. Sanctify them by the truth (God's Word) (v. 17).

Jesus also said something that may have shocked you. He said, *"I pray for them. I am not praying for the world, but for those you have given me, for they are yours"* (John 17:9). Jesus said He was *not* praying for the lost world but for His disciples.

➡ **5. In your opinion, why did Jesus pray for His disciples and not for the lost world? Check your response or write your own.**
- ❑ a. Jesus didn't care about the lost world. He loved His disciples.
- ❑ b. Jesus didn't have any hope for the lost world.
- ❑ c. Jesus knew the Father would use godly men to draw a lost world to salvation through Christ.

❑ d. Other: _____

_____

John 17:20–26

20 "My prayer is not for them alone. I pray also for those who will believe in me through their message, 21that all of them may be one, Father, just as you are in me and I am in you. May they also be in us so that the world may believe that you have sent me. 22I have given them the glory that you gave me, that they may be one as we are one: 23I in them and you in me. May they be brought to complete unity to let the world know that you sent me and have loved them even as you have loved me.

24 "Father, I want those you have given me to be with me where I am, and to see my glory, the glory you have given me because you loved me before the creation of the world. 25 "Righteous Father, though the world does not know you, I know you, and they know that you have sent me. 26I have made you known to them, and will continue to make you known in order that the love you have for me may be in them and that I myself may be in them."

Jesus knew that the quality of the disciples' lives would deeply affect the lost world. He wanted the disciples to be filled with His joy (v. 13). He also wanted them to be protected from evil and the evil one. He wanted them to live holy and godly lives separated from the evil things and ways of the world. He wanted them to withstand the pressures when the world hated them for being Christlike. In the remainder of Jesus' prayer, we'll see more clearly why the godly lives of the disciples would be so important to God's plan for redemption. In the following verses, you'll notice that Jesus prayed for us—the ones who have believed because of the message of those first disciples.

➡ **6. As you read the remainder of Jesus' prayer in the margin (John 17:20–26), underline the things Jesus wanted to be true of His disciples. We've underlined one for you.**

Jesus prayed for us. He prayed for all His followers from the original twelve to the end of the world. Here is what Jesus wanted to be true of His disciples (followers):
- Jesus wanted all His disciples to be one, just as He and the Father are one (v. 21).
- Jesus wanted them to be in the Father and in Christ so that the world would believe the Father sent Christ (v. 21).
- Jesus wanted them to be brought to complete unity to let the world know that the Father sent Christ and loves the disciples as He has loved Christ (v. 23).

• Jesus wanted the disciples to be with Him and see His heavenly glory (v. 24).

The reason Jesus prayed for His disciples and not for the lost world is this: The future of His redemptive work depended on the disciples' revealing Him as God's Son to the lost world. Christ's glory (v. 22) and love (v. 26) would be in them. Christ Himself would be in them (v. 26). If the disciples were the people God created them to be, the lost world would come to know Christ as God's Son. God would use their *"sanctified"* lives to reveal Christ and draw the lost to saving faith in Him.

If the disciples were the people God created them to be, the lost world would come to know Christ as God's Son.

➥ **7. Based on this prayer of Jesus, how important is it for the followers of Christ to be one and in complete unity? Check your response or write your own.**
   ❑ a. Unity is of great importance. Revealing Christ to be God's Son to a lost world depends on our spirit of oneness in Christ.
   ❑ b. Unity is fairly important, but it's optional. Christian unity is not the key to people coming to know Jesus.
   ❑ c. Unity is not important. What people believe about Jesus doesn't depend on whether Christians can get along with each other.

   ❑ d. Other: _____

   _____

Jesus clearly identified unity among His disciples as a critical factor in the lost world's coming to understand that He was God's Son.

Whatever your opinion, Jesus knew unity was of great importance. It was the dominant theme of this prayer He prayed just before going to the cross. He clearly identified unity among His disciples as a critical factor in the lost world's coming to understand that He was God's Son.

➥ **What, if anything, do you sense God has said to you through today's lesson? Write *one* of the most meaningful things He has said below.**

   _____

   _____

➥ **Conclude today's lesson by joining Jesus in His prayer for unity.**
   • Ask the Father to protect you from evil and the evil one.
   • Ask Him to make you holy, Christlike, and sanctified (separated) for His service.
   • Ask the Father to bring the Christians in your church; denomination, association, or tradition; city; nation; and the world to the spirit of complete unity for which Jesus prayed in John 17.
   • Ask Him to begin revealing to you what you need to do to experience that spirit of unity in all your Christian relationships.

LESSON 4 THE BASIS OF OUR UNITY

Scripture for Meditation
"There is neither Jew nor Greek, slave nor free, male nor female, for you are all one in Christ Jesus" (Galatians 3:28).

A Beginning Prayer
Father, being one in Christ Jesus is a wonderful thought. I believe I have lived below the reality of that statement. Please help me understand the basis of the unity You want us to have. Where does it come from? What must I do to begin experiencing this unity with brothers in Christ from other races, ethnic groups, or denominations? Amen.

➡ **Read and think about the Scripture for Meditation in the left margin, and begin the lesson with prayer.**

❖ ❖ ❖

A church seemed to be divided on every major vote taken by the church body. The deacons decided something must be done to restore unity. Someone suggested that the lack of unity was due to having two worship services on Sunday morning. "If everyone worshiped in one service," they argued, "we would function more like a single unit." So the deacons recommended dropping the early service. In the church conference, however, the senior adults were angry because the rest of the church was taking away "their" service. This human attempt to create unity resulted in creating even greater division. Unity is not something that can be achieved by a vote or other human endeavor alone.

When Jesus prayed that we be brought to complete unity, He also revealed the *basis* of that unity. Knowing that will help us understand right ways of seeking and maintaining the unity of which He speaks.

➡ **1. Where do you think most people in your church would look to attain unity? Check your opinion.**
❑ a. The denominational headquarters would send down the order.
❑ b. The pastor and deacons or elders would order it.
❑ c. We would work until everyone believed the same doctrines.
❑ d. The congregation would vote and expect everyone to get in line with the decision.
❑ e. We would find it in our common relationship to Christ and by living in a Christlike relationship to God and each other.

Let's look again at Jesus' prayer to see where the unity would come from. Some would suggest that common beliefs or doctrines provide the source of our unity. Jesus said something about that: *"I gave them the words you gave me and they accepted them. They knew with certainty that I came from you, and they believed that you sent me"* (John 17:8). *"I have given them your word"* (John 17:14). His disciples did have a common belief that He was the divine Son of God. That was important because it led to a right relationship with Christ. James, however, wrote, *"You believe that there is one God. Good! Even the demons believe that"* (James 2:19). Common beliefs alone—even the belief that Jesus is the Son of God—do not produce the unity that Jesus prayed for. Let's look a little deeper.

➡ **Read the Scriptures in the margin, and answer the questions related to each.**

➡ **2. (John 17:11–12) What did Jesus do while He was with the disciples?**

_____

➡ **3. What did Jesus ask the Father to do "so that they may be one"?**

_____

John 17:11–12
"Holy Father, protect them by the power of your name . . . so that they may be one as we are one. While I was with them, I protected them and kept them safe."

John 17:20–23
"I pray . . . that all of them may be one, Father, just as you are in me and I am in you. May they also be in us so that the world may believe that you have sent me. I have given them the glory that you gave me, that they may be one as we are one: I in them and you in me. May they be brought to complete unity."

➡ **4. Based on John 17:20–23, which of the following statements most clearly describes the basis of our unity? Check one.**
❑ a. Our unity comes by belonging to the same church structure with common church practices and a common creed (statement of beliefs).

❑ b. Our unity comes through a common relationship to God through Christ. When we are in Christ and Christ is in us, we can experience unity together.
❑ c. Our unity comes by common agreement, even if we have to agree to disagree.

In John 17:11, Jesus asked the Father to protect the disciples so they would be one. Then Jesus said He had protected them while He was with them. Now that He was returning to heaven, Jesus asked the Father to protect them.

In verses 20–23, Jesus prayed that we would be in Him and He would be in us so that we could experience the same kind of unity He shares with the Father—they are One. God reveals Himself in diversity as Father, Son, and Holy Spirit. Yet He is One God. The Trinity exists in perfect unity. Christ prayed that His followers would be one just as God is One. Our unity comes through our common relationship to God through Christ.

Our unity comes through our common relationship to God through Christ.

A Relationship to Jesus Christ
Seventy thousand men gather in a football stadium for a Promise Keepers conference:
- red, yellow, black, brown, and white men;
- African Methodist Episcopal, Assemblies of God, Baptist, Brethren, Catholic, Church of Christ, Church of God in Christ, Episcopalian, Evangelical Free, Pentecostal, and Presbyterian men;
- men of all kinds of ethnicity and denominational heritage.

They've come together because they have a common Savior. These men want to be faithful to their Lord, and they've come for help and encouragement. The singing of praise and worship begins, and they realize, *We're worshiping the same Lord.* They meet in a huddle to pray and realize they have many of the same struggles as Christians. They talk together and realize, *These guys really do know my Lord, and they love Him, too!* In the middle of great diversity, these men experience a taste of Christian unity, because the Lord is present to bind their hearts together in Christian love.

➡ **5. In your own words, write a statement that describes the basis for our unity as Christian brothers.**

_____

_____

The Holy Spirit of Christ who dwells in believers produces a unity that can't be produced by any human effort.

The Holy Spirit of Christ who dwells in believers produces a unity that can't be produced by any human effort. We are one *in Christ.* We'll see in future lessons that our job is to keep or maintain the unity that the Spirit produces (Ephesians 4:3). Our right relationship to Christ is the foundation for right relationships with other Christians.

➡ **What, if anything, do you sense God has said to you through today's lesson? Write *one* of the most meaningful things He has said below.**

_____

_____

Ephesians 4:3
"Make every effort to keep the unity of the Spirit through the bond of peace."

➡ **Conclude today's lesson by praying.**
- Thank the Lord for providing for your salvation.
- Thank the Father for sending the Holy Spirit to live in you.
- Pray for the small group with whom you're going to be studying.
- Ask the Lord to allow you to experience the unity the Spirit produces as you build relationships with these other men.

LESSON 5   BARRIERS TO UNITY

Scripture for Meditation

"Once you were alienated from God and were enemies in your minds because of your evil behavior. But now he has reconciled you by Christ's physical body through death to present you holy in his sight, without blemish and free from accusation" (Colossians 1:21–22).

A Beginning Prayer

Father, how can I begin to thank You for sending Christ to pay my sin debt? I cannot. You sought me and brought me into a right relationship with Yourself. I praise and thank You for what You have done through Christ. Please reveal to me anything in my current attitudes or actions that is displeasing to you. I want to get those things right as well. Amen.

P = Pleased

S = Satisfied

N = Neutral/Doesn't Care

D = Dissatisfied

B = Brokenhearted

A = Angry

➡ **Read and think about the Scripture for Meditation in the left margin, and begin the lesson with prayer.**

❖ ❖ ❖

You've been studying about God's desire for unity among His people. Do you see that kind of unity among God's people you know?

➡ **1. Think about the unity and oneness you see between followers of Christ today. How would you evaluate the quality of that unity in the following areas? Write a letter from the list below beside each of the categories that follow.**

A. Very united; one in heart, mind, and spirit.
B. Unity is growing; signs of cooperation and fellowship are improving.
C. Little unity; a few encouraging signs can be seen, but differences and disagreements are far more visible.
D. Very divided; can't get along; disagree and even fight each other.

____ Your local church
____ Your denomination, church tradition, or association of churches
____ Christian churches in your town or city
____ Christian churches in your nation
____ Christian churches worldwide

➡ **2. If Jesus is praying for our unity in the body of Christ, how do you think He feels about the following? Write a letter from the list in the margin beside each item below based on what you think Jesus feels.**

____ a. A church splits because members can't agree.
____ b. Churches publicly criticize each other in the news media.
____ c. Churches display envy and jealousy as they compete for members.
____ d. A denomination judges other Christian believers as being less spiritual or even lost.
____ e. A Christian leader constantly puts down and criticizes as wrong most other Christian leaders and groups.
____ f. A church denies membership to a person because of his skin color or economic status.
____ g. Christians from one ethnic group refuse to have any dealings with other Christians who are different.
____ h. A Christian couple divorces.
____ i. Christians or Christian organizations file lawsuits against each other and take each other to court.
____ j. Sunday morning in churches is probably the most segregated time of the week.

A person could understand if these kinds of things happened between non-Christians. That's just the way our sinful world is. But when Christ takes up residence in a person and makes him or her a new creature, everything should be different.

When Christians can't get along with each other, Jesus is grieved and brokenhearted. At times His righteous anger may be expressed, but because of His love His response will more likely be weeping over the brokenness. He died on a cruel cross to make our unity possible. He wants us to experience the mutual love and

> When Christians can't get along with each other, Jesus is grieved and brokenhearted.

unity that He died to provide. Members in the body of Christ need to please God by living out their faith in a right relationship with each other. We need to be reconciled with each other. We need to display unity to a watching world.

Sin Creates Barriers

Sin not only separates us from God, but it can also separate us from brothers and sisters in Christ. When we sin against another person, we can create a barrier that keeps us from a right relationship with him or her. The following list includes some of the ways we may sin and build a barrier between ourselves and other believers.

➡ **3. Read the following list of sins. Underline those you believe are major causes of division and broken relationships between Christians.**

• anger	• anxiety	• arguing	• arrogance
• bitterness	• blasphemy	• boasting	• competition
• complaining	• conceit	• coarse talking	• covetousness
• critical spirit	• cursing	• deception	• unforgiveness
• discord	• disorder	• divisiveness	• envy
• factions	• faultfinding	• fear	• fits of rage
• gossip	• greed	• grumbling	• hatred
• hypocrisy	• impatience	• impurity	• independence
• injustice	• insensitivity	• jealousy	• lack of love
• lies	• malice	• oppression	• persecution
• prejudice	• pride	• quarreling	• resentment
• revenge	• rudeness	• slander	• stereotyping
• strife	• unbelief	• self-seeking	• acts of violence

• intolerance of differences	• judgmental spirit
• keeping a record of wrongs	• lawsuits among believers
• party spirit (factions)	• protecting "turf"
• provoking one another	• self-centeredness
• self-righteousness	• a controling spirit
• selfish ambition	• struggle for control
• spirit of superiority	• delighting in downfall of a brother

➡ **4. Now look back over the ones you underlined. Which do you think are the top three causes of broken relationships in the Christian community? In the left margin, write your top three on the lines provided.**

Fruit Sins and Root Sins

Suppose you planted a fruit tree in your backyard. As that tree grew and matured, you would expect it to bear fruit for you to eat. Though the Bible does not describe them as such, two types of sins may be evidenced in our lives. One is fruit sin and the other is root sin. When root sins mature, they produce fruit sins. Many of the sins in the list above are fruit sins. We may choose to act like that because of a more serious root sin our lives.

A fruit sin is one that shows. It's evident in our actions and words. A root sin is one that may be hidden deep in our minds or hearts. Let's take a look at three root sins.

➡ **3. Read Jude 5–7 in the left margin. It gives three examples of sins that are serious in God's sight. Write the sin described beside the group who sinned.**

A. The people God delivered out of Egypt: _____

B. The angels of darkness: _____

C. The people of Sodom and Gomorrah: _____

My List of Top Three Causes

1. _____

2. _____

3. _____

Jude 5–7

"Though you already know all this, I want to remind you that the Lord delivered his people out of Egypt, but later destroyed those who did not believe. And the angels who did not keep their positions of authority but abandoned their own home—these he has kept in darkness, bound with everlasting chains for judgment on the great Day. In a similar way, Sodom and Gomorrah and the surrounding towns gave themselves up to sexual immorality and perversion. They serve as an example of those who suffer the punishment of eternal fire."

God delivered the people of Israel out of Egypt. But they didn't trust Him when He commanded them to enter the promised land. They sinned in their *unbelief*. The angels were given assignments (positions or places of authority). Instead of doing what God assigned them, they *rebelled* and did what they wanted to do. Sodom and Gomorrah were guilty of sexual immorality and the perversion of homosexuality (see Genesis 19:1–28). The Bible, however, tells us there is a root sin behind their sexual sin.

➡ **4. Read Ezekiel 16:49–50 in the left margin. What seems to be the root sin of Sodom's *"detestable things"*?**

_____

The people of Sodom were arrogant and self-centered. They overfed themselves and weren't concerned about others. They took care of themselves but not the poor and needy. They were haughty and did detestable things before God. The root sin of Sodom was their *pride*—their arrogance.

Pride produces all kinds of fruit sins. In Jude, we see some of them described: *"reject authority and slander celestial beings"* (v. 8), *"speak abusively against whatever they do not understand"* (v. 10), *"shepherds who feed only themselves"* (v. 12), *"harsh words"* (v. 15), *"grumblers and faultfinders"* (v. 16), *"they boast about themselves and flatter others for their own advantage"* (v. 16), *"scoffers"* (v. 18), and *"These are the men who divide you, who follow mere natural instincts and do not have the Spirit"* (v. 19).

Racism and Sectarianism Are Fruit Sins
Though we may describe these two sins differently, racism and sectarianism—the two giants—are fruit sins. We bear fruit sin when we:
• treat others as inferior while we act superior
• judge others with a higher standard than we use to judge ourselves
• use our tongues to slander, demean, lie about, criticize, or put down others
• show insensitivity toward others' feelings and needs
• reject brothers Christ has accepted
• demonstrate jealousy, envy, or selfish competition
• express hatred or desire for revenge

Many of these sins may be born in pride: *"Do not think of yourself more highly than you ought"* (Romans 12:3). Pride is a root sin of racism and sectarianism.
➡ **Read the two Scriptures on pride in the margin.**
❖ ❖ ❖
➡ **5. Ask the Lord if pride causes you to treat others in wrong ways. Ask Him if some of the sins in your life grow out of a root sin of pride.**
❖ ❖ ❖
➡ **6. Which of the following do you think best describes the sin of pride in your life? Check your opinion.**
❑ a. I have a regular battle with pride, but God gives me grace to keep it under control.
❑ b. I'm proud and proud of it! Humility and a lowly spirit are not traits I want. I don't care what God has to say about it.
❑ c. I do have a root sin of pride in my life, and I sin too often because of it. I often mistreat others in words and actions because of my pride.
❑ d. I don't believe pride is one of my problems.

If you realize that pride is a problem and it's yielding fruit sin in your life, now is the time to break down this wall. *"He who conceals his sins does not prosper, but whoever confesses and renounces them finds mercy"* (Proverbs 28:13).
➡ **7. Humble yourself before the Lord and confess any pride or other sin**

Ezekiel 16:49–50
"'Now this was the sin of your sister Sodom: She and her daughters were arrogant, overfed and unconcerned; they did not help the poor and needy. They were haughty and did detestable things before me. Therefore I did away with them as you have seen.'"

Root Sins
unbelief
rebellion
pride

Pride is a root sin of racism and sectarianism.

Pride
"Pride goes before destruction, a haughty spirit before a fall. Better to be lowly in spirit and among the oppressed than to share plunder with the proud" (Proverbs 16:18–19).

"All of you, clothe yourselves with humility toward one another, because, 'God opposes the proud but gives grace to the humble.' Humble yourselves, therefore, under God's mighty hand, that he may lift you up in due time. Cast all your anxiety on him because he cares for you" (1 Peter 5:5–7).

that may separate you from Him or His people. Ask Him for mercy and forgiveness. Ask Him to help you develop a spirit of humility.

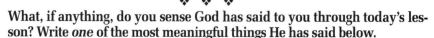

➡ What, if anything, do you sense God has said to you through today's lesson? Write *one* of the most meaningful things He has said below.

_____

_____

➡ For each lesson this week, you've been recording what you sense God has said to you. Review the final activity for each of the previous lessons on pages 20, 23, 26, and 28. What is the major emphasis of what you sense God wants you to do in response to this unit's lessons? Pray and ask Him what He wants you to do. Then write notes below, in the margin, or in a separate notebook. You might use these questions in your prayer:

1. What do You want me to do in my personal relationship to You?
2. What do You want me to do in relationship to other people in my church or denomination?
3. What do You want me to do in relationship to Christians in other denominations or Christian traditions?
4. What do You want me to do in relationship to Christians of other races or ethnic backgrounds?

_____

_____

_____

➡ **Conclude today's lesson by praying.**
- Ask the Lord to give you the courage to experience the broader dimensions of what it means to be His people.
- Thank Him for the people from other Christian denominations or traditions or other ethnic groups who have been a spiritual blessing to your life.
- Ask Him to guide you to relationships with other members of your spiritual family who will bless you and to whom you can be a blessing.
- Pray for your upcoming small-group session.

UNIT 2 — A HEALTHY BODY OF CHRIST

Scripture Memory Verse

"He himself is our peace, who has made the two one and has destroyed the barrier, the dividing wall of hostility."

—Ephesians 2:14

The Body of Christ

GOD'S TROPHY

Unit Learning Goal

You will understand the kind of relationships God wants you to experience in the body of Christ, and you will adjust your life to His in order to experience health in the body through unity and reconciliation.

Overview of Unit 2

Lesson 1: Jesus Provided for Unity
Lesson 2: Three Illustrations of Unity
Lesson 3: The Body of Christ
Lesson 4: No Divisions Among You
Lesson 5: Becoming Christlike in the Body

Key Summary Statements from Unit 2

- Neither Jews nor Gentiles brought down the dividing wall—Christ did it!
- When they were reconciled to God, they were also reconciled to each other.
- Christ has already provided for our unity. Our problem is that we're not living in the reality of what He has provided.
- We're never commanded to produce unity. . . . We are to keep or maintain the unity the Spirit has produced.
- If you have erected "walls" through your own actions, you bring pain to the body of Christ.
- The things we have in common (like the Spirit of Christ) are far greater and more important than the things on which we differ.
- Our oneness in God's family is because we all have the same heavenly Father, and He has placed the Spirit of His Son in each of us. We share a family resemblance.
- Our experiences together with Christians who are different can enrich our lives and widen our experience of God's grace in Christ.
- The greatest display of God's glory comes when He brings together those of great diversity and causes them to function in unity.
- Only one opinion is important, and that is God's.
- Every member of the body needs all the other members.
- God wants the church to be a trophy for Christ. He wants to be able to point to the unity and love in a very diverse church, and say, "That's what I can do through My Son, Jesus Christ."
- Renewed people of God will rebuild old ruins, restore places that are devastated, and renew ruined cities. They will display God's splendor to a watching world.
- Christians, churches, and denominations that are willing to give themselves away in ministry for God's kingdom will experience a fullness of life that the Lord gives to those who place His interests over their own.

FROM HATRED TO INTERDEPENDENCE

by H. C. Warfield as told to Glen Kehrein

I grew up believing there were two gods—one for black people and one for white people. I don't mean this figuratively; I mean it literally. I learned about the God of black people from my grandfather, who was a loving man. He taught me that God was love. Even though white people didn't like us much, treated us mean, abused us, and might even kill us if they wanted, God taught us to love and forgive. While I loved my grandfather, sometimes his God didn't make sense.

Even so, I thought the black folks' God was better than the white folks' God. The plantation owner, his overseer, and all the other white folks in our town worshiped a different God. I figured that because they all went to church every Sunday. Many were church leaders. But they never showed any love that I could see. Instead they seemed to like to inflict pain. So it seemed to me that one God taught love and the other hate. As incredible as it seems, I would be forty-three years old before I realized there was only one God, and it was His children who didn't do right.

Even though Mississippi was home to racial oppression in the 1950s and '60s, I hardly saw it as a child. Segregation was a way of life. Black folks were poor and picked cotton. They ran the cotton gin and made five dollars a day. And that's the way it was. My first realization of strong racism came when I was fifteen years old. Up until then, my good friend was a white boy I would play with every day. He was the son of the family my grandma cooked and cleaned for. Being the same age, it was quite natural. One day, however, I was told we could never play together again, and we never did. In fact, I never saw him again. My grandma never explained why. It just was the way it was.

At sixteen, I left home to join the Job Corps, a federal program that offered skills training. For the first time in my life, I found myself outside Mississippi. I discovered a new world in Washington state. It was a world where I wasn't called a nigger and people addressed me like an equal. For the first time, I was treated like a human being. I hadn't recognized oppression until I experienced freedom. It was something! But it didn't last. I returned to Mississippi as a certified welder, but I couldn't find a job. Good-paying jobs like welding (which paid five dollars an hour, not a day) were not for black folks. At age 19, I decided I wasn't going to be put down anymore. I kept after "the man" until I got one of those jobs. I learned that the good money I earned wasn't enough. I was despised and given the worst jobs. My white bosses resented me and weren't afraid to show it. I began to get angry, and hatred grew in my heart. Because I "had a chip on my shoulder" and wasn't afraid to stand up for myself, my family was afraid for my life. While not afraid, I was growing bitter and angry. I returned to the cotton fields.

I now realized I was protected as a child from the horrors and realities of racist Mississippi by adults who knew that little could be done about it. Then as a young adult, I began to hear the stories—like the story of the black guy who did the wrong thing and was tied behind

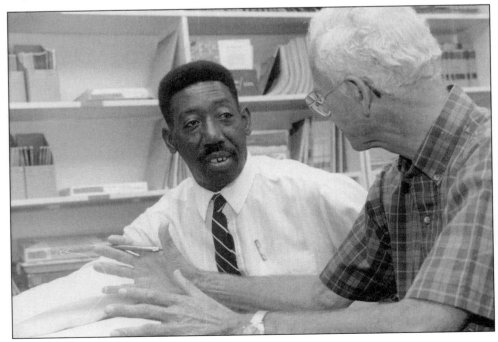

a pickup truck and dragged through town. Meaning to teach a lesson, the "good old boys" made a point to drive to the local plantation store, where it was payday and black folks were picking up their checks. The odds were three hundred black people to four white people, but not one person rose to that poor man's rescue. That's how stomped down we were. When I heard about that, it tore me up inside, and my hatred blossomed. I flat-out hated white people.

The plantation overseer was a God-fearing churchgoer on Sunday. On Monday he cursed, abused, and called us all manner of foul-mouthed names. His greatest fun was to sneak up on a worker who was relieving himself and kick him with his steel-pointed cowboy boots, then howl with laughter. I despised him. Why did we have to take that? Anger was seeping down into my soul, and I wasn't hiding it. When hate gets a hold on you, it seems you get blind to everything else. I developed a reputation as a troublemaker. Once I got in trouble for trying to organize a union. Other times I confronted white boys who thought they could do anything to any black person they happened upon. It was such an incident that drove me from Mississippi.

One day outside a nightclub, a car full of white boys decided to humiliate an older black man. I was inside the club. I got into a minor skirmish that ended with me getting in a few good punches that put the white boys on the run. The next day, the sheriff came looking for me, but there was no way I would let him find me. The day after, a mob came. Hiding in a grain hopper, I could hear the threats of the lynch mob just a few feet away. The men cursed and bragged about what they were going to do to me when they found me. If they had brought their dogs, I would have been discovered for sure. But they hadn't, and they eventually gave up and left for the time being. My family knew a trip north was the only thing that would save my life.

While Chicago provided well-paying jobs, its racial climate was not a lot better. My bitterness grew when I worked in the city's famous stockyards in a racist neighborhood. Friends warned me that to stay there past dark might cost a black man his life. One family in the community said it all by hanging a dummy of a black man from their rear porch. The message was clear: "You might work here, but don't stay here." I learned that North or South, the white folks were all the same, and I hated every one. But somewhere far away, I could hear my grandfather's voice saying, "Don't be like that. God loves you." At the time, however, it was too faint.

Alcohol provided my escape. I could drown myself from reality, but each morning I awoke to the same world. Alcohol took me away, but it left me on a downer when I returned. Marijuana gave me a lift, only to let me down, too. I drank every day to cope. It wasn't until I discovered the drug subculture and hippies that I interacted with whites as peers. We were all hooked on the same escape, I guess.

Finally, it was crack cocaine that removed any of my remaining dignity. Though I got drunk every night, I could still function. I always worked and had even run a little business. But crack took it all. Wasted by alcohol and drugs, I lost my children, my home, and my business. My life was a pitiful existence. Eventually I felt only anger, bitterness, and hatred. I was a powder keg ready to explode. I carried hate in my heart and a gun in my pocket. Yet God kept me from ever killing a white guy in spite of every desire I had to do just that.

Hunger brought me to God. I had gone to churches all over Chicago for food, but it wasn't until I came to the food pantry of Circle Urban Ministries on the West Side that I was filled. While waiting for a bag of groceries, I heard the gospel. Those were the words of my grandfather from forty years before. Now his voice grew stronger.

Circle Urban Ministries and Rock Church were holding week-long revival meetings called Harvestfest. I couldn't have cared less what they called it, but I knew they served meals, so I went. There was one problem. Though Circle was in the middle of the black community, there were white people there. I keep thinking, *You know how you feel about white folks.* But my hunger overcame my hatred, and I returned. Again I heard the gospel, and this time I responded. My heart was completely broken by God's love. On top of that, a white guy from Hershey, Pennsylvania, stepped up and counseled me. God's love overcame my hatred as Bruce talked with me. That was the beginning of a new life. It was also then that I realized there is only one God, and that we're all His children. God also knew that to heal my heart, He needed to put me in a church that was committed to racial reconciliation. At Rock and Circle, I found black and white folks loving each other and serving God. But it was my relationship with Bruce that made it real. For four years and in spite of hundreds of miles that separate us, our friendship has grown.

Through the relationship with Bruce, and with the many other white men around the ministry, God has healed me. Accepting Christ brought a power into my life. I realized I am not controlled by my feelings or my circumstances. Today, I'm controlled by the Holy Spirit—the Spirit of the one and only God. Bruce and I have been through a lot. A couple of years after God moved in my heart and taught me about love, Bruce's life fell apart when his wife left him. I found myself reaching out to him and telling him that God could give him the strength to overcome his bitterness and anger. We walked through that time together. Today we're both wounded and healed ambassadors of reconciliation.

Five years ago, I was totally consumed by hatred of white people. I felt justified because of what I had experienced. Today I can honestly say that God has taken away that hatred and given me love. I can't really explain it better than that. It's a miracle. I would even like to go back and ask to be forgiven for hating those men down in Mississippi. God supplies the power to do just that.

LESSON 1 JESUS PROVIDED FOR UNITY

Scriptures for Meditation

"He himself is our peace, who has made the two one and has destroyed the barrier, the dividing wall of hostility" (Ephesians 2:14).

"[Caiaphas] did not say this on his own, but as high priest that year he prophesied that Jesus would die for the Jewish nation, and not only for that nation but also for the scattered children of God, to bring them together and make them one" (John 11:51–52).

A Beginning Prayer

Father, through Your Son, Jesus, and the working of the Holy Spirit, You have provided a way for me to experience unity with my brothers in Christ. I realize the absence of unity in the Christian community is an evidence of sin. I pray You will reveal how we can experience and maintain the unity You have already provided. Amen.

Ephesians 2:11–13

"Formerly you who are Gentiles by birth . . . remember that at that time you were <u>*separate from Christ,*</u> *excluded from citizenship in Israel and foreigners to the covenants of the promise, without hope and without God in the world. But now in Christ Jesus you who once were far away have been brought near through the blood of Christ."*

Neither Jews nor Gentiles brought down the dividing wall; Christ did it!

➡ Read and think about the Scriptures for Meditation in the left margin. Notice the relationship to Christ that brings us together. Ephesians 2:14 is your Scripture memory verse for this unit. Remove the perforated card for unit 2 from the back of your book and begin memorizing it. Then start the lesson with prayer.

❖   ❖   ❖

Our lack of unity in the body of Christ is an evidence of sin. When we cause factions in the body, we're sinning against the Lord. When we resurrect the hostility between races, denominations, or Christian traditions, we're sinning against the Lord and His body. This is not the way Christians are supposed to relate to each other.

The Dividing Wall Between Jew and Gentile Came Down

In the first century, the greatest wall of division for God's people was between Jews and Gentiles (all non-Jews). This was a racial barrier, a social barrier, a cultural barrier, and a religious barrier. As the church spread across those barriers, believers debated about what was happening. Some thought Gentiles could not become Christians without first becoming Jews. Others wanted to keep the walls up. But God had a different plan.

➡ **1. Read Ephesians 2:11–13 in the margin below, and underline words or phrases that describe what the Gentiles were before coming to salvation by faith in Christ. We have underlined one for you.**

The Gentiles were separated, excluded, and aliens without hope and without God. Some Jews had plans to keep it that way. But Jesus Christ did something for Jews and Gentiles alike that they couldn't do for themselves. He brought them near by His blood.

➡ **Read the following passage to see what Christ did to this dividing wall.**

14For he [Jesus Christ] himself is our peace, who has made the two one and has destroyed the barrier, the dividing wall of hostility, 15by abolishing in his flesh the law with its commandments and regulations. His purpose was to create in himself one new man out of the two, thus making peace, 16and in this one body to reconcile both of them to God through the cross, by which he put to death their hostility. 17He came and preached peace to you who were far away and peace to those who were near. 18For through him we both have access to the Father by one Spirit (Ephesians 2:14–18).

➡ **Based on this Scripture, mark the following T for true or F for false.**

_____ 1. The Jews destroyed the barrier, the dividing wall of hostility.
_____ 2. Jesus' purpose was to create one new man and make peace in His body.
_____ 3. Gentiles had to become Jews before they could come near.
_____ 4. Jews and Gentiles became one when they were both reconciled to God.
_____ 5. Christ put to death the hostility between these two groups.
_____ 6. Both Jews and Gentiles have access to God the Father by one Spirit.

Neither Jews nor Gentiles brought down the dividing wall—Christ did it! He did something they couldn't. It was an impossible task for man, but not

When they were reconciled to God, they also were reconciled to each other.

for God. He put their hostility to death. He brought together people who were very different, and He gave them equal standing as one new man. When they were reconciled to God, they both became part of this new body of Christ. When they were reconciled to God, they also were reconciled to each other. Because of Christ, they both had access to God. (Answers: True=2, 4, 5, 6; False=1, 3) Do you realize this is God's peace plan for the Middle East and any other place where conflict exists? Without Christ, there can be no lasting peace. In Christ, hostility can be put to death, and different people can become one new man in Christ.

As you think about the divisions present in the body of Christ today, you may get discouraged and think change is impossible. But what is impossible with man is possible with God. Trust Him to do what Jesus is already praying for Him to do. The truth is that Christ has already provided for our unity. Our problem is that we're not living in that reality.

Christ has already provided for our unity. Our problem is that we're not living in the reality of what He has provided.

Maintaining the Unity of the Spirit

No divisions between people today are any greater than the one between Jew and Gentile in the first century. Christ has already done the work of removing the dividing walls of hostility between us. Unity is not something we must create; Christ has already provided for it. Jesus prayed for our unity in John 17 *before* He went to the cross. On the cross, He finished the work that brought down the walls. That's why we're never commanded to *produce* unity. Paul said we're to *keep* or *maintain* the unity the Spirit has produced:

We're never commanded to *produce* unity. We're to *keep* or *maintain* the unity the Spirit has produced.

I urge you to live a life worthy of the calling you have received. Be completely humble and gentle; be patient, bearing with one another in love. Make every effort to keep the unity of the Spirit through the bond of peace (Ephesians 4:1–3).

➡ **8. Which attitude or trait in each pair below can help maintain the unity the Spirit produces? Check one word or phrase in each pair.**

arrogant and haughty	❏ or ❏	completely humble
harsh	❏ or ❏	gentle
short tempered, impatient	❏ or ❏	patient
intolerant and hateful	❏ or ❏	tolerant and loving

Did you check items only in the right column? Good! Those are some of the traits God wants to produce in you in relationship to other brothers and sisters in Christ. These are ways you can help maintain or restore the unity the Spirit produces.

If you've demonstrated arrogance, harshness, impatience, prejudice, a judgmental spirit, or intolerance toward Christians of other races or denominations (or even members of your own church or denomination), these actions tarnish and undermine the unity the Spirit has provided. Such actions are not *"worthy of the calling you have received."* If you have erected "walls" through your own actions, you bring pain to the body of Christ. You need to break down those walls of sin through repentance.

If you have erected "walls" through your own actions, you bring pain to the body of Christ.

➡ **What, if anything, do you sense God has said to you through today's lesson? Write *one* of the most meaningful things He has said below.**

_____

_____

A Prayer for Unity
"May the God who gives endurance and encouragement give you a spirit of unity among yourselves as you follow Christ Jesus, so that with one heart and mouth you may glorify the God and Father of our Lord Jesus Christ" (Romans 15:5–6).

➡ **Conclude today's lesson by praying for unity. Use Paul's prayer for the church at Rome in the left margin.**
 • Pray this for your church.
 • Pray this for your study group.
 • Pray this for Christians you know from other races, denominations, or Christian traditions.

LESSON 2 — THREE ILLUSTRATIONS OF UNITY

Scripture for Meditation
"Consequently, you are no longer foreigners and aliens, but fellow citizens with God's people and members of God's household, built on the foundation of the apostles and prophets, with Christ Jesus himself as the chief cornerstone. In him the whole building is joined together and rises to become a holy temple in the Lord. And in him you too are being built together to become a dwelling in which God lives by his Spirit" (Ephesians 2:19–22).

A Beginning Prayer
Father, I'm beginning to understand a little more about unity in the body of Christ. Thank You for making that unity possible. Please reveal more clearly what that unity would look like in my relationships with others. Help me to begin experiencing the kind of relationships that will honor You and bring glory to Christ in my church and my city. Amen.

Ephesians 2:11–12
"Formerly you who are Gentiles by birth . . . remember that at that time you were separate from Christ, excluded from citizenship in Israel and foreigners to the covenants of the promise, without hope and without God in the world."

➡ **Read and think about the Scripture for Meditation in the left margin, and begin the lesson with prayer.**

❖ ❖ ❖

➡ **1. Read again the Scripture for Meditation in the left margin. As you read it, underline what the believing Gentiles (together with believing Jews) became. Hint: One is "fellow citizens with God's people."**

The New Testament describes several relationships between God's people. These will help us better understand what unity might look like in our day. Let's see what God has created His people to be. In Ephesians 2:11–12 (margin below), Paul described the Gentiles as separated from Christ, excluded from citizenship, and aliens without hope and without God. Then Christ removed the dividing wall.

When people come to faith in Christ, they become citizens of a nation (God's people). They become members of God's family (household). And they are built together to become a holy temple for the Lord. Peter said some similar things about God's people (see 1 Peter 2:9–10, margin on the next page). This holy nation was chosen to declare God's praises. Let's look at these three relationships.

A Holy Nation
God's people are *"a holy nation, a people belonging to God."* Christians are fellow citizens in that nation. In the Old Testament, Israel was this holy nation belonging to God. In the church, God has created a new covenant with a new people—those who turn to Him through faith in Jesus Christ.

In the old Israel, there were twelve tribes. Each was unique. Members traveled and camped with their tribe in the wilderness. They had a banner that indicated their unique identity. They maintained and celebrated their uniqueness as a tribe. They were never asked to give up their tribal heritage. However, they also were a nation—Israel. As such, they were one people. When they went to battle, they went out *"as one man."* Thus, Israel had both diversity as tribes and unity as a nation.

➡ **2. In the box to the right, draw a picture that represents the nation Israel as a single unit made up of twelve tribes. It can be a simple drawing.**

Israel and the Twelve Tribes:

1 Peter 2:9–10

"You are a chosen people, a royal priesthood, a holy nation, a people belonging to God, that you may declare the praises of him who called you out of darkness into his wonderful light. Once you were not a people, but now you are the people of God; once you had not received mercy, but now you have received mercy."

The things we have in common (like the Spirit of Christ) are far greater and more important than the things in which we differ.

CHILDREN OF GOD
Galatians 4:4–7

"God sent his Son . . . to redeem those under law, that we might receive the full rights of sons. Because you are sons, God sent the Spirit of his Son into our hearts, the Spirit who calls out, 'Abba, Father.' So you are no longer a slave, but a son; and since you are a son, God has made you also an heir."

John 1:12–13

"Yet to all who received him, to those who believed in his name, he gave the right to become children of God—children born not of natural descent, nor of human decision or a husband's will, but born of God."

Romans 8:14–17

"Those who are led by the Spirit of God are sons of God. For . . . you received the Spirit of sonship. And by him we cry, "Abba, Father." The Spirit himself testifies with our spirit that we are God's children. Now if we are children, then we are heirs—heirs of God and co-heirs with Christ."

A HOLY TEMPLE
1 Corinthians 3:16

"Don't you know that you yourselves are God's temple and that God's Spirit lives in you?"

You may have drawn a circle or square divided into twelve parts. That's the idea we're studying. The new nation Christ has created can have a similar combination of diversity and unity. We can maintain our uniqueness as a denomination, association, or Christian tradition. We can celebrate and experience joy together as a unique people created by God. But we can also be united as a spiritual nation. The things we have in common (like the Spirit of Christ) are far greater and more important than the things in which we differ. The most important thing we share in common is our King. Our common relationship to Him and His indwelling presence in our lives is the source of our unity.

Our many "tribes" can labor as a united nation to see the kingdom of God come on earth as it is in heaven. We can learn from each other. We can help each other by working together. We can help each other follow Christ more perfectly. We can celebrate the unique contributions different "tribes" make to the larger nation. We can all serve the same King and contribute to His kingdom.

➡ **3. What are some ways you've seen God's people function like this? Check any in the list below that you've seen or heard about. Write others in the margin.**

❑ a. Billy Graham evangelistic crusade
❑ b. Citywide concert of prayer
❑ c. Citywide Easter sunrise service
❑ d. Citywide Thanksgiving service
❑ e. Gideon Bible distributions
❑ f. Interdenominational ministerial association
❑ g. March for Jesus
❑ h. National Day of Prayer gathering
❑ i. Promise Keepers conference

God's Family

We are also described as members of God's household. In other passages (see the margin), we're called *"children of God," "sons of God," "heirs of God,"* and other names indicating we're part of His family. *"God sent the Spirit of his Son into our hearts"* (Galatians 4:6). We have the same Spirit of Christ in us. We've been adopted into His family by His divine choice. He chose each one of us. We need to accept the ones our Father has chosen. The truth is that none of us deserve to be in the family. Only His mercy and grace have made it possible.

➡ **4. One illustration of our oneness is unity as a holy nation. What's a second illustration of our unity?**
We belong to God's . . . _____

Human families often have members who are very different. They probably disagree on many concerns. But they can function in unity as a family. That's an imperfect example of what God intends His family to be. Our oneness in God's family is because we all have the same heavenly Father, and He has placed the Spirit of His Son in each of us. We share a family resemblance. One of the great joys of being in God's family is going to a "family reunion" and meeting parts of the family we haven't met before. We can be enriched by the contribution of other family members and their ethnic or denominational heritage.

➡ **5. Our oneness is illustrated by our being a holy nation and part of God's family. What's a third illustration of our unity?**

We're being built into a . . . _____

Paul also described our relationship to each other as a holy temple. We're

The Temple Complex

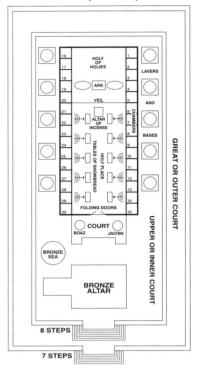

being built together. This is a dwelling where God lives. The Jerusalem temple was not a single building but a complex of different courts and smaller structures that combined to make up the temple complex. Some scholars see this spiritual building as a complex of smaller buildings, each growing up to become a grand temple for God's dwelling. Whether we're one building or a complex of buildings, God is present. Again we see the illustration of many different parts being brought together to form a single unit.

> **The greatest display of God's glory comes when He brings together those of great diversity and causes them to function in unity.**

➡ What, if anything, do you sense God has said to you through today's lesson? Write *one* of the most meaningful things He has said below.

_____

_____

➡ Conclude today's lesson by praying.
- Thank the Lord for making you a citizen of His kingdom.
- Thank Him for adopting you into His family.
- Thank Him for building you into a holy temple where He chooses to dwell.
- Ask Him to help you live in relationship with other believers in such a way that He will be honored by the testimony of your lives together.

LESSON 3   THE BODY OF CHRIST

Scripture for Meditation
"By this all men will know that you are my disciples, if you love one another" (John 13:35).

A Beginning Prayer
Father, You have placed me in the body of Christ. I'm not sure I have really experienced what it would be like to belong to a healthy body. Please teach me how to do my part to be a healthy member. Please help me experience unity and reconciliation in my church and in the larger Christian community for Your glory. Amen.

➡ Read and think about the Scripture for Meditation in the left margin, and begin the lesson with prayer.

❖ ❖ ❖

In the last lesson, you studied three illustrations of our unity as God's people.

➡ **1. See if you can use the hints below to recall the three illustrations of unity. You can check your answers (or peek for help).**

a. (hint: Israel had twelve tribes.) _____

b. (hint: We are adopted into it.) _____

c. (hint: Jesus is the cornerstone.) _____

We are a holy nation, members of God's family, and a spiritual building—a holy temple for the Lord. One more description of God's people is that we're the body of Christ. Though we are many members and very different, we're added by God to that body (a local congregation and the broader community of faith).

➡ **2. Read Romans 12:3–5 in the margin on the next page. Which of the following best describes the way you should think about your relationship to the other members of the body of Christ? Check one.**
- ❑ a. I am special, gifted, and have great knowledge. I can do pretty well all by myself. I don't need anybody else. I don't want to be dependent on anyone else.

Romans 12:3–5

"Do not think of yourself more highly than you ought, but rather think of yourself with sober judgment, in accordance with the measure of faith God has given you. Just as each of us has one body with many members, and these members do not all have the same function, so in Christ we who are many form one body, and each member belongs to all the others."

❑ b. God has given me grace and a measure of faith. But I can't make it alone. I'm only one part of the body. I need all the other members in order to be whole.

We hope you checked *b*. One of the big obstacles to unity in the body of Christ is pride and a judgmental spirit toward others. If you or your church or denomination thinks more highly of yourself than you ought, the body won't be as healthy as it should be. Another need in the body is a recognition that members belong to each other and need each other. The lost world out there is big. None of us can do all that needs to be done. We need each other.

A large church in a growing city was criticized by the smaller churches of their denomination. The smaller churches resented the fact that the large church was reaching people for Christ in every area of town. The smaller churches felt the large church was encroaching on "their territory." The large-church pastor responded by saying, "This is like a bunch of ants arguing about who will get to eat the elephant." The task for Christ's kingdom is so great that none of us can do it alone. We're on the same side carrying light into the darkness. Rather than compete with each other, we should be encouraging each other—cheering each other on to the goal and rejoicing with each other when the kingdom grows.

➡ **3. Which of the following is a way you could "cheer" for other churches and Christians in your city? Check one that's most meaningful, or write one of your own.**

    ❑ a. Pray that God would use other churches and denominations to bring people to Christ and help them mature as disciples.

    ❑ b. Rejoice with others when I hear that God has done a good work through them, and encourage them to keep up the good work.

    ❑ c. Share a love offering with another church or group in need just to say, "We love you, and we're in this battle together."

    ❑ d. Other: _____

The Head of the Body

Paul described the relationship of the body of Christ to Christ Himself:

➡ **Read Ephesians 1:22–23 and Colossians 1:18 in the margin.**

➡ **4. Who is the head of the body?** _____

➡ **5. Who is given the supreme authority to govern the body?**

_____

Ephesians 1:22–23

"God placed all things under his [Christ's] feet and appointed him to be head over everything for the church, which is his body."

Colossians 1:18

"He [Christ] is the head of the body, the church; he is the beginning and the firstborn from among the dead, so that in everything he might have the supremacy."

Christ is Head of the body. No man is the head. A healthy body of Christ will always look to the Head for its instructions, and He calls us to function in unity rather than division. One lesson we all need to learn is that our personal opinions are not important.

> **Only one opinion is important, and that is Christ's.**

As we study together, prayer and reading God's Word are essential. During these times, we will receive instructions from our Head. We must trust Christ to give us guidance to overcome the two giants of racism and sectarianism. The good news is that He wants us to gain the victory. Let's seek Him for the answers.

God's Assignment to Leaders

God has given some structure to the body of Christ, beginning with the provision of leaders. As you read Paul's statement about the body, look for the assignment God has given the leaders. Watch also for ways in which we may reach a spirit of unity.

➡ **6. Read Ephesians 4:11–16 in the margin, and fill in the blanks below:**
   a. God has given apostles, prophets, evangelists, pastors and teachers *"to prepare God's people for . . .*

   _____ _____ _____*."*

   b. Why? *". . . so that the body of Christ may be* _____ _____

   until we all reach _____ *in the* _____*."*

Leaders are given to the body to prepare God's people for works of service. Can you imagine what your own body would be like if half your limbs and organs didn't do anything? When a physical body is paralyzed, we consider it a tragedy. That's also true of the body of Christ. Every member needs to be involved. Our goal is that the body will be built up and become mature in faith and knowledge. We will experience unity when we grow into the maturity of Christ's fullness.

Relationship of the Members

Christlikeness in our actions and relationships will contribute to unity in the body. To the Corinthian church, Paul described the relationship of its members:

> The body is a unit, though it is made up of many parts. . . . So it is with Christ. For we were all baptized by one Spirit into one body—whether Jews or Greeks, slave or free—and we were all given the one Spirit to drink. . . .
> The eye cannot say to the hand, "I don't need you!" And the head cannot say to the feet, "I don't need you!" On the contrary, those parts of the body that seem to be weaker are indispensable. . . . But God has combined the members of the body and has given greater honor to the parts that lacked it, so that there should be no division in the body, but that its parts should have equal concern for each other. If one part suffers, every part suffers with it; if one part is honored, every part rejoices with it (1 Corinthians 12:12–13, 21–22, 24–26).

➡ **7. How much concern should you have for other members of the body?**

   _____

➡ **8. If one part of the body of Christ is suffering, how should you respond?**

   _____

➡ **9. If one part is honored or successful, how should you respond?**

   _____

Every member of the body needs all the other members. We should have equal concern for each other. God intends that there be no division. He

---

Ephesians 4:11–16

"It was he who gave some to be apostles, some to be prophets, some to be evangelists, and some to be pastors and teachers, to prepare God's people for works of service, so that the body of Christ may be built up until we all reach unity in the faith and in the knowledge of the Son of God and become mature, attaining to the whole measure of the fullness of Christ.

"Then we will no longer be infants, tossed back and forth by the waves, and blown here and there by every wind of teaching and by the cunning and craftiness of men in their deceitful scheming. Instead, speaking the truth in love, we will in all things grow up into him who is the Head, that is, Christ. From him the whole body, joined and held together by every supporting ligament, grows and builds itself up in love, as each part does its work."

Every member of the body needs all the other members.

has given each of us His Spirit. Won't it be wonderful when we care about each other in such a way that we suffer when others suffer and rejoice when others are honored? Paul gave us specific instruction for behavior that will help the body function in a healthy way.

➥ **10. Read the following instructions for the body of Christ from Romans 12:9–21. Grade yourself for each item, using the scale in the margin. Write a letter or question mark beside each item.**

E = Excellent

I = Improving

? = Don't Know

S = Satisfactory

N = Needs Improvement

_____ "Love must be sincere."
_____ "Hate what is evil; cling to what is good."
_____ "Be devoted to one another in brotherly love."
_____ "Honor one another above yourselves."
_____ "Never be lacking in zeal, but keep your spiritual fervor, serving the Lord."
_____ "Be joyful in hope, patient in affliction, faithful in prayer."
_____ "Share with God's people who are in need."
_____ "Practice hospitality."
_____ "Bless those who persecute you; bless and do not curse."
_____ "Rejoice with those who rejoice; mourn with those who mourn."
_____ "Live in harmony with one another."
_____ "Do not be proud, but be willing to associate with people of low position."
_____ "Do not be conceited."
_____ "Do not repay anyone evil for evil."
_____ "Be careful to do what is right in the eyes of everybody."
_____ "If it is possible, as far as it depends on you, live at peace with everyone."
_____ "Do not take revenge."
_____ "'If your enemy is hungry, feed him; if he is thirsty, give him something to drink.'"
_____ "Do not be overcome by evil, but overcome evil with good."

➥ **What, if anything, do you sense God has said to you through today's lesson? Write *one* of the most meaningful things He has said below.**

_____

_____

➥ **Conclude today's lesson by praying.**
• Ask the Lord to teach you how to be a healthy and faithful member of His body.
• Ask Him to teach you what that would mean in relationship to your local church.
• Ask Him to show you what that would mean in relationship to other churches or Christian groups.

LESSON 4 NO DIVISIONS AMONG YOU

Scripture for Meditation

"I appeal to you, brothers, in the name of our Lord Jesus Christ, that all of you agree with one another so that there may be no divisions among you and that you may be perfectly united in mind and thought" (1 Corinthians 1:10).

A Beginning Prayer

Father, I receive this appeal for unity as a word from You for me and the Christians with whom I have fellowship. Teach us how to come to this kind of agreement so that we may live in perfect unity of mind and thought. Teach me today what I need to do to eliminate any divisions of which I may be a part. Amen.

➡ **Read and think about the Scripture for Meditation in the left margin, and begin the lesson with prayer.**

Because of their sinful human nature, people have conflict with others. Satan and his followers take pleasure in the strife they see all over the earth. They know it's an indication that God hasn't gained victory in those lives. For example, Satan finds:
• Tribal conflict throughout Africa
• National conflict in Europe and Asia
• Ethnic conflict in the republics of Eastern Europe
• Religious conflict in Ireland and India
• Racial conflict in the United States . . .
The list could go on and on. Just change the names of the country or continent.

A Trophy for Christ
Only lives radically changed by Jesus Christ can overcome the sinful human tendency for destructive conflict. But God has a plan for reconciliation, and He intends for the church to be a part of this beautiful and needed process. Paul said:

> *I became a servant of this gospel by the gift of God's grace . . . to preach to the Gentiles the unsearchable riches of Christ, and to make plain to everyone the administration of this mystery, which for ages past was kept hidden in God, who created all things. **His intent was that now, through the church, the manifold wisdom of God should be made known** to the rulers and authorities in the heavenly realms, according to his eternal purpose which he accomplished in Christ Jesus our Lord* (Ephesians 3:7–11, emphasis added).

God has a plan to reveal His *"manifold wisdom"* to *"rulers and authorities in the heavenly realms."* In the book of Job, we see an interesting heavenly meeting. The angels—including the fallen angels and Satan—presented themselves before the Lord for a meeting. *"The LORD said to Satan, 'Have you considered my servant Job? There is no one on earth like him; he is blameless and upright, a man who fears God and shuns evil'"* (Job 1:8). God pointed to Job as a great example of a man who loved and served God faithfully. Satan couldn't believe a man could love God that way without an impure motive. After Satan's severe testing, the Scripture says, *"In all this, Job did not sin by charging God with wrongdoing"* (Job 1:22). Job's life was a trophy of God's grace at work in a man. God could use Job to reveal His wisdom to rulers and authorities in heavenly realms.

In a similar way, God wants to put the church on public display to the *"rulers and authorities in the heavenly realms."* He wants to offer the church as a living testimony of what He can accomplish through Christ—a trophy for Christ. He wants to be able to point to the unity and love in a diverse church and say, "That's what I can do through My Son, Jesus Christ." He wants to take Fatherly pride in the church when the rulers and authorities in heavenly realms gather for a meeting.

➡ **1. In the margin on the next page are pictures of four trophies. Circle the one you think might best represent Christianity in your country**

The Body of Christ

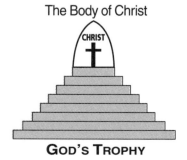

GOD'S TROPHY

A   **B**

C   **D**

1 Corinthians 1:10

"I appeal to you, brothers, in the name of our Lord Jesus Christ, that all of you agree with one another so that there may be no divisions among you and that you may be perfectly united in mind and thought."

Agree
No Divisions
Perfectly United

today. Draw a star beside the one with which you think God would be most pleased.

We believe that today, God is calling the larger body of Christ to display the kind of unity that will reveal Christ to a watching world. We believe God wants the body of Christ in every country to be a beautiful trophy for Christ.

Divisions Abound

A missionary living in Slovenia saw the ravages of revenge and ethnic hatred in the regions of the former Yugoslavia. He began working on a project to teach forgiveness and reconciliation to the people. He knew that only the love and power of Jesus Christ could bring any lasting change in their hearts. When he started teaching, he realized they had no word in their language for "reconciliation." Their culture taught a "code of blood" that required revenge. That cycle of revenge has been growing more fierce and devastating over the years.

Racial divisions are a sinful response to people around us. In various countries, the skin colors, languages, and ethnic or religious backgrounds that divide people are different. But every nation on earth faces human conflict because of sin. When these divisions are not overcome in the body of Christ, however, something is seriously wrong.

➡ **2. Read again the words of Paul in 1 Corinthians 1:10 (in the margin). Then circle *one* phrase under each group below that Paul used to describe God's desire for His people.**

Group 1	Group 2	Group 3
a. disagree	a. a few factions	a. perfectly united
b. argue	b. no divisions	b. almost united
c. agree	c. one or two splits	c. somewhat united
d. fight	d. some dissensions	d. united a little bit

God's Standards for the Body

Paul said we need to *"agree with one another so that there may be* no divisions *among you and that you may be* perfectly united *in mind and thought"* (1 Corinthians 1:10, emphasis added) (Answers: 1-c; 2-b; 3-a). Those are high goals. "Few," "little bit," or even "almost" are not the standards, but *"no divisions"* and *"perfectly united."*

➡ **3. If God were to rate your local church on a scale of 1 to 10 regarding unity, what number do you think He would give you? Circle your answer on the following line.**

About to Split		In Agreement
Fighting	1—2—3—4—5—6—7—8—9—10	No Divisions
Arguing		Perfect unity

If you realize your church is not where God wants it to be, you're not alone. Many churches lack unity to some degree. But God wants to bring health to the body of Christ—on a local level and on a worldwide level as well. Now is a time for you to begin or to continue praying for your church and your pastor as God calls you to His standards of unity and agreement.

➡ **Pause for a moment and pray for your church and pastor. As you pray, ask the Lord how you can support your pastor's role of guiding the church to be a trophy for Christ in your community.**

➡ **Read the following Scriptures, and answer the questions that follow each set.**

1 Corinthians 1:10–13, 17: *"I appeal to you, brothers, in the name of our Lord Jesus Christ, that all of you agree with one another so that* *there may be no divisions among you and that you may be perfectly united in mind and thought. My brothers, some from Chloe's household have informed me that there are quarrels among you. What I mean is this: One of you says, 'I follow Paul'; another, 'I follow Apollos'; another, 'I follow Cephas'; still another, 'I follow Christ.'*

"Is Christ divided? . . . Christ did not send me to baptize, but to preach the gospel—not with words of human wisdom, lest the cross of Christ be emptied of its power."

➥ **4. Why did Paul want the brothers to agree with one another? Underline the reason.**

➥ **5. What's one of the dangers if the body of Christ becomes divided by following personalities and words of human wisdom? What happens to the message of the cross?**

_____

1 Corinthians 3:1–3: *Brothers, I could not address you as spiritual but as worldly—mere infants in Christ. I gave you milk, not solid food, for you were not yet ready for it. Indeed, you are still not ready. You are still worldly. For since there is jealousy and quarreling among you, are you not worldly? Are you not acting like mere men?*

➥ **6. When Christian brothers are jealous, quarrel, and can't get along with each other, how are they acting? Check one.**
❑ a. As mature born-again Christians are supposed to act
❑ b. Immature and worldly, like mere men who are not related to Christ

Paul wrote to the church at Corinth the following words: *"I am afraid that when I come I may not find you as I want you to be. . . . I fear that there may be quarreling, jealousy, outbursts of anger, factions, slander, gossip, arrogance and disorder"* (2 Corinthians 12:20).

➥ **7. If Paul were to visit your church or city, which of the following sinful actions would he find among the Christians and churches there? Check those you *know* he would find.**
❑ quarreling ❑ jealousy ❑ outbursts of anger ❑ factions
❑ slander ❑ gossip ❑ arrogance ❑ disorder

Galatians 5:19–21

"The acts of the sinful nature are obvious: . . . hatred, discord, jealousy, fits of rage, selfish ambition, dissensions, factions and envy . . . and the like. I warn you, as I did before, that those who live like this will not inherit the kingdom of God."

Paul clearly described such actions as *"acts of the sinful nature"* (Galatians 5:19–21). Continuing to live this way may well indicate that a person has never become a new creation in Christ (see 2 Corinthians 5:17). A church filled with people who act like this will show the world what an unhealthy body of Christ is like.

➥ **What, if anything, do you sense God has said to you through today's lesson? Write *one* of the most meaningful things He has said below.**

_____

_____

2 Corinthians 5:17

"If anyone is in Christ, he is a new creation; the old has gone, the new has come!"

➥ **Conclude today's lesson by praying.**
• Confess to the Lord any division you're aware of in your church or in the Christian community in your city.
• Seek the Lord's forgiveness for any ways you may have contributed to that division.
• Join Christ in praying for unity among His followers.

LESSON 5 BECOMING CHRISTLIKE IN THE BODY

Scriptures for Meditation

"We know that in all things God works for the good of those who love him, who have been called according to his purpose. For those God foreknew he also predestined to be conformed to the likeness of his Son, that he might be the firstborn among many brothers" (Romans 8:28–29).

"Put on the new self, which is being renewed in knowledge in the image of its Creator" (Colossians 3:10).

A Beginning Prayer

Father, You desire that I be conformed to the image of Christ. You want the body of Christ on earth to look and act like Jesus. Open my mind and my eyes to understand how I can act more like Jesus in my life and through my church. Amen.

Isaiah 61:1–3

"The Spirit of the Sovereign LORD is on me, because the LORD has anointed me to <u>preach good news to the poor.</u> He has sent me to bind up the brokenhearted, to proclaim freedom for the captives and release from darkness for the prisoners, to proclaim the year of the LORD's favor and the day of vengeance of our God, to comfort all who mourn, and provide for those who grieve in Zion—to bestow on them a crown of beauty instead of ashes, the oil of gladness instead of mourning, and a garment of praise instead of a spirit of despair."

➥ **Read and think about the Scriptures for Meditation in the left margin, and begin the lesson with prayer.**

❖ ❖ ❖

Jesus' Assignment = Our Assignment

God the Father sent Jesus with a mission to reconcile the world to Himself. Before Jesus returned to heaven, He said to His followers, *"As the Father has sent me, I am sending you"* (John 20:21). If we want to understand our assignment as the body of Christ, we need to hear what Jesus said about His calling. In Luke 4:18–21, Jesus opened the scroll of Isaiah and read a passage in the synagogue. Then He said, *"Today this scripture is fulfilled in your hearing."* Let's look at the larger passage in Isaiah and see the assignment Jesus—the Anointed One—had from the Father.

➥ **1. Read Isaiah 61:1–3 in the margin below. As you read, underline words and phrases that describe the work of God's Anointed One. We've underlined one for you.**

The assignments the Father anointed Jesus to carry out have something in common. He started with people who were broken, wounded, in bondage, or needy. Then He ministered to their need and brought them to health. Notice the contrasts summarized below.

Jesus started with:
- the poor
- the brokenhearted
- captives
- prisoners of darkness
- mourners
- the grieving

Jesus responded by:
- preaching good news to them
- binding up their broken hearts
- proclaiming freedom
- releasing them from darkness
- comforting them
- providing for them

To this day, Jesus continues to carry out those assignments. For ashes He gives a beautiful crown. Instead of mourning, He gives the oil of gladness. Instead of a spirit of despair, He gives a garment of praise. And He calls the body of Christ to join Him in that work. When we become Christlike in our actions, we can expect God to produce the same kind of results Jesus expected and received. God's Servant in Isaiah 61 expected to see people experience renewal.

➥ **Read the following Scripture, and then answer the questions that follow.**

They will be called oaks of righteousness, a planting of the LORD for the display of his splendor. They will rebuild the ancient ruins and restore the places long devastated; they will renew the ruined cities that have been devastated for generations. Aliens will shepherd your flocks; foreigners will work your fields and vineyards. And you will be called priests of the LORD, you will be named ministers of our God (Isaiah 61:3–6).

➥ **2. Which of these two descriptions better charactierizes *"oaks of righteousness"*?**
☐ a. weak, frail, temporary, and evil
☐ b. strong, firm, long-lasting, and wholesome

47

➡ **3. What trait of the Lord's will these *"plantings"* display?**

His _____

➡ **4. What three actions will God's renewed people take that will produce renewal around them? Fill in the blanks:**

- They will _____ the ancient ruins.

- They will _____ the places long devastated.

- They will _____ the ruined cities.

When God changes a life through Christ, He takes old things and makes them new. Human governments and social organizations make all kinds of attempts to renew our ruined cities. They invest huge amounts of money to try to revive a decaying society. But these human efforts often are ineffective and short-lived. When Christ changes lives, however, permanent changes take place that can have long-lasting effects on society. Renewed people of God will rebuild old ruins, restore places that are devastated, and recreate ruined cities. They'll display God's splendor to a watching world.

As the body of Christ becomes healthy and Christlike, the Father can work through it to draw a lost world to be reconciled with Him. One great hope for any nation is that God's people will get right with Him and with each other. Then He will have a body through which to work to renew what has been ruined by sin (see 2 Chronicles 7:14).

As you've learned during this unit, the members of the body need each other. We can help each other come to health. Christians need other Christians; churches need other churches. And even denominations, associations, and various Christian traditions need each other from time to time. You and your small group will want to begin watching to see how God may work through you to see the body of Christ become more healthy for His glory.

➡ **5. Suppose you became aware of an unhealthy, hurting, or needy part of the body of Christ like those listed below. How might God work through other believers to help that part of the body be restored to health and wholeness? Match the needs below with appropriate responses in the left margin. Write a number on the line provided by each need.**

Needs

____ A. A new Christian in the inner city has no job skills and is not able to provide adequately for his family's needs.

____ B. An African-American church was burned down by an arsonist because of his racial hatred.

____ C. An old mainline denomination is facing some potentially divisive issues in its upcoming annual conference. The news media are building up the conflict, and tensions are growing.

____ D. Pastors and churches in the city have a jealous and competitive spirit. Consequently, the Christian community is splintered and isolated.

These responses to the needs may not be the responses to which God would call you. But they should give you the general idea: When a part of the body is needy or hurting, the rest of the body needs to step in to help bring the whole body to health and wholeness. (A-3; B-4; C-1; and D-2) Too often our response is that we're too busy to help, or we may just admit that we don't care what happens to them.

---

2 Chronicles 7:14

"If my people, who are called by my name, will humble themselves and pray and seek my face and turn from their wicked ways, then will I hear from heaven and will forgive their sin and will heal their land.'"

Responses

1. Mobilize your church and denomination to pray for the leaders and decision makers. Send a prayer team to conduct spiritual warfare in the prayer room at the meeting.

2. Begin to model Christlike acceptance, forgiveness, love, and service toward other Christians and churches. Call together spiritual leaders who also are weary of the brokenness. Begin meeting, talking, and praying together and follow the Lord's directions toward healing.

3. Provide job training along with training in discipleship. Help him network with other Christians to find a job and encourage him to live out his faith on the job.

4. Form a partnership between your church and the other one. Share facilities. Jointly sponsor men's and women's retreats to comfort during the grief and fear stage. Develop understanding and caring relationships. Take an offering and provide work crews to help with clean-up and rebuilding.

When a part of the body is needy or hurting, the rest of the body needs to step in to help bring the whole body to health and wholeness.

These common reactions don't come from Jesus, the Head of the body. He wants His body to be healthy. When God causes us to be aware of a need, we should seek direction from Christ for if and how we should become involved. A spiritual principle for individuals, churches, and denominations says,

> *"Whoever wants to save his life will lose it, but whoever loses his life for me will save it."*
> —Luke 9:24

Christians, churches, and denominations that are willing to give themselves away in ministry for the kingdom of God will experience a fullness of life that the Lord gives to those who place kingdom interests over their own.

Christians, churches, and denominations that are willing to give themselves away in ministry for the kingdom of God will experience a fullness of life that the Lord gives to those who place the interests of the kingdom over their own.

➥ **What, if anything, do you sense God has said to you through today's lesson? Write *one* of the most meaningful things He has said below.**

_____

_____

➥ **For each lesson this week, you've been recording what you sense God has said to you. Review the final activity for each of the previous lessons on pages 37, 40, 43, and 46. What's the major emphasis of what you sense God wants you to do in response to this unit's lessons? Pray and ask Him what He wants you to do. Then write notes below, in the margin, or in a separate notebook.**

_____

_____

➥ **Conclude today's lesson in prayer.**
  • Ask the Lord to show you ways you need to adjust your life to become like Christ in your attitudes and actions.
  • Ask the Lord to give you spiritual eyes to see needs within the body of Christ and the wisdom and resources to help meet those needs.
  • Ask the Lord to teach you to receive help and ministry from members of the body of Christ who may be different from you.
  • Thank the Lord for the unity He makes possible.

UNIT 3 — CALLED TO RECONCILIATION

Scripture Memory Verse
"God was reconciling the world to himself in Christ, not counting men's sins against them. And he has committed to us the message of reconciliation."
—2 Corinthians 5:19

Unit Learning Goal
You will understand God's call to a ministry of reconciliation, and you'll demonstrate your intention to be reconciled with God and your brothers.

Overview of Unit 3
Lesson 1: Reconciled to God
Lesson 2: The Ministry of Reconciliation
Lesson 3: The Principle of Call
Lesson 4: Reconciled to My Brothers
Lesson 5: Special Assignments from God

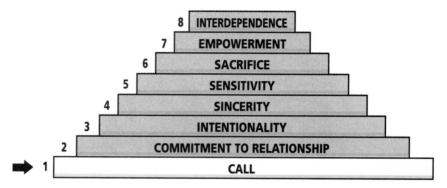

8 INTERDEPENDENCE
7 EMPOWERMENT
6 SACRIFICE
5 SENSITIVITY
4 SINCERITY
3 INTENTIONALITY
2 COMMITMENT TO RELATIONSHIP
1 CALL

PRINCIPLE 1
Call: We are all called to a ministry of reconciliation, and we're all commanded to be reconciled with our brothers across racial, cultural, and denominational barriers.

Key Summary Statements from Unit 3
- Our assignment is to carry a message to others on Christ's behalf. That message is: *"We beg you: be reconciled to God."*
- Reconciliation means being committed to seeing love win out over alienation and division.
- As ambassadors of Christ and reconcilers, we should seek opportunities to cross barriers, as Jesus did.
- When you're reconciled to God, He begins the process of reconciling you to others.
- Without a right relationship with each other, we may miss what God wants to do through us in those relationships.
- Without right relationships, the body cannot function as it should to correct, encourage, strengthen, exhort, and *"spur one another on toward love and good deeds."*
- A special calling to be a reconciler indicates that God wants to reconcile people. He just wants to give you the privilege of joining Him in His wonderful work.
- If God calls you to a ministry across human boundaries, it's because He's getting ready to do something there, and He wants you involved!

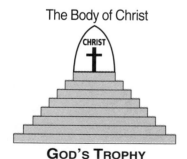

The Body of Christ

CHRIST

GOD'S TROPHY

"LET'S KILL 'EM ALL!"[1]

by Dave and Neta Jackson

It's summer, and 400 African Americans have gathered in the 100 degree heat for a dinner in a gymnasium. They've come to the annual "Harvest Banquet" at Rock of Our Salvation Church and Circle Urban Ministries on Chicago's West Side. Most of the women are single parents and come from nearby apartments such as the notorious "Murder Building," where, in one week, three people had died in drug-related killings. The young men, many unemployed, are angry and hold little hope for a better life. Most are convinced that their desperate struggle to survive is still resisted by the oppressive "white man."

In planning for the banquet, Pastor Raleigh Washington of Rock Church and Glen Kehrein, executive director of Circle Urban Ministries, decided to speak on the subject of bitterness and the need for black/white reconciliation, a reconciliation they've experienced in their own relationship.

As a child in Jacksonville, Florida, Pastor Washington, an African American, had only known white people as the insurance man who came to collect the bill and the policeman who arrested a friend's father. Meanwhile, Glen, of German descent, grew up in Ripon, a town of 6,000 in central Wisconsin. His first conversation with a black person took place when he moved to Chicago to attend college. But now the two men work together in a remarkable interracial relationship.

After the sumptuous feast, Pastor Washington stands up and taps on the mike. Chairs still scrape; some people keep talking. Several people look uncertain, not sure what they're in for.

After describing his childhood in the public housing projects in Jacksonville, Pastor Washington begins to open up his life to these Harvest guests. "I escaped the ghetto by getting a baseball scholarship in college," the former army officer booms in his strong voice. "The ROTC program commissioned me as a second lieutenant in the U.S. Army when I graduated from college. Then the army assigned me to the Adjutant General's Corps, a predominantly white, elite, administrative branch. In the military, I did exceedingly well. The army promoted me to captain, then major, and finally to lieutenant colonel—all ahead of my contemporaries. I was on the fast track to becoming the first black general in that branch of the army."

The shuffling and small talk stop. The people are listening. A black man who has succeeded in a white arena always captures attention in the 'hood (neighborhood).

"I supervised white personnel and even fired some of them. Oh, yeah, I fired a whole lot of white folks!" Washington grins broadly. Then his tone becomes serious. "But a black man does not climb the ladder of success so fast without making enemies. The white officers I climbed past—and sometimes over—and those I fired, they were not about to forget. Eventually, a conspiracy of jealous officers began telling lies about me. Two white colonels—one from Mississippi and the other from Alabama—investigated those lies, and you know what they were thinking."

Heads nod, and some in the audience respond, "Uh-huh." "You got that right."

"They conducted eleven different investigations. I was never informed about any of them. It took a year, and they spent over a million dollars going anywhere and talking to anybody who had any contact with me since I'd become a major. All the charges ended without basis; they couldn't find a thing to pin on me. Finally, the army found some minor technicalities to stick me with, like using the government telephone for a personal call—even though my post commander had given me permission—or having my driver pick up my boots on his way back from another official errand. That was considered 'misappropriating a government vehicle.'

"Such minor matters would not have done me any damage if the army had specifically charged me. Instead, they said I was guilty of 'conduct unbecoming an officer'—without explanation. Then I was given a choice: Sign a paper admitting guilt and take mandatory retirement, or be discharged after nineteen years, eleven months, and twenty-nine days of service—one day before I was eligible for full retirement benefits."

An angry murmur travels around the room. Heads are really shaking now.

"If I would have signed, the government would have given me full retirement pay as a lieutenant colonel. But I would not sign that lie. So they kicked me out of the army—no fond farewells, no medical benefits, no nothin'—one day short of full retirement eligibility!"

The dinner guests are really with him now, punctuating every sentence with their own retorts. A layer of anger fills the air as the crowd listens to the story of racial injustice.

"But I didn't want to retire," Washington continues. "Soon I would have been making full colonel; I was on my way to becoming a general. But because of a conspiracy of white people, because of their lies, because of racism and prejudice, they kicked me out of the army. It was white folks who kicked me out of the army. It was white folks who took away my retirement."

A black man at a table near the front of the gymnasium suddenly jumps to his feet. With a face contorted by rage, he raises his fist in a black power salute and roars, "Then let's kill 'em all!" A cheer goes up from hundreds of African-American guests. The sixty white volunteers in that hot gymnasium, standing around the perimeter, freeze with terror. They've come from various churches in the suburbs to help cook and serve a meal, not to become the targets of an angry mob.

Pastor Washington continues his story. "You've only heard half of my story," he tells the Harvest guests. "Several years later, a white Jewish lawyer named Jeff Strange found out about my experience and offered to take on my case without charging a penny. For nine years he battled the army, and finally he got them to reverse their decision. I was called to active duty to serve one more day so that I could retire."

The crowd yells and claps.

"Fort Sheridan—the same base that had drummed me out of the army—had to roll out the band to give me a retirement parade. I put on my lieutenant colonel's uniform—after fasting for two weeks—and Glen's dad, Pa Kehrein, picked me up in a limousine he borrowed from his work. I returned to active duty in style."

The crowd roars louder. These people understand Washington's pain and struggle with racism and prejudice; they love the victory story. But in a way, it's as alien as a Superman tale. This man's triumph came not by "any means necessary" but through the intercession of white people who cared about him.

In the middle of their cheers, Pastor Washington says, "Wait! Don't shout now about my victory, because I heard the same kind of shouting a few minutes ago when the brother down front here yelled, 'Let's kill 'em all!'

"The truth is, you are bitter and you focus your bitterness on white people. You have just faced that bitterness in yourselves. It's there, brother; it's there, sister. Now let me tell you what Jesus Christ did for my bitterness."

As the volunteers quietly clear away the remains of the Harvest feast, Pastor Washington begins to declare the gospel.

"I had to forget what was behind—as the Bible says—and reach for what lies ahead. Only Jesus Christ, who died on the cross to reconcile us to God and to break down the walls of hate and bitterness between us, can help a person do that. That's the only way I can be a partner with my brother Glen Kehrein here today." The former army officer then points out that it was a white church that had given Rock Church a sound system and hymnals; it was white people who, because of the love of Christ, had been providing food for the Harvest events all that week. "White people cooked it and are here serving you right now. All this is only possible because of the gospel of Jesus Christ."

When Pastor Washington gives an invitation, people start coming forward to give their lives to Christ. The eighth person to come forward is the man who wanted to "kill 'em all." With the crowd bursting into spontaneous applause, Pastor Washington embraces Timmy as a new brother in Christ. Tears flow from the eyes of the volunteers ringing the perimeter over this visible display of the power of the gospel to change lives.

---

[1] Adapted from *Break Down the Walls,* by Raleigh Washington and Glen Kehrein with Dave and Neta Jackson (Chicago: Moody Press, 1993), 23-28.

LESSON 1 RECONCILED TO GOD

Scripture for Meditation

"God was reconciling the world to himself in Christ, not counting men's sins against them. And he has committed to us the message of reconciliation" (2 Corinthians 5:19).

A Beginning Prayer

Father, I know that the body of Christ is not what it should be. I confess we have sinned against You by our divisions. Bringing the body to health and wholeness seems impossible. I know I can't do it, but I believe You can and will. Help me in the areas of my unbelief. Encourage me today to walk by faith and to trust in You. Amen.

➡ Second Corinthians 5:19 (in the left margin) is your Scripture memory verse for this unit. Remove the perforated card from the back of your book, and begin memorizing it. Read and think about this verse, and begin the lesson with prayer.

❖ ❖ ❖

Perhaps, as you've studied Christian unity, you feel it's an impossibility in our day. At a point when the disciples lacked faith, Jesus said, *"With man this is impossible, but not with God; all things are possible with God"* (Mark 10:27). As you think about the great barriers to unity around you, consider the following testimony.

The Walls of Jericho Came Down

God delivered Israel from Egypt through Moses' leadership. Because of their unbelief, however, the Israelites wandered in the wilderness for forty years while the adult generation died out. Then God took the new generation into the promised land under Joshua's leadership. Their first military assignment was to take the great walled city of Jericho.

Some of the people probably looked at the tall walls and said, "It can't be done." Considering their own strength, they saw it as an impossible assignment. They didn't have the power or know-how to bring down those walls. But they did know God could do it, so they turned to Him.

Then the LORD said to Joshua, "See, I have delivered Jericho into your hands, along with its king and its fighting men. March around the city once with all the armed men. Do this for six days. Have seven priests carry trumpets of rams' horns in front of the ark. On the seventh day, march around the city seven times, with the priests blowing the trumpets. When you hear them sound a long blast on the trumpets, have all the people give a loud shout; then the wall of the city will collapse and the people will go up, every man straight in" (Joshua 6:2–5).

➡ **1. If you were given this military strategy for bringing down a walled city, how do you think you would respond to the Lord? Check one.**
- ❑ a. Lord, You don't understand the nature of a walled city. Marching and blowing trumpets won't bring down the wall. What else should we do to *really* get the job done?
- ❑ b. Lord, we must be hearing the voice of Satan here. Surely You wouldn't give us such a ridiculous assignment. We'll keep waiting until we hear something more reasonable.
- ❑ c. Lord, the small city of Ai nearby doesn't have a wall. Could we start working there first?
- ❑ d. Lord, this battle belongs to You. We trust that You know what You're doing and that You can bring it to pass. We'll obey and trust You.

Some people would check *a* above. They think God's work depends on them. They believe God only helps those who help themselves. They have far more confidence in themselves than they have faith in God. They may try to accomplish God's work, but in man's ways. They work hard but will see little, if any, lasting fruit.

Other people would check *b*. God keeps calling them to walk by faith, and they want to walk by sight. They don't walk closely enough to God to know His voice clearly. They trust more in their human reason than in God's revelation. When God invites them to join Him, they miss the opportunity while waiting for something more reasonable to come along. Others with similar reasoning will try to make their own suggestions to God (like answer *c*). They think they know a better way.

> God is looking for people of faith.

But God is looking for people of faith—people who trust Him and will obey His directions. He wants people to trust in His wisdom, knowledge, and abilities. Israel had learned during forty years in the wilderness to walk by faith instead of their earlier unbelief. They followed God's instructions in confidence.

➡ **Read Joshua 6:15, 20 in the margin to see what God did.**

> **Joshua 6:15, 20**
> *"On the seventh day, they got up at daybreak and marched around the city seven times. . . . When the trumpets sounded, the people shouted, and at the sound of the trumpet, when the people gave a loud shout, the wall collapsed; so every man charged straight in, and they took the city."*

God had a plan for Israel to destroy Jericho. He was going to bring down the walls. He gave the people His instructions. But His plan required faith and obedience. When the people walked by faith and obeyed, God brought down the walls.

➡ **2. Do you have that much faith to believe that God can produce unity among God's people in our day?**
❑ yes ❑ no ❑ probably not, but I want to have it

> Jesus Christ has provided for the unity we need. This unity, however, is possible only for those who are rightly related to Him.

Jesus Christ has provided for the unity we need. This unity, however, is possible only for those who are rightly related to Him. If you're low on faith, ask Him to increase your faith or help your unbelief. Today's lesson focuses on how God has reconciled us to Himself.

Reconciled: Bringing into Agreement

Banking is big business in America. Many people put their money in a checking account and write checks to pay bills and buy things. Once a month, their banks send a statement so they can make sure their records agree with the banks'.

Suppose you failed to record several checks during the month or your wife wrote checks and forgot to tell you. Your records would not agree with your bank's. If you didn't correct your records, you would soon begin to bounce checks due to lack of funds. Bringing your records into agreement with the bank's is called "reconciling" your bank statement.

➡ **3. Suppose you lost your job and got into debt way beyond your ability to pay. The stress from the debt kept getting heavier and heavier. Then suppose a wealthy person came along and paid off all your debts—every penny. Then he offered you a wonderful job. How do you think you would feel? Check your response, or write your own.**
❑ a. I'd feel great and free. I couldn't believe anyone would do that for me. I would do my best in my new job to say thank you.
❑ b. I would resent somebody sticking his nose in my business. I would tell him to take his money and job and get out of my life.

❑ c. Other: _____

If you would turn down an offer like that, most people would say you're crazy. The offer seems too good to be true. But that's what Christ has done for you spiritually. Believers have been reconciled to God by Jesus Christ. This is a far deeper and more significant work than just correcting your bank records or paying off your bills.

From God's perspective and because of sin, all people became debtors and

Romans 6:23
"The wages of sin is death."

Ephesians 2:1–3
"As for you, you were dead in your transgressions and sins, in which you used to live when you followed the ways of this world. . . gratifying the cravings of our sinful nature and following its desires and thoughts. Like the rest, we were by nature objects of wrath."

Colossians 1:21
"Once you were alienated from God and were enemies in your minds because of your evil behavior."

slaves to sin. Our sin debt is so big we could never repay it. What we deserve for our sin is death (see Romans 6:23). In fact, before we became Christians we were *"dead in [our] transgressions and sins"* and *"objects of wrath"* (Ephesians 2:1–3). We had sinned against God and become His enemies (see Colossians 1:21). But then God did something too wonderful to believe:

God demonstrates his own love for us in this: While we were still sinners, Christ died for us.
    Since we have now been justified by his blood, how much more shall we be saved from God's wrath through him! For if, when we were God's enemies, we were reconciled to him through the death of his Son, how much more, having been reconciled, shall we be saved through his life! Not only is this so, but we also rejoice in God through our Lord Jesus Christ, through whom we have now received reconciliation (Romans 5:8–11).

➥ **4. Based on the passage above, how did God demonstrate His love for us?**

_____

➥ **5. Fill in the following blanks from Romans 5:8–11 above.**

a. *"We have now been justified by his* _____.*"*

b. *"Much more shall we be saved from God's* _____.*"*

c. *"through our Lord Jesus Christ . . . we have now* _____ *reconciliation."*

His gift of reconciliation is available to you, but it must be received.

God showed His love by sending His Son, Jesus, to pay our sin debt with His death on the cross. We've been justified (made right with God—just as if we had never sinned) by Christ's blood. We've been saved from God's wrath! His gift of reconciliation is available to you, but it must be received. God has worked through Christ to reconcile you to Himself.

➥ **6. Are you confident that you have experienced this process of reconciliation and been made right with God?**
❏ yes ❏ no ❏ I'm not sure

➥ **If you realize you've never been reconciled with God (or if you're not sure), turn to page 170 and read "How to Be Reconciled to God." *Now* is the time to get that settled.**

The following summarizes what God has done to reconcile you to Himself.

> **Reconciled to God**
> 1. You were separated and estranged from God because of sin.
> 2. You were helpless to return to a right relationship with God by yourself.
> 3. God took the initiative to restore you to a right relationship with Himself.
> 4. Christ is the agent of reconciliation. He made it possible by His death on the cross.
> 5. Reconciliation is a completed work. God waits on you to claim (receive) what Christ has already provided.
> 6. You receive God's reconciliation by faith.
> 7. When you are reconciled to God, you're forgiven, made holy, and placed in right standing with God.

➥ **What, if anything, do you sense God has said to you through today's lesson? Write *one* of the most meaningful things He has said below.**

_____

_____

➥ **Conclude today's lesson by praying.**
- Think about what you were before you turned your life over to Christ, and thank the Lord for changing your life.
- Think about the suffering your sins caused Christ to suffer on the cross. Express your love to God for what He has done for you.

LESSON 2 THE MINISTRY OF RECONCILIATION

Scripture for Meditation

"God . . . reconciled us to himself through Christ and gave us the ministry of reconciliation. . . . And he has committed to us the message of reconciliation. We are therefore Christ's ambassadors. . . . We implore you on Christ's behalf: Be reconciled to God" (2 Corinthians 5:18–20).

A Beginning Prayer

Father, thank You for Your Son, Jesus, and for what He did for me on the cross. I realize I could not carry the burden of my own sins. Thank You for not counting my sins against me. Your forgiveness is so freeing. How can I ever repay You? I can't.

I realize, however, that You have given me a message and ministry of reconciliation. I pray that You will reveal to me what I need to do to be faithful to that calling. Amen.

Our assignment is to carry a message to others on Christ's behalf. That message is: *"We beg you: Be reconciled to God."*

➥ **Read and think about the Scripture for Meditation in the left margin, and begin the lesson with prayer.**

❖ ❖ ❖

Yesterday you learned that God reconciled us to Himself through Christ. He paid our sin debt and brought us into agreement and right relationship with Himself.

➥ **1. After we were reconciled to God through Christ, what did God give us? (See 2 Corinthians 5:18–20 in the margin.)**

the ministry and message of . . . _____

Once God brings us into a right relationship with Himself, He calls us into active duty for His kingdom. We're given a ministry of reconciliation. Before you jump to a conclusion about what that ministry is, let's look one more time at 2 Corinthians 5:18–20 in the margin.

➥ **2. What office or position are we given?**

"We are therefore Christ's _____."

➥ **3. As ambassadors, what is the message we've been given to deliver to others?** *"We implore you on Christ's behalf: . . .*

_____

Our assignment is to carry a message to others on Christ's behalf. That message is: *"We beg you: Be reconciled to God."* Here's the way the ministry of reconciliation works:

The Ministry of Reconciliation

1. God has provided a way for people to be reconciled to Himself through Christ.
2. When you receive reconciliation to God through faith in Christ, God calls you to join Him in the ministry of reconciliation.
3. You help others find peace with God by being reconciled to Him through faith in Christ.
4. When you're right with God and others get right with God, you will experience right relationships with each other. This is biblical unity.

Your Primary Assignment

He works through you to bring others to a right relationship with Himself.

Do you see the process? First, God brings you to a right relationship with Himself. Then He works through you to bring others to the same relationship. Because of what Christ has done to destroy the wall between His people, those who are right with God will be reconciled to each other. We'll study more about how we are right with each other in lesson 3.

➡ **4. What is the first and *primary* assignment you've been given in the ministry of reconciliation? Check your response.**
  ❑ a. I'm to use political and social pressure to change the way people treat each other.
  ❑ b. I'm to allow God to work through me by calling people to get right with Him.
  ❑ c. I'm to tell people all the ways they need to change so we can have a right relationship with each other.
  ❑ d. I don't have an assignment. That's just for preachers and evangelists.

We hope you didn't check *d*, because that might indicate we're not doing our job of teaching you God's Word! *All* Christians are called to be involved in the ministry of reconciliation. We're going to learn more about that call in lesson 4. Your human reasoning may have caused you to lean toward checking *a* or *c*. Those approaches focus on what we do rather than what God can do. We do have a role to play in living out the fruits of reconciliation. God may call you to work for peace in the church and/or justice in society. He may guide you to offer correction to those who aren't living rightly toward others. But those are secondary assignments that God must direct.

The first and primary assignment in the ministry of reconciliation is to join God's work by calling people to get right with Him.

The first and *primary* assignment in the ministry of reconciliation is to join God's work by calling people to get right with Him (*b*). If people aren't right with God, the possibilities for peace and reconciliation are slim to none. Our sinful human nature will always tend toward conflict. You could spend your entire life trying to change people apart from God and end in utter failure. When you begin by helping people get right with God, they will want your help in learning to live in a right relationship with others.

Jesus Was a Reconciler

In the first century, a major racial division existed between Jews and Samaritans. Samaritans were "half-breeds"—a mixture of Jews and Assyrians. Because of the Jewish rejection and their own sin, the Samaritans also worshiped God differently from the Jews. Jews would take a much longer route to go around rather than through Samaria when they traveled north and south. In that kind of racist environment, Jesus showed us what the ministry of reconciliation would look like:

➡ **Begin reading about the woman at the well in the margin. Watch to see where Jesus focused His attention. Was it on her changing her actions toward Jews and others, or was it on the woman's need to get right with God through Him (the Messiah)? Answer the questions below as you read each section of the story.**

THE WOMAN AT THE WELL
John 4:3–9

³ "The Lord . . . left Judea and went back once more to Galilee.

⁴ "Now he had to go through Samaria. ⁵So he came to a town in Samaria called Sychar. . . . ⁶Jacob's well was there, and Jesus, tired as he was from the journey, sat down by the well. It was about the sixth hour.

⁷ "When a Samaritan woman came to draw water, Jesus said to her, 'Will you give me a drink?' ⁸(His disciples had gone into the town to buy food.)

⁹ "The Samaritan woman said to him, 'You are a Jew and I am a Samaritan woman. How can you ask me for a drink?' (For Jews do not associate with Samaritans.)"

➡ **5. (John 4:3–9) How did Jesus relate to this person who normally would have been hated by a Jew? Check one.**
  ❑ a. Jesus did His best to avoid contact with her.
  ❑ b. Jesus made the best of a bad situation.
  ❑ c. Jesus intentionally pursued this opportunity for reconciliation.

➡ **6. Now read John 4:10, 13–15 in the margin on the next page. What topic did Jesus first turn to in His conversation with the woman?**

John 4:10, 13–15

10 *"Jesus answered her, 'If you knew the gift of God and who it is that asks you for a drink, you would have asked him and he would have given you living water. . . .'*

13 *"'Everyone who drinks this water will be thirsty again,* 14 *but whoever drinks the water I give him will never thirst. Indeed, the water I give him will become in him a spring of water welling up to eternal life.'*

15 *"The woman said to him, 'Sir, give me this water so that I won't get thirsty and have to keep coming here to draw water.'"*

John 4:16–24

16 *"He told her, 'Go, call your husband and come back.'*

17 *"'I have no husband,' she replied.*

"Jesus said to her, 'You are right when you say you have no husband. 18 *The fact is, you have had five husbands, and the man you now have is not your husband. What you have just said is quite true.'*

19 *"'Sir,' the woman said, 'I can see that you are a prophet.* 20 *Our fathers worshiped on this mountain, but you Jews claim that the place where we must worship is in Jerusalem.'*

21 *"Jesus declared, 'Believe me, woman, a time is coming when you will worship the Father neither on this mountain nor in Jerusalem.* 22 *You Samaritans worship what you do not know; we worship what we do know, for salvation is from the Jews.* 23 *Yet a time is coming and has now come when the true worshipers will worship the Father in spirit and truth, for they are the kind of worshipers the Father seeks.* 24 *God is spirit, and his worshipers must worship in spirit and in truth.'"*

Jesus crossed significant racial, cultural, social, and religious barriers.

❑ a. He began to talk to her about her need to be right with God.
❑ b. He talked about unimportant things like the heat, weather, and water.
❑ c. He told her how wrong and sinful she was and what she would have to do to change her ways.

➡ **7. Read John 4:16–24 in the margin below. When opportunities came to sidetrack Jesus from His emphasis on a right relationship with God, how did He respond?**
❑ a. He condemned her for her multiple divorces and talked about the importance of marriage to one partner for life.
❑ b. He began to argue about the ignorant worship practices of the Samaritans.
❑ c. He directed her attention to the need she had for a right and personal relationship with God the Father.

➡ **Now read the rest of the story:**

25 *The woman said, "I know that Messiah" (called Christ) "is coming. When he comes, he will explain everything to us."*

26 *Then Jesus declared, "I who speak to you am he."*

27 *Just then his disciples returned and were surprised to find him talking with a woman. But no one asked, "What do you want?" or "Why are you talking with her?"*

28 *Then, leaving her water jar, the woman went back to the town and said to the people,* 29 *"Come, see a man who told me everything I ever did. Could this be the Christ?"* 30 *They came out of the town and made their way toward him. . . .*

39 *Many of the Samaritans from that town believed in him because of the woman's testimony, "He told me everything I ever did."* 40 *So when the Samaritans came to him, they urged him to stay with them, and he stayed two days.* 41 *And because of his words many more became believers.*

42 *They said to the woman, "We no longer believe just because of what you said; now we have heard for ourselves, and we know that this man really is the Savior of the world"* (John 4:25–30, 39–42).

➡ **8. (Based on John 4:25–30, 39–42 above) Once the Samaritans believed in Jesus as the Christ and Savior of the world, what kind of relationship do you think they had with Him? Check your opinion, or write your own.**
❑ a. They hated Him because He was a Jew. That would never change.
❑ b. They used Him to get what they wanted, and then they ran Him out of town.
❑ c. They enjoyed their relationship and wanted Him to stay longer. They didn't care that He was a Jew.
❑ d. Other: _____

In this encounter, Jesus crossed significant racial, cultural, social, and religious barriers. He didn't try to avoid this experience but pursued it intentionally. He didn't allow the woman to sidetrack His message. He kept the focus on her need to experience a right and personal relationship with God the Father through Christ (Himself). He *didn't* focus on her sexual lifestyle or her religious ignorance. He knew that her first and greatest need was for a right relationship with God; He would take care of correcting the other things in His timing.

When the Samaritans encountered God through Christ, they didn't let their racial and religious differences separate them. They wanted to keep Jesus around. Did you notice, too, how the woman became involved in the ministry of reconciliation with Jesus? She helped lead many in her town to the Lord. That's the way God wants us involved in the ministry of reconciliation.

In the middle of this experience with the woman at the well, Jesus instructed His disciples about the importance of this ministry of reconciliation.

➡ **Read the following passage. Underline what Jesus said about His Father's will and about the harvest.**

> *Meanwhile his disciples urged him, "Rabbi, eat something."*
> *But he said to them, "I have food to eat that you know nothing about." . . .*
> *"My food," said Jesus, "is to do the will of him who sent me and to finish his work. Do you not say, 'Four months more and then the harvest'? I tell you, open your eyes and look at the fields! They are ripe for harvest. Even now the reaper draws his wages, even now he harvests the crop for eternal life, so that the sower and the reaper may be glad together. Thus the saying 'One sows and another reaps' is true. I sent you to reap what you have not worked for. Others have done the hard work, and you have reaped the benefits of their labor"* (John 4:31–32, 34–38).

For Jesus, the Father's will was like food that nourishes. His will was for Jesus to help reap the spiritual harvest that was ready. The harvest is ripe and ready around us as well. Others have already been working, and God has been working. Now we have God's invitation to join Him in the harvest.

➡ **What, if anything, do you sense God has said to you through today's lesson? Write *one* of the most meaningful things He has said below.**

_____

_____

➡ **Conclude today's lesson by praying. Ask the Lord to give you confidence, boldness, and direction as you join Him in a ministry of reconciliation.**

"Open your eyes and look at the fields! They are ripe for harvest."

LESSON 3 THE PRINCIPLE OF CALL

Scripture for Meditation

"Christ's love compels us . . . that those who live should no longer live for themselves but for him who died for them and was raised again.

"So from now on we regard no one from a worldly point of view. . . . If anyone is in Christ, he is a new creation; the old has gone, the new has come! All this is from God, who reconciled us to himself through Christ and gave us the ministry of reconciliation: that God was reconciling the world to himself in Christ, not counting men's sins against them. And he has committed to us the message of reconciliation. We are therefore Christ's ambassadors, as though God were making his appeal through us. We implore you on Christ's behalf: Be reconciled to God. God made him who had no sin to be sin for us, so that in him we might become the righteousness of God" (2 Corinthians 5:14–21).

A Beginning Prayer

Father, because of Christ's love for me, I am compelled to love You and serve You in any way You ask. I realize I'm a new creation in Christ. I thank You for reconciling me to Yourself. Being an ambassador for Christ is an awesome challenge. Train and use me to help others be reconciled to You. Please help me to know exactly what my part is in the call to be a reconciler. Amen.

PRINCIPLE 1

Call: We are all called to a ministry of reconciliation, and we're all commanded to be reconciled with our brothers across racial, cultural, and denominational barriers.

➡ If you haven't already done so, remove the memory card for principle 1 from the back of your book. During the course, we want you to be able to state the eight principles in your own words. Read the statement of the principle of call two or three times to get familiar with the message.

❖   ❖   ❖

➡ Read and think about the Scripture for Meditation in the left margin, and begin the lesson with prayer.

❖   ❖   ❖

➡ 1. What's the first principle of reconciliation and unity?

The Principle of _____

➡ 2. What are the two main ideas in the Principle of Call?

All are called to a ministry of _____

We are _____ to be reconciled with our brothers.

All Are Called to the Ministry of Reconciliation

Reconciliation is not just one good cause among many from which Christians can choose. It's a lifestyle commanded by our Lord. Reconciliation is the heart of the good news of the gospel: We can be reconciled with God, and we can be reconciled with others. As you've already learned, we all have a role in the ministry of reconciliation as ambassadors of Christ. The principle of call to be ambassadors of Christ is included in one of the Seven Promises of a Promise Keeper:

Promise 7: A Promise Keeper is committed to influence his world, being obedient to the Great Commandment (Mark 12:30–31) and the Great Commission (Matthew 28:19–20).

➡ 3. Read the two greatest commandments below, and see if you can write a summary in ten words or less.

The Great Commandments

"'Love the Lord your God with all your heart and with all your soul and with all your mind and with all your strength.' The second is this: 'Love your neighbor as yourself.' There is no commandment greater than these" (Mark 12:30–31).

My ten-word summary of the two greatest commandments:

_____

_____

We're commanded to love God with all our being and to love our neighbor. In other words, be reconciled to God and be reconciled to each other.

Where love and unity exist in the body, God is being honored.

Reconciliation means being committed to see love win out over alienation and division. Unity and love are the "right stuff" of our Christian walk. Where they exist in the body, God is being honored. Our enemy's goal for Christians is just the opposite. Where division and strife (exemplified by sectarianism and racism) exist in the body of Christ, Satan is having his way.

➥ **4. Who has the following goals for the body of Christ? Write Christ or Satan on the line beside the goal.**

_____ a. My goal is to keep the members of the body of Christ separated from each other, fighting, arguing, rejecting, and mistreating each other and divided along racial and denominational lines.

_____ b. My goal for the body of Christ is for the members to come together in unity of mind and thought, to get along with each other, and to care for and show love to each other.

Satan has the goal of keeping us divided (a). Christ has a goal for us to love one another and be united (b). Not only are we to demonstrate love for God and to others, but we're also to be intentional witnesses for Christ—His ambassadors.

➥ **5. Read the Great Commission in the margin, and write a brief summary in your own words. My summary of the Great Commission:**

_____

_____

The Great Commission
"Go and make disciples of all nations, baptizing them in the name of the Father and of the Son and of the Holy Spirit, and teaching them to obey everything I have commanded you. And surely I am with you always, to the very end of the age" (Matthew 28:19–20).

The opening words of this commission could be literally translated, "as you are going, make disciples." Some believers will be more intentional in going to the nations, but we all can be witnesses for Christ as we go about our daily lives. *None of us is exempt from the Great Commission.*

As ambassadors of Christ and reconcilers, we should seek opportunities to cross barriers, as Jesus did: to Samaritans, women, sinners, the poor, and others.

As ambassadors of Christ and reconcilers, we should seek opportunities to cross barriers as Jesus did: to Samaritans, women, sinners, the poor, and others. We can do this as we go through daily life, helping point and call all kinds of people to turn to the Lord. To embrace this calling in a Christlike way will require us to cross human boundaries with the gospel. Christians must reach beyond the mold of the world and refuse to conform. We need to be agents of transformation. As we reach out and break down walls in relationships, people will be drawn by the Father to ask about the hope we have (see 1 Peter 3:15).

1 Peter 3:15
"In your hearts set apart Christ as Lord. Always be prepared to give an answer to everyone who asks you to give the reason for the hope that you have. But do this with gentleness and respect."

As men and women are reconciled with God, He will work in them so they will be reconciled with their fellow man and with brothers and sisters in Christ. If we had to accomplish this task alone, we would quickly realize we couldn't do it alone. But Christ has good news for us. As His ambassadors, He promises us:

"You will receive power when the Holy Spirit comes on you; and you will be my witnesses in Jerusalem, and in all Judea and Samaria, and to the ends of the earth" (Acts 1:8).

➥ **6. Where does your power come from to be a witness for Christ? Check one.**
❑ a. From me; I can do it myself.
❑ b. From others; I can do it with the encouragement of my brothers.
❑ c. From God the Holy Spirit; He works in and through me in great power.

We're all called to be involved in the ministry of reconciliation. That calling

As we all grow in our obedience, we'll be reconciled to one another.

requires us to point people to Christ and then help them learn to obey all God has commanded. As we all grow in our obedience, we'll live out the reconciliation Christ has provided. The Holy Spirit in us empowers us to carry out that ministry as we go about our daily lives.

➡ **What, if anything, do you sense God has said to you through today's lesson? Write *one* of the most meaningful things He has said below.**

_____

_____

➡ **Conclude today's lesson by praying.**
  • Ask God to empower your witness to others.
  • Ask Him to remind you of this calling daily as you go about your every-day activities.
  • Ask Him to give you a particular burden for people around you who need Jesus Christ as their Savior.

LESSON 4 RECONCILED TO MY BROTHERS

Scriptures for Meditation

"If you are offering your gift at the altar and there remember that your brother has something against you, leave your gift there in front of the altar. First go and be reconciled to your brother; then come and offer your gift" (Matthew 5:23–24).

"Brothers, if someone is caught in a sin, you who are spiritual should restore him gently. But watch yourself, or you also may be tempted. Carry each other's burdens, and in this way you will fulfill the law of Christ" (Galatians 6:1–2).

A Beginning Prayer

Father, reconciliation is a calling You have given me. According to Your Word, I *must* be reconciled to my brothers in order to be right with You. Reveal to me the brothers to whom I need to be reconciled, and enable me for reconciliation. Amen.

➡ **Read and think about the Scriptures for Meditation in the left margin, and begin the lesson with prayer.**

You've learned that God has called us all to a ministry of reconciliation. The first and primary assignment is to call people to get right in their relationship with God. But that's not the end of God's plan; it's the beginning. When God adds members to the body of Christ, He wants them to be one in Christ. That requires that brothers in Christ live out reconciliation with each other as well.

➡ **1. In Matthew 5:23–24 in the margin, Jesus gave us a prerequisite for worship (bringing an offering or gift to God). Check which of the following we must do to be right with God and ready for worship.**
  ❑ a. All I have to do is ask God to forgive me for any sin against my brother.
  ❑ b. All I have to do is confess my sin against my brother to some other Christian and ask him to pray for my forgiveness.
  ❑ c. I don't have to do anything but make sure my heart is sincere.
  ❑ d. I must be reconciled with any brother whom I have offended or with whom I have a broken relationship.

You may want to shout, "No way! Surely God wouldn't require that before He'll accept my worship!" But we don't make the rules; God does. God in Jesus Christ has commanded that we must be reconciled with our brother in order to be acceptable to Him.

➡ **2. Stop and pray about this matter right now. Ask God to reveal any relationship with another person that isn't right. Before the Lord, review the following areas:**

  • family
  • neighbors
  • relatives
  • friends
  • police
  • people of another denomination

  • coworkers
  • church members
  • competitors
  • group members
  • government officials

  • supervisors/management
  • pastor or church staff
  • people in other churches
  • recreation partners
  • people of another race
  • business associates

  • workers who serve you in a local store, gas station, business, etc.

➡ **3. Did anyone come to mind? more than one? Write in the margin the names of any persons who came to mind as you prayed. Assume that these may be people the Lord has brought to mind. As you study today, ask the Lord to reveal how you should respond to them.**

When you're reconciled to God, He then begins the process of reconciling you to others.

When you're reconciled to God, He begins the process of reconciling you to others. His desire is that you experience unity in the body of Christ. The fellowship you have with God will be reflected in the kind of relationship you have with brothers in Christ. In fact, the kind of relationship you have with those brothers is one of the best indicators of the quality of your relationship with God. If one isn't right, the other isn't, either.

➡ **4. Read the following Scriptures from 1 John. Circle the words *brother* and *brothers* each time they occur. Watch to see how your relationship with your brother is a direct indicator of your relationship with God.**

1 John 1:7—*If we walk in the light, as he is in the light, we have fellowship with one another, and the blood of Jesus, his Son, purifies us from all sin.*

1 John 2:9–11—*Anyone who claims to be in the light but hates his brother is still in the darkness. Whoever loves his brother lives in the light, and there is nothing in him to make him stumble. But whoever hates his brother is in the darkness and walks around in the darkness; he does not know where he is going, because the darkness has blinded him.*

1 John 3:14–18—*We know that we have passed from death to life, because we love our brothers. Anyone who does not love remains in death. Anyone who hates his brother is a murderer, and you know that no murderer has eternal life in him.*
   This is how we know what love is: Jesus Christ laid down his life for us. And we ought to lay down our lives for our brothers. If anyone has material possessions and sees his brother in need but has no pity on him, how can the love of God be in him? Dear children, let us not love with words or tongue but with actions and in truth.

1 John 4:19–21—*We love because he first loved us. If anyone says, "I love God," yet hates his brother, he is a liar. For anyone who does not love his brother, whom he has seen, cannot love God, whom he has not seen. And he has given us this command: Whoever loves God must also love his brother.*

➡ **5. Based on these Scriptures, how would you describe your need to be in right relationship with your brothers in Christ? Write a brief answer below.**

_____

_____

_____

_____

_____

_____

➡ **6. Based on the same Scriptures, which of the following brothers in Christ can you hate, refuse to love, carry a grudge against, or maintain a broken relationship with? Check all that apply. Fellow Christians who are:**

❑ Asian	❑ black	❑ charismatic
❑ Cuban	❑ fundamentalist	❑ German
❑ Hispanic	❑ Japanese	❑ Korean
❑ liberal	❑ Mexican	❑ Catholic
❑ Puerto Rican	❑ Vietnamese	❑ mainline Protestant
❑ white	❑ Pentecostal	❑ Native American
❑ Southerners	❑ Northerners	❑ None of the above

This may be another tough question for you. Keep in mind that we're talking about people who have come to faith in Christ and are adopted into God's family. These are brothers.

• You may have served in a war and learned to hate those who killed your comrades.
• You may have had a hurtful experience with a person of another race and find that you have difficulty loving people from that race.
• You may have developed a judgmental spirit toward Christians whose worship practices or doctrines are different from yours.

All these experiences can lead to broken relationships within the body of Christ. These walls must come down if we're to function as a healthy body for the cause and honor of Christ. Members of His body need each other. Without a right relationship with each other, we may miss what God wants to do through us in those relationships. That's why Christ has commanded us to be reconciled to our brothers, even before we come to worship Him.

The Lord might, for example, put together a fundamentalist and a charismatic in a relationship. The fundamentalist may realize he has missed out on some of the joy and spontaneity of worship because of his traditions. God may challenge him to be more open to His divine power and the movement of the Holy Spirit in worship. The charismatic, on the other hand, may realize his focus on spontaneity and emotion in worship has left him without a solid knowledge of God's Word. He may sense God's call to give greater attention to a study and mastery of the Scriptures and turn to his brother for encouragement and help. As they learn to talk and pray together, they may each find ways that they've gone to extremes and need to return to a closer walk with the Lord.

Without right relationships, the body cannot function as it should to correct, encourage, strengthen, exhort, and *"spur one another on toward love and good deeds"* (Hebrews 10:24).

➡ **What, if anything, do you sense God has said to you through today's lesson? Write *one* of the most meaningful things He has said below.**

_____

_____

➡ **Conclude today's lesson by praying. Reflect on what God may have said to you about the need for reconciliation with a brother in Christ. Ask Him what you need to do to be right with your brothers.**

Without a right relationship with each other, we may miss what God wants to do through us in those relationships.

Without right relationships, the body cannot function as it should to correct, encourage, strengthen, exhort, and "spur one another on toward love and good deeds."

SPECIAL ASSIGNMENT

by Raleigh Washington

I retired from the army and felt God's call to pastor. After my training at seminary, one of my professors suggested I consider starting a new church in the inner-city Austin community of Chicago. He got me together with Glen to discuss linking a new church with Circle Urban Ministries.

I considered this pioneering effort without a deep call to serve the poor. When my wife, Paulette, and I first came to Austin, I just wanted to preach. My first preference for planting a church would have been an integrated, middle-class community—not Austin with its terrible poverty, gang graffiti everywhere, and drug traffic. I'd had enough of the ghetto growing up; why in the world would I want to go back?

But we listened to Glen and Lonni Kehrein—these white folks, after all—talk about their call and commitment to racial reconciliation between black and white. We saw their call and commitment to the poor, the oppressed, and the needy.

They chose to live in Austin when they could live much more comfortably somewhere else. The more we listened and observed their lives, the more God was working on our hearts.

"You know," I told Paulette, "if people like us don't return to bring God's hope and resources back into the ghetto, how are we going to facilitate change? I'm a product of the ghetto. Now, I need to go back to live out God's reconciling power." If Glen and Lonni could—how could we not?

Glen found an abandoned building complex that could house a church and Circle Urban Ministries. By that time, God had begun to build deep within Paulette and me an unmistakable call. We already had been called to a ministry of reconciliation to bring people to Christ—as all Christians are called. During seminary, God had called us to a cross-cultural ministry across racial barriers. But now God was confirming our calling across other barriers to be Christ's ambassadors to the poor, oppressed, and needy in the ghetto.

LESSON 5 SPECIAL ASSIGNMENTS FROM GOD

Scripture for Meditation
"'This man is my chosen instrument to carry my name before the Gentiles and their kings and before the people of Israel. I will show him how much he must suffer for my name'" (Acts 9:15–16).

A Beginning Prayer
Father, I thank You for calling Paul to cross barriers with the gospel. I'm sure the spread of Christianity over the past 2,000 years has been, in part, because Paul was faithful to his special assignment. As I study today, help me to appreciate any special calling You have for some of Your ambassadors. Help me to know if I have a special calling from You. Amen.

➡ **God gives some believers a special calling to be trailblazers across different barriers. Read and think about the Scripture for Meditation in the left margin, where God describes His assignment for the apostle Paul. Then begin the lesson with prayer.**

❖ ❖ ❖

➡ **Using your memory cards, review the first four principles for reconciliation and unity.**

➡ **1. In your own words write a summary of the Principle of Call:**

_____

_____

All Christians have been reconciled to God, and *all* have been called to be ambassadors for Christ as they go about their everyday lives. But some have a special assignment that goes above and beyond the ordinary call. When God gives such an assignment to a person, He also equips him to accomplish it. The call to be a reconciler may extend further for you than for other Christians. God may want you to make it the primary focus of your life and ministry—to become a trailblazer.

God Called Paul to the Gentiles

God issued that call to the apostle Paul. Though he was a devout Jew, Paul had grown up as a Roman citizen in a Gentile city (Tarsus). In many ways, God had prepared him to carry the gospel to the Gentiles.

➥ **Read again what God had to say about Saul (later called Paul) in the Scripture for Meditation at the beginning of this lesson.**

After his conversion, Paul spent several years reorienting himself to God through Christ. Then in a prayer meeting at the church in Antioch:

> *"While they were worshiping the Lord and fasting, the Holy Spirit said, 'Set apart for me Barnabas and Saul [Paul] for the work to which I have called them.' So after they had fasted and prayed, they placed their hands on them and sent them off"* (Acts 13:2–3).

➥ **2. Who called Paul and Barnabas to a special assignment? Check one.**
❑ a. Paul and Barnabas decided it sounded like a great challenge to serve the Lord and called themselves.
❑ b. The leaders at the church at Antioch decided someone needed to go to the Gentiles and called Barnabas and Paul to do the job.
❑ c. God, through the Holy Spirit, called out Paul and Barnabas to the assignment He had for them.

God is the only one who has a right to your life. He alone can call you to be a trailblazer who goes beyond what He calls all Christians to do in reconciliation. And even when He gives the assignment, you'll need to wait until He says, "Now is the time to go." Paul waited several years before God gave Him the specific assignment to go start new churches among the Gentiles.

Peter Was Called to Cross Boundaries
Peter was a Jew—evidently a fairly strict one. His saw his job as taking the message of reconciliation to other Jews. He didn't feel right about crossing the boundary to work with Gentiles.

➥ **3. Where is your comfort zone denominationally, ethnically, and socioeconomically? Check *one in each column* below, or describe your comfort zone in your own words.**

Denomination/ Tradition	Ethnicity	Socioeconomic group
❑ Baptist	❑ white	❑ poor
❑ Charismatic	❑ black	❑ middle class
❑ Methodist	❑ Hispanic	❑ upper class
❑ Pentecostal	❑ Native American	❑ Other:
❑ Presbyterian	❑ Asian (specify)	
❑ Other:	❑ Other:	_____
_____	_____	

➥ **4. If God were to call you to cross the *most difficult* boundary in each of those three categories, which would it be? Circle one in each column, or write your own in the margin.**

One day, however, God called Peter to cross major cultural barriers for Christ. You may want to turn in your Bible and read the full story in Acts 10:1–48. We're only going to look at part of the story. It begins with a Gentile:

> *"At Caesarea there was a man named Cornelius, a centurion. . . . He and all his family were devout and God-fearing; he gave generously to those in need and prayed to God regularly"* (Acts 10:1–2).

God was getting ready to do a special work in this Gentile's life and family. But God needed an ambassador who would bring Cornelius the message about Jesus

God is the only one who has a right to your life.

He alone can call you to be a trailblazer who goes beyond what He calls all Christians to do in reconciliation.

God needed an ambassador who would bring Cornelius the message about Jesus Christ.

Peter's Assignment

"About noon the following day as they were on their journey and approaching the city, Peter went up on the roof to pray. He became hungry and wanted something to eat, and while the meal was being prepared, he fell into a trance. He saw heaven opened and something like a large sheet being let down to earth by its four corners. It contained all kinds of four-footed animals, as well as reptiles of the earth and birds of the air. Then a voice told him, 'Get up, Peter. Kill and eat.'

"'Surely not, Lord!' Peter replied. 'I have never eaten anything impure or unclean.'

"The voice spoke to him a second time, 'Do not call anything impure that God has made clean.'

"This happened three times, and immediately the sheet was taken back to heaven.

"While Peter was wondering about the meaning of the vision, the men sent by Cornelius found out where Simon's house was and stopped at the gate. They called out, asking if Simon who was known as Peter was staying there.

"While Peter was still thinking about the vision, the Spirit said to him, 'Simon, three men are looking for you. So get up and go downstairs. Do not hesitate to go with them, for I have sent them'" (Acts 10:9–20).

Christ. Through an angel, God told Cornelius to send for Peter. So Cornelius sent messengers to get Peter. Now God had to get Peter ready! To understand the call of Peter, keep in mind that Jews ate only approved (kosher) foods.

➡ **5. Read the next part of the story in the margin. As you read, underline the key statement by the "voice" that would help Peter consider crossing the boundary to work with Gentiles.**

❖ ❖ ❖

The voice said, *"Do not call anything impure that God has made clean."* Peter found out what the visitors wanted, and he went with them.

Cornelius was expecting them and had called together his relatives and close friends. As Peter entered the house, Cornelius met him and fell at his feet in reverence. But Peter made him get up. "Stand up," he said, "I am only a man myself."

Talking with him, Peter went inside and found a large gathering of people. He said to them: "You are well aware that it is against our law for a Jew to associate with a Gentile or visit him. But God has shown me that I should not call any man impure or unclean. So when I was sent for, I came without raising any objection. . . .

"I now realize how true it is that God does not show favoritism but accepts men from every nation who fear him and do what is right" (Acts 10:24–29, 34–35).

➡ **6. According to God's instructions to Peter, how many groups of people are common, unclean, and unacceptable to God? Check the correct answer.**
❏ a. None. God shows no favoritism. He accepts people from every nation, so I should accept them, too.
❏ b. God has given me a brain to use. I can decide which people are not acceptable to God, and He gives me permission to refuse to fellowship with them.

If you checked *b*, you had better read the Scriptures again. God does not show favoritism, and He accepts people from every nation. Peter told Cornelius and his Gentile household about God's plan for salvation through Jesus. Then:

While Peter was still speaking these words, the Holy Spirit came on all who heard the message. The circumcised believers who had come with Peter were astonished that the gift of the Holy Spirit had been poured out even on the Gentiles. For they heard them speaking in tongues and praising God.

Then Peter said, "Can anyone keep these people from being baptized with water? They have received the Holy Spirit just as we have." So he ordered that they be baptized in the name of Jesus Christ. Then they asked Peter to stay with them for a few days (Acts 10:44–48).

God called Peter to cross this major boundary because He (God) was getting ready to reconcile a whole household (probably including servants and other workers) to Himself. More than that, God was getting ready to open the door of missions to the Gentiles. God had called Paul and equipped him to be the first primary missionary to them. After Peter's experience with Cornelius, Paul was used by God to start churches among the Gentiles. When some Jews objected, God used Peter and his experience with Cornelius to verify that God was the author of this work.

➡ **7. If God were to call you to a special assignment as a trailblazer, what do you suppose He would have in mind? Check your opinion, or write your own.**

❏ a. I guess He would want to give me a chance to see what I can do.
❏ b. He must not like me and would want to give me a tough assignment just to punish me.
❏ c. He would have a plan to touch people's lives, and I would have the privilege of working with Him to see their lives changed for good.
❏ d. Other: _____

A Special Assignment

God does have a special assignment for some of His people. When He calls people to such a task, He has a plan in mind. What God purposes, He brings to pass. A special calling to be a trailblazer indicates that God wants to reconcile people, and He wants to give you the privilege of joining Him in His wonderful work. This special calling may mean making the message of reconciliation your primary lifelong ministry focus. It may mean being on the front lines, showing the way for your brothers in Christ, by:

- becoming part of a multiracial church
- taking the lead in building a bridge between your church and a church of another denomination or racial mix
- serving as a counselor to help couples and families be reconciled
- working with other nationalities or language groups as a missionary
- settling disputes between fellow believers as a Christian arbitrator
- reaching out on your job to people of other races
- working in a multicultural community to see people of all types be reconciled to God and each other

> *A special calling to be a trailblazer indicates that God wants to reconcile people, and He wants to give you the privilege of joining Him in His wonderful work.*

If God calls you to a ministry across human boundaries, it's because He's getting ready to do something there, and He wants you involved!

➥ **8. Is He calling you to be a "wall buster" in your community or somewhere else in the world?** ❏ yes ❏ no ❏ I'm not sure

➥ **If you're not sure, ask Him. Take a moment to pray. If He's calling you to a special assignment, He'll let you know at just the right time!**

> *If God calls you to a ministry across human boundaries, it's because He's getting ready to do something there, and He wants you involved!*

Equipped, Too

God doesn't call you to a task without providing help. He's present in your life to enable you to do what He has called you to do. His Holy Spirit will give you the needed gift or gifts.

Trailblazers have a special grace that shows itself in a greater-than-usual desire to cross barriers. Melting racial or social barriers "comes more naturally" to them than to most of us, even though we all share the goal of reconciliation, and they refuse to remain within cultural confines. They're comfortable and at ease in mixed settings. There's no fear, but love abounds. They have an extra ability to absorb pain inflicted by others without retaliating. They can forgive quickly when offended. They enjoy the "spice" of differences found in the mixture of people.

> *Trailblazers have a special grace that shows itself in a greater-than-usual desire to cross barriers.*

The trailblazer with God's call is gifted, driven, and committed to follow after God's heart of reconciliation. It's his passion in ministry. He's compelled by Christ's love for the people with whom he works. The dangers of the inner city, which intimidate many, will not stop him if that is where God has called him. The suspicious rejection of people will challenge him but not defeat him. The anger of others will call forth love; their despair will generate compassion. He will learn to carry the pain of others, and he'll be able to overlook offenses and differences.

The world has yet to see the incredible power that could be unleashed if God's people faithfully "took up the cross" of reconciliation and lived out the love of the gospel.

The world has yet to see the incredible power that could be unleashed if God's people faithfully "took up the cross" of reconciliation and lived out the love of the gospel. We're all called to play a part in this symphony of God's kingdom. Each of us has a part to play. And some will be especially called in this area to be God's trailblazers.

➡ **9. Do you sense that God already may be calling you to be a trailblazer across significant human boundaries like denominational, racial, or socioeconomic walls? If so, briefly describe:**
  • what you sense He's calling you to do or
  • how He has equipped and prepared you to cross barriers and love people who are different

_____

_____

_____

➡ What, if anything, do you sense God has said to you through today's lesson? Write *one* of the most meaningful things He has said below.

_____

_____

1. What do You want me to do in my personal relationship to You?
2. What do You want me to do in relationship to other people in my church or denomination?
3. What do You want me to do in relationship to Christians in other denominations or Christian traditions?
4. What do You want me to do in relationship to Christians of other races or ethnic backgrounds?

➡ For each lesson this week, you've been recording what you sense God has said to you. Review the final activity for each of the previous lessons on pages 56, 59, 62, and 64. What's the major emphasis of what you sense God wants you to do in response to this unit's lessons? Pray and ask Him what He wants you to do. Then write notes in the margin or in a separate notebook. You might use the questions in the margin in your prayer.

➡ Conclude today's lesson by praying the prayer of Francis of Assisi—one who had a special assignment to cross boundaries as a trailblazer for Christ's kingdom.

The Prayer of Francis of Assisi
Lord, make me an instrument of your peace,
Where there is hatred, let me sow love,
Where there is injury, pardon,
Where there is doubt, faith,
Where there is despair, hope,
Where there is darkness, light,
Where there is sadness, Joy.

Oh Divine Master,
Grant that I may not so much seek
To be consoled as to console
To be understood as to understand
To be loved as to love.

For it is in giving that we receive.
It is in pardoning that we are pardoned.
It is in dying that we are born to eternal life!

UNIT 4 COMMITMENT TO RELATIONSHIP

Scripture Memory Verse

"A new command I give you: Love one another. As I have loved you, so you must love one another."

—John 13:34

Unit Learning Goal

You will understand the nature and importance of committed relationships, and you'll demonstrate your commitment to build God-honoring relationships with others in the body of Christ.

Overview of Unit 2

Lesson 1: The Principle of Commitment to Relationship
Lesson 2: Committed Relationships
Lesson 3: God's Model for Relationships
Lesson 4: Accepting One Another for Relationships
Lesson 5: Loving One Another

PRINCIPLE 2
Commitment to Relationship: Loved by God and adopted into His family, we are called to committed love relationships with our brothers.

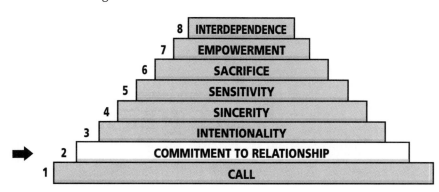

8	INTERDEPENDENCE
7	EMPOWERMENT
6	SACRIFICE
5	SENSITIVITY
4	SINCERITY
3	INTENTIONALITY
2	COMMITMENT TO RELATIONSHIP
1	CALL

The Body of Christ

CHRIST

GOD'S TROPHY

Key Summary Statements from Unit 4

- When we desire to be reconciled across racial lines or denominational barriers, we start on the personal level and seek out a person to become a friend.
- When relationships form, stereotypes quickly fall, and understanding grows.
- Genuine reconciliation happens when a relationship has a commitment to resolve differences.
- "Divorce is not an option," and we must lean on our commitment to our brother to resolve that difference.
- If we hang in there and resolve our differences, the resolution will bring us closer.
- We're to accept one another the way Christ has accepted us.
- The way Christians love each other is the best way to tell if they're disciples (followers) of Jesus Christ.
- *Love* is a verb. It calls for action that demonstrates its reality.
- God's love for us is a perfect love. It's not based on changing circumstances.
- When you see a person or group with a need, the way to demonstrate love is to help meet that need. Meeting needs of Christian brothers is one way for healing to come to the body of Christ.

God's Model for Relationships

- Accept one another as Christ has accepted you.
- Forgive one another as Christ has forgiven you.
- Love one another as Christ has loved you.
- Serve one another as Christ has served you.
- Comfort one another as Christ has comforted you.

KIOWA SON[1]

I sat looking at the white man seated a few feet from me. My heart was cold toward this man, and I assumed he felt the same way about me. It seemed this was the way it had always been and the way it would always be—the Indian and the white man as enemies, facing each other in anger and suspicion.

This man, Sonny, had taken me into his home to help me overcome my addiction to alcohol. Sonny had opened his home to other men who needed help, and now I realized I had placed myself in the midst of the very thing I hated most: white men. I could have left, but I didn't have any other options.

Things had gone well at first. I kept to myself and just tried to do what was required of me. But then one day we were all out building fences, and one of the other men began to antagonize me. Cold fury started to well up within me, and before I knew it, I was beating him mercilessly with my fists. He had fallen to the ground, moaning in pain, and I continued to kick him, again and again, until blood was flowing from his face and ears. I had intended to crush the life from him, but for some reason I stopped. Later, when we arrived back at Sonny's house, I still couldn't understand what had kept me from murdering the other man.

Sonny called me into his office, and I thought, *If this white man provokes me, I'm going to hurt him.* He didn't say anything at first but just sat there looking at me, incredulous at the amount of anger and hatred he had seen pouring out of me. He kept shaking his head in disbelief, and finally he said, "I just can't understand why you reacted that way!" He paused for a moment, and then a look of realization slowly spread across his face. He blurted out, "Spencer, you have hatred and bitterness in your heart toward all white people!"

I looked at him and said coldly, "Yeah, you're right. And I don't think I like you that much, either." I wanted him to react to my words, but he did nothing. I had expected Sonny to try to intimidate me as other white men had always done. Instead, he had unexpectedly confronted me with the bitterness in my own heart. I felt strangely uneasy.

"Why?" he pleaded. "Why are you so angry?"

In that moment, my mind wandered back to my childhood days in Oklahoma . . . and to my father.

My father was a Kiowa Indian who loved Jesus. As a young man, he had been an alcoholic, but he was miraculously saved on a skid-row street in Los Angeles. He came home to Oklahoma, married my mother, and said to himself, *To live in this white man's world, I will need to be like the white man.* So he went off to college and got his degree in accounting.

He came back to Oklahoma again, but no one would hire him because he was an Indian. He tried and tried to find work, but no one would even talk to him. So he took a job as a dishwasher. My father had a college degree, yet he worked in that kitchen washing dishes until he died. My father would always go to church at the Indian mission down the street, but most of the time he'd be the only one there. Preachers to the Indians were few and far between. I remember my father would sit on the front porch of our house in the evenings and sing hymns to Jesus. When I walked by him, I was afraid to say a word because the presence of God was all around him. Yet I saw him consistently looked down upon because of the color of his skin.

One particular incident that tore at my heart happened when I was twelve years old. My father and I had been standing in a hardware store for what seemed like an eternity. We had been waiting alone at the counter, but the clerk just ignored us. We waited and waited, but when the door swung open and a few white men came in, the clerk came alive. He greeted them with a warm smile and within a few minutes had taken care of their every need. When the store was once again empty except for us, he turned to my father, and his smile disappeared. "Well, what do you want?" he demanded impatiently. I'll never forget how it felt to see my father humiliated before me. But the painful memories didn't stop there.

My thoughts wandered back to another day I couldn't forget: the day my sisters and brother and I convinced our parents to let us go with them to town. Our family lived out in the country, so going to town was a rare treat. It was a big deal for us to be able to play in the park while they went grocery shopping. But when they dropped us off at the park and drove away, the four of us were suddenly surrounded by a group of older white children who began to beat us and call us "redskin" and "dirty Indian."

I watched the kids jerk my sister around by her braids as I screamed in frustration, powerless to help her. I watched my baby brother get pushed to the ground while my older sister kept pleading with them to stop slapping her in the face. When at last they left us alone, I cried softly and wondered why being an Indian made us so different.

But all these wounds I hid in my heart. As I grew older and more bitter, I began to get into fights. I took martial arts classes, and I started drinking more and more. There seemed to be no end to the anger inside me. After one particular late-night brawl with a bunch of cowboys, I came home, walked inside the front door, and heard the unmistakable sound of weeping. I looked down the hall and saw that it was coming from my father. He was praying for me. When he saw me, he ran and hugged me. Just like the father of the prodigal son, he fell on my neck and wept. Then he looked up to heaven and said, "Thank You, Lord, for bringing my son home safely to me."

All of a sudden, I wanted to know this Jesus who could fill a man with such deep love for his family, even in the midst of humiliation and hardship. I had seen a lot of Christian tracts and heard a lot of preachers, but I saw a living example of Christ in my father, and I wanted to be like him. So when I was seventeen, I met Jesus.

I went back to high school with a Bible in my hand. I started preaching, and people began to get saved. My father was overjoyed. He came to me and said, "Son, God is going to use you. But if you get a burden, get a burden for the Indian people. The white people have plenty of preachers, but the Indians have nothing."

I looked at him, and it was then I realized I was ashamed of who I was. I had no intention of going to that Indian mission. Instead, my wife and I married right after high school, and we started going to a white church. But I felt pressured to change all kinds of things about myself in order to fit in. I was trying to be a young white man and to be successful in the white man's world, but I was living a lie.

I saw my poor father continually going to the mission church, and still there were no preachers. I kept trying to live up to the standard of my church, cutting my hair short and wearing all the nice clothes. I got my associate degree from Bible school and started talking the language young preachers talked. But my soul was in deep conflict. I was still attempting to be something I wasn't.

When I was nineteen years old and just about to be ordained as a minister, my church split apart. Right then the conflict in my soul reached a breaking point. I laid down my Bible and said to my wife, "I'm not going back. The white folks don't have any more truth than we have."

For the next two years, I walked in rebellion. I drank and became worse. I shamed myself and brought reproach upon my family. And right in the middle of that time, my father passed away. A couple of months before he died, he said to me, "Son, you're breaking my heart. I'm not going to live to see next year, but I've prayed for you. You and all my family will be saved, but I'll not live to see it."

He died soon after that. When we buried him, I looked

at his body in that casket and said quietly, without anybody listening, "Dad, I'll see you there." And that's when I turned my heart back to Jesus.

But I still couldn't quit drinking. There was an incredible emptiness inside me, and I was drinking up to a fifth of liquor a day. By this time, I was totally addicted. I ended up in the Native American Detoxification Center, but I could stay there only a few months.

I began looking for a rehabilitation program to help me stay sober. I heard about a little ministry in east Texas called "Gates of Life" and run by an ex-longshoreman named Sonny Jaynes. I prayed and decided that this was the place to which God was directing me. Little did I know that my long and bitter journey would soon be coming to an end.

It seemed as if an eternity had passed that day as I looked up at Sonny's face. He was quietly waiting for my answer, and his eyes still reflected the confusion: "Why?" Waves of pain washed over me as I poured out memories of my past. I couldn't hold it back. I just sat there and cried. I cried for my mother, my brothers, and my sisters. I cried for my father, and I cried for myself.

Then I heard something I had never heard before. I looked up, and Sonny was crying, too, and praying, "Lord, forgive us for how we have treated the Indian people. Lord, please forgive us." His head went down, and his shoulders were shaking as he wept. My heart began to break as I realized he was weeping for my people.

"Lord, O Lord, please forgive us," he prayed again. Then he looked up at me with tears streaming down his face and said, "Spencer, I can't speak for every white man, but I can speak on behalf of myself and my family. I'm sorry for what's been done to the Indian people. Will you forgive me?"

I knew then, deep in my spirit, that Jesus was real. Nobody but a God of love could fill a man with the kind of love and acceptance that was emanating from Sonny at that moment. Looking up at him, I knew that I would follow Jesus, too.

"For Jesus' sake," I replied, "I forgive you." Peace flooded my being from that day on. My relationship with Jesus began to take me to a place of deep love for my fellowman. There would come a day when I would look into the eyes of white men and say, "My brothers, I love you.'"

---

[1]Adapted from *Healing America's Wounds,* by John Dawson (Ventura, Cal.: Regal Books, 1994), 166-72.

LESSON 1

THE PRINCIPLE OF COMMITMENT TO RELATIONSHIP

Scriptures for Meditation
"A new command I give you: Love one another. As I have loved you, so you must love one another" (John 13:34).

"If we walk in the light, as he is in the light, we have fellowship with one another, and the blood of Jesus, his Son, purifies us from all sin" (1 John 1:7).

A Beginning Prayer
Father, as I walk in the light of Christ, I do have a deep love relationship with You. I also have a love relationship with other brothers and sisters in Christ. Help me to experience that kind of committed relationship with those in the body of Christ who are different from me. Amen.

PRINCIPLE 2
Commitment to Relationship: Loved by God and adopted into His family, we are called to committed love relationships with our brothers.

➡ John 13:34 (in the margin) is your Scripture memory verse for this unit. Remove the perforated card from the back of your book, and begin memorizing it. Read and think about the Scriptures for Meditation in the left margin, and begin the lesson with prayer.

❖ ❖ ❖

➡ Remove the memory card from the back of your book for the second principle of reconciliation and unity. Read it two or three times. In the margin to the left, you'll see the same text. Memorize the three words that are underlined. Write those words below:

_____

➡ 1. In John 13:34 in the margin above, how are we commanded to relate to brothers and sisters in Christ? We are to . . .

_____

A Relationship Changed a Life
Thomas Tarrants wrote the following in a book chapter entitled "How I Learned to Hate":

There were plenty of black people in Mobile, [Alabama] . . . But I did not want them as my next-door neighbors or best friends, and I certainly did not want to go to school with them. White was white, and black was black, and never the twain should mix.[1]

And he grew good at hating—so good that he joined the Ku Klux Klan and served faithfully with a vengeance until it landed him in a Mississippi state prison death row. Cracks in his white supremacist ideology began to form when he was forced to work with a black fellow prisoner—a doctor who "was a genuinely compassionate man. . . . He treated me the same way he treated everyone else, respectfully and cordially, and I found myself liking him immensely, almost in spite of myself."[2] What the relationship began, the power of Scripture completed as Tom soon thereafter accepted Christ, and his racist beliefs dissolved.

Committed Relationship to God
The greatest chasm ever to exist was created by what we call sin. Adam's sin and consequently our fallen nature brought the inevitable consequence of spiritual death, or separation from God. *"Your iniquities have separated you from your God; your sins have hidden his face from you, so that he will not hear"* (Isaiah 59:2). No greater alienation of any two parties has ever existed than the absolute separation brought on by sin. The separation was so great that the whole human race was alienated from God, and the entire earthly creation was polluted. But God sought to redeem His creation and reconcile us to himself through His Son, Jesus Christ:

God was pleased to have all his fullness dwell in him [Christ], and through him to reconcile to himself all things, whether things on earth or things in heaven, by making peace through his blood, shed on the cross.
Once you were alienated from God and were enemies in your minds because of your evil behavior. But now he has reconciled you by Christ's physical body through death to present you holy in his sight, without blemish

---

[1] *He's My Brother*, by John Perkins and Thomas A. Tarrants, III with David Wimbish. (Grand Rapids, Mich.: Chosen Books, 1994), p. 39.

[2] Ibid., p. 118.

and free from accusation (Colossians 1:19–22).

The sacrificial work was completed by Christ on the cross. This reconciliation becomes effective in our individual lives as we enter a personal committed relationship with God through the finished work of Jesus. God, therefore, has given us the foundation for reconciliation: committed relationships.

➡ **2. What is a foundation for reconciliation?**

_____

You can't be reconciled with your brother without a committed relationship.

God demonstrated His commitment to relationship with us by sending His Son. We can't be reconciled apart from a relationship with Jesus. The same will be true of reconciliation with brothers who are different from you. You can't be reconciled with your brother without a committed relationship.

➡ **3. Read again the second Scripture for Meditation at the beginning of today's lesson (1 John 1:7). If we walk in the light of a right relationship with God, how will we be related to brothers in Christ?**

_____

The word *fellowship* is an intimate sharing of common life between believers. In a right relationship with each other, the blood of Jesus will continually cleanse us of sin. How can you have that kind of committed relationship with people who are different from you?

Where to Start

When we desire to live out reconciliation across racial lines or denominational barriers, we start on the personal level and seek out a person to become our friend.

Where Do I Start

When the greatness of the divisions in the body of Christ is discussed, we almost always are asked, "But where do I start?" We start where God started. When we desire to live out reconciliation across racial lines or denominational barriers, we start on the personal level and seek out a person to become our friend. As that relationship grows, false prejudices (or prejudgments) that created walls of separation will fall in the face of interpersonal reality.

➡ **4. Which of the following best describes a way to begin overcoming racial and denominational barriers? Check one, or write your own.**
❏ a. I would ask my pastor what I ought to believe about those people.
❏ b. I would read a book about them but keep my distance.
❏ c. I would cultivate a personal friendship with a person who is different.
❏ d. Other: _____

Seeking counsel from your pastor is not a wrong answer. There are cults and false religions in the world that he might be able to help you avoid. Later we'll talk about developing sensitivity, and reading a book about people who are different is one way of becoming sensitive to others. But the best place to begin reconciliation is by cultivating a personal friendship with another person in the body of Christ who is different from you.

"Birds of a feather flock together"?

Ephesians 2:14
"For he himself is our peace, who has made the two one and has destroyed the barrier, the dividing wall of hostility."

"Birds of a feather flock together" is true for birds, and sometimes for people. It sounds innocent enough, and it does describe a natural tendency of human beings. We tend to feel most comfortable around people who are just like us. But have you ever stopped to think that our enemy might have a purpose in this "natural" tendency? We know from Scripture that human barriers are not supposed to exist between believers (Ephesians 2:14). The early church was a cultural and racial mixture, visibly demonstrating Christ's commandment to the disciples to be unified. God's goal is to see Christians united in love, as brothers and sisters. Satan's goal is to separate us.

Historically, racial strife is rooted first in separation. In the United States, Jim

Crow laws in the South and racial ghettos in the North created a separate society, divided by race and racism. Satan can get us to believe a lie about people we don't know. Blacks might believe, "Those suburban white people hate us." Whites might believe, "Black people are killing each other, and they just don't care." Similar conflict can exist between Native Americans and whites or between Hispanics and blacks.

➡ **5. What's the major danger in separation from our brothers? Check one.**
❑ a. I don't think there's any danger in separation. I think it's a good idea.
❑ b. I might be tempted to believe a lie or accept stereotypes as true for all people different from myself.
❑ c. I might miss opportunities to offer and receive ministry from my brothers.

Overcoming Ignorance

The greatest danger in separation is believing an untruth due to ignorance. When relationships form, stereotypes quickly fall, and understanding grows. Separation will also cause us to miss opportunities to offer and receive ministry, but that's not so much a danger as a missed opportunity. People who would like to maintain separation in the body of Christ don't realize God is working in just the opposite direction. Their resistance is resistance against God's efforts to make us one in Christ. The separation keeps us from revealing God's heart to the world through a unified body of Christ.

Native Americans challenge us to "Walk a mile in my moccasins" before drawing conclusions about them. We can show great ignorance based on lack of personal contact and involvement. Personal experience remains the best teacher. That's why learning through relationships is foundational to reconciliation.

➡ **6. Suppose you wanted to understand why alcoholism and suicide are so prevalent among Native Americans on reservations. Which of the following would be the best way to come to that understanding? Check one answer below, or write your own in the margin.**
❑ a. Get together with your white friends and discuss the problems.
❑ b. Spend time with a Native American friend on the reservation, and experience the sense of despair up close and personal.
❑ c. Wait until they have a program about it on The Discovery Channel.
❑ d. Read a book about the problems written by a black sociologist.

You probably could come up with a good way of your own. But keep in mind that secondhand discussions, books, or television programs won't help you understand nearly as well as experiencing the problems with a friend.

➡ **What, if anything, do you sense God has said to you through today's lesson? Write *one* of the most meaningful things He has said below.**

_____

_____

➡ **Conclude today's lesson by praying.**
• Pray about the small group God has placed you in for this study.
• Talk with the Lord about any weaknesses you have that might cause you to run away from the relationships.
• Ask the Lord to increase your love for and commitment to others.
• Ask Him to help you "Walk a mile in their shoes" and come to understand each group member better.
• Pray for each group member by name, and pray for specific needs you know of in each life.

When relationships form, stereotypes quickly fall, and understanding grows.

People who would like to maintain separation in the body of Christ don't realize God is working in just the opposite direction.

"Walk a mile in my moccasins."

LESSON 2 COMMITTED RELATIONSHIPS

Scripture for Meditation

"Don't urge me to leave you or to turn back from you. Where you go I will go, and where you stay I will stay. Your people will be my people and your God my God. Where you die I will die, and there I will be buried. May the LORD deal with me, be it ever so severely, if anything but death separates you and me" (Ruth 1:16–17).

Beginning Prayer

Father, You have created me to need relationships with others. I confess I have shied away from some relationships just because I enjoyed staying in my comfort zone. Reveal to me the kind of relationships that would be best for my life. Amen.

➡ **Read and think about the Scripture for Meditation in the left margin, and begin the lesson with prayer.**

❖ ❖ ❖

An Example of a Committed Relationship

One of Jesus' and King David's ancestors has a whole book in the Bible devoted to telling her story. Ruth was not a Hebrew (later called Jews). She was a Moabite woman. During the period when judges ruled Israel, a Hebrew family moved to Moab because of a famine in Israel. The father died, and the two sons married Moabite women. Ten years later, the two sons died. Naomi, the mother, determined to return to Israel and encouraged her widowed daughters-in-law to return to their families. One did, but Ruth did not.

➡ **1. Read again the words of Ruth to Naomi in your Scripture for Meditation in the margin. In each pair of words below, check the one that you think best describes Ruth's committed relationship with her mother-in-law.**

❑ a. permanent   or   ❑ b. temporary
❑ c. unfaithful   or   ❑ d. faithful
❑ e. shaky   or   ❑ f. firm
❑ g. selfish   or   ❑ h. giving

Ruth's determination to move to a foreign land with her mother-in-law revealed a committed relationship that was permanent, faithful, firm, and giving. It caught the attention of others who saw it. Ruth was commended by Naomi's relative Boaz:

> *"I've been told all about what you have done for your mother-in-law since the death of your husband—how you left your father and mother and your homeland and came to live with a people you did not know before. May the LORD repay you for what you have done. May you be richly rewarded by the LORD, the God of Israel, under whose wings you have come to take refuge"* (Ruth 2:11–12).

God honored Ruth by giving her Boaz as a new husband. Together they became the great-grandparents of Israel's King David. Because of her commitment to Naomi, she also became an ancestor of Jesus the Messiah. What a reward!

Committed to Resolving Differences

Genuine reconciliation happens when a relationship has a commitment to resolve differences. The analogy of a marriage is helpful. A marriage is, above all else, a commitment to another person. Successful marriages are not those in which conflict never arises—no such marriage exists. A solid marriage is one in which the partners share a commitment to resolve conflict. The commitment says, "I'm going to hang in there and resolve this problem."

The greater the natural differences of gender, culture, and life experience between people, the greater is the potential for conflict. Racial struggle causes a unique dynamic. To think that friendships with people of other races should be effortlessly filled with joy, peace, and success is unrealistic. We accept the fact that gender conflict is inevitable in a marriage. Why, then, do we bristle when racial conflict arises in a cross-cultural relationship?

We should understand that Satan is a roaring lion who is prowling around, seeking to destroy the unity God desires to build. Satan will use our cultural differences and past racial pain against us. We may verbally wound each other. We'll

Genuine reconciliation happens when a relationship has a commitment to resolve differences.

The commitment says, "I'm going to hang in there and resolve this problem."

be tempted to "cut and run" quickly when a relationship encounters its first struggle. This is where commitment comes in. We must understand that "divorce is not an option," and we must lean on our commitment to our brother to resolve that difference. If we respond with, "I don't need this, I'm out of here," Satan wins a victory, and our faith is impotent. If we hang in there and resolve our differences, the experience will bring us closer. Just as the resolution of conflict strengthens a marriage, it also strengthens a committed relationship across racial or denominational lines.

Divorce is not an option.

If we hang in there and resolve our differences, the resolution will bring us closer.

➡ **Answer the following questions as True (T) or False (F).**

___ 1. In a committed relationship, I should not run away just because differences arise.

___ 2. "Divorce," or cutting off a relationship, is a good option if conflict arises.

___ 3. Resolving conflict will weaken a relationship and lead to a breakup.

___ 4. The greater the differences between two people, the greater is the potential for conflict.

The principle of commitment to relationship will call for patience and determination to stay connected even when the going gets tough. (Answers: true=1, 4; false=2, 3)

➡ **What, if anything, do you sense God has said to you through today's lesson? Write *one* of the most meaningful things He has said below.**

_____

_____

➡ **Conclude today's lesson by praying for lasting relationships with other Christians, especially with those who are different. Think about problems or concerns you might encounter with the people in your small group, and ask the Lord to enable you to "hang in there" and work through any difficulties for His glory.**

LESSON 3   GOD'S MODEL FOR RELATIONSHIPS

Scripture for Meditation
"God has chosen to make known . . . this mystery, which is Christ in you, the hope of glory" (Colossians 1:27).

A Beginning Prayer
Father, You have planned from the beginning that I should be like Jesus—Your Son. You want me to share the family likeness. I do, too. Please work in me to conform me to look like Jesus in the way I relate to others, especially those in the body of Christ. Teach me God-honoring ways to relate to my brothers. Amen.

➡ **Read and think about the Scripture for Meditation in the left margin, and begin the lesson with prayer.**

❖ ❖ ❖

Unity and reconciliation in the body of Christ cannot be experienced apart from relationships. God has given us a perfect model for right relationships in the body. Jesus was and is fully God. He's divine. Yet in His earthly life, He was fully and perfectly human as well. He lived a sinless life in every relationship. He's our model for right relationships—relationships that will honor God. As you experience new relationships in your small group and in the larger Christian community, your best hope for success is to be like Jesus.

➡ **1. Think about developing relationships across racial or denominational lines in a manner like Christ's. What's your first thought about your potential for success? Check your opinion.**

❑ a. Hey, I can do it—no problem!

❑ b. No way. I can't do it, and I couldn't even come close.

❑ c. It's a big challenge, but with Christ's help, I can come close.

❑ d. The best I can expect is average success: win some and lose some.

If you're thinking from a human perspective, you might be depressed and see

Colossians 1:27
"God has chosen to make known . . . this mystery, which is Christ in you, the hope of glory."

little hope for success. If you look at the possibilities from God's perspective, however, you'll see much greater potential. The good news is that Jesus isn't just your model; He's also present and living in you.

➡ **2. Read again Colossians 1:27 in the margin. Where is Christ in relation to you?**

He is _____

The Spirit of Christ is in you! If you will let self die, Christ will live out His life through you. When people encounter you, they'll encounter Christ through you! That's the way Paul described his life:

I have been crucified with Christ and I no longer live, but Christ lives in me. The life I live in the body, I live by faith in the Son of God, who loved me and gave himself for me (Galatians 2:20).

As you enter into relationships with other brothers in Christ, look to Him for the correct model for those relationships. Deny the ways your human nature might choose to respond to others. Allow His Spirit to guide you and enable you to live correctly in relationship to others. *"For it is God who works in you to will and to act according to his good purpose"* (Philippians 2:13).

➡ **3. Which of the following best describes the way you can live in God-honoring relationship to other members in the body of Christ? Check one.**

❏ a. I will study the life and ways of Christ. Then I'll do my best to live the way He lived in relationship to others.

❏ b. I will study the life and ways of Christ so I can identify the human ways in me that are not like Him. Then I'll deny my sinful ways and allow Christ to live through me in right relationship to others.

Romans 15:1–9, 13
"We who are strong ought to bear with the failings of the weak and not to please ourselves. Each of us should please his neighbor for his good, to build him up. For even Christ did not please himself but, as it is written: 'The insults of those who insult you have fallen on me.' For everything that was written in the past was written to teach us, so that through endurance and the encouragement of the Scriptures we might have hope.

"May the God who gives endurance and encouragement give you a spirit of unity among yourselves as you follow Christ Jesus, so that with one heart and mouth you may glorify the God and Father of our Lord Jesus Christ.

"Accept one another, then, just as Christ accepted you, in order to bring praise to God. For I tell you that Christ has become a servant of the Jews on behalf of God's truth, to confirm the promises made to the patriarchs so that the Gentiles may glorify God for his mercy. . . .

"May the God of hope fill you with all joy and peace as you trust in him, so that you may overflow with hope by the power of the Holy Spirit."

You may be able to summarize this truth better, but *b* is our best attempt. The Holy Spirit of Christ is present in the life of a believer. He wants to live out His life through you. He can do that in a way that an unbelieving human being never could. The Gospels (Matthew, Mark, Luke, and John) are filled with illustrations of Jesus Christ's relationships to others. In future lessons, we'll study some of them.

Several passages in the Bible tell us to treat others the way we've been treated by God. In this lesson, we want to identify five of the ways we're to treat others as God treated us.

➡ **4. Read Romans 15:1–9, 13 in the margin. Then, on the line below, write a title for this passage to describe the way you are to treat one another as Christ treated you.**

_____ one another as Christ _____ you.

➡ **5. Read Colossians 3:13 and Ephesians 4:29–32 below. Then write a title for them on the line that follows.**

Colossians 3:13: *Bear with each other and forgive whatever grievances you may have against one another. Forgive as the Lord forgave you.*

Ephesians 4:29–32: *Do not let any unwholesome talk come out of your mouths, but only what is helpful for building others up according to their needs, that it may benefit those who listen. And do not grieve the Holy Spirit of God, with whom you were sealed for the day of redemption. Get rid of all bitterness, rage and anger, brawling and slander, along with every form of malice. Be kind and compassionate to one another, forgiving each other, just as in Christ God forgave you.*

_____ one another as Christ _____ you.

6. Read John 13:34–35 and 1 John 4:7–12 below. Then write a title for them on the line that follows.

John 13:34–35: *A new command I give you: Love one another. As I have loved you, so you must love one another. By this all men will know that you are my disciples, if you love one another.*

1 John 4:7–12: *Dear friends, let us love one another, for love comes from God. Everyone who loves has been born of God and knows God. Whoever does not love does not know God, because God is love. This is how God showed his love among us: He sent his one and only Son into the world that we might live through him. This is love: not that we loved God, but that he loved us and sent his Son as an atoning sacrifice for our sins. Dear friends, since God so loved us, we also ought to love one another. No one has ever seen God; but if we love one another, God lives in us and his love is made complete in us.*

_____ one another as Christ _____ you.

7. Read Galatians 5:13 and Matthew 20:26–28 in the margin. Then write a title for them on the following line.

_____ one another as Christ _____ you.

8. Read 2 Corinthians 1:3–4 in the margin. Then write a title for the passage on the following line.

_____ one another as Christ _____ you.

9. Now, without looking back, see if you can list the five ways you're instructed to treat others following the model of Christ.

① _____ one another. ② _____ one another.

③ _____ one another. ④ _____ one another.

⑤ _____ one another.

Check your answers in the boxed list in the lower left margin. We'll study these five ways in more detail in lessons to come. Jesus is our best example for committed relationships.

What, if anything, do you sense God has said to you through today's lesson? Write *one* of the most meaningful things He has said below.

_____

_____

Conclude today's lesson by praying for the people in your small group, especially those who are most different from you. As you pray, review the five instructions, and ask God if there are specific ways He wants you to carry them out toward one or more group members this week.

Galatians 5:13
"You, my brothers, were called to be free. But do not use your freedom to indulge the sinful nature; rather, serve one another in love."

Matthew 20:26–28
"'Whoever wants to become great among you must be your servant, and whoever wants to be first must be your slave—just as the Son of Man did not come to be served, but to serve, and to give his life as a ransom for many.'"

2 Corinthians 1:3–4
"Praise be to the God and Father of our Lord Jesus Christ, the Father of compassion and the God of all comfort, who comforts us in all our troubles, so that we can comfort those in any trouble with the comfort we ourselves have received from God."

God's Model for Relationships
- Accept one another as Christ has accepted you.
- Forgive one another as Christ has forgiven you.
- Love one another as Christ has loved you.
- Serve one another as Christ has served you.
- Comfort one another as Christ has comforted you.

LESSON 4 ACCEPTING ONE ANOTHER FOR RELATIONSHIPS

Scripture for Meditation
"Accept one another, then, just as Christ accepted you, in order to bring praise to God" (Romans 15:7).

A Beginning Prayer
Father, thank You for accepting me into Your family. You didn't have to, but You did.

I pray that You will give the body of Christ a spirit of unity. Teach us to follow Christ and accept one another as He has accepted us. I pray You will enable us to do this in a way that will bring You praise and glory. Amen.

➡ **Read and think about the Scripture for Meditation in the left margin, and begin the lesson with prayer.**

❖ ❖ ❖

One of the reasons Christians don't experience the unity God intended is that they don't accept one another. We have a tendency to reject, despise, or refuse fellowship to those who are different or don't measure up to our standards. We've accepted many of the world's prejudices, "prejudging" others based on stereotypes rather than facts and personal knowledge. Lacking relationships, we often believe what we've heard from others. Sometimes we allow a previous negative experience to permanently affect our responses. But prejudice creates a wall that harms fellowship and unity. The antidote is a committed relationship. Reconciliation can't occur without a relationship, and relationship can't develop without acceptance of the other person or group.

➡ **1. What are some reasons that Christians might not accept others who claim to be Christian? Check any reasons that might be common in the Christian community you know.**
❑ I've been told by parents or church leaders not to associate with their kind.
❑ I'm afraid they may lead me astray or corrupt my doctrine.
❑ They approve of things that I disapprove of.
❑ They're lazy and don't want to work. I don't want my children around them.
❑ They're a violent people, and I'm afraid of them.
❑ They have bad habits like smoking and drinking.
❑ They're in a different social class (poor, rich, etc.).
❑ They're not like me racially, ethnically, or culturally.
❑ They don't belong to my denomination.
❑ They don't have a good reputation in the community.
❑ They have religious practices with which I disagree.
❑ They hold to beliefs and doctrines that I believe are wrong.
❑ They work in jobs that Christians shouldn't have.

➡ **2. What people do you have the greatest difficulty accepting as fellow Christians? From all the groups listed below, pick the three that you have the greatest difficulty accepting for fellowship as a Christian brother or sister (if there are any). Write a 1 beside the group that's most difficult for you, a 2 beside the second most difficult, and a 3 beside the third most difficult. If one of your toughest groups to accept isn't in this list, write it in the margin.**

Others:

_____

_____

_____

__ Asians	__ Protestants	__ fundamentalists
__ blacks	__ Catholics	__ liberals
__ Hispanics	__ charismatics	__ conservatives
__ Native Americans	__ Pentecostals	__ Republicans
__ whites	__ evangelicals	__ Democrats

➡ **3. If you do have difficulty accepting others as brothers or sisters in Christ, why do you think that's so?**

_____

_____

Romans 15:7
"Accept one another, then, just as Christ accepted you, in order to bring praise to God."

➡ **4. Read Romans 15:7 in the margin. How are we to accept one another?**

_____

God Accepts People of All Nations

We're to accept one another the way Christ has accepted us. Without a relationship, we won't be able to know a person's walk with the Lord. With one heart and mouth, we're to glorify God and bring praise to Him by our unity. When God called Peter to cross over the Jew-Gentile barrier to present the gospel to Cornelius, Peter had to learn to accept those whom God accepted. He said:

> *I now realize how true it is that God does not show favoritism but accepts men from every nation who fear him and do what is right* (Acts 10:34–35).

➡ **5. In the above verses, what is the opposite of accepting others?**

_____

➡ **6. In the same passage, what are two characteristics of those God does accept?**

_____

Favoring one type of people over another is the opposite of accepting them. God accepts those who fear Him and do what's right.

God Accepts Us as Sons

The writer of Hebrews reminded us that God accepts us as children even when we sin and require discipline:

> *"My son, do not make light of the Lord's discipline, and do not lose heart when he rebukes you, because the Lord disciplines those he loves, and he punishes everyone he accepts as a son. . . .*
>
> *"God disciplines us for our good, that we may share in his holiness. No discipline seems pleasant at the time, but painful. Later on, however, it produces a harvest of righteousness and peace for those who have been trained by it"* (Hebrews 12:5–6, 10–11).

Matthew 7:3–5
"'Why do you look at the speck of sawdust in your brother's eye and pay no attention to the plank in your own eye? How can you say to your brother, "Let me take the speck out of your eye," when all the time there is a plank in your own eye? You hypocrite, first take the plank out of your own eye, and then you will see clearly to remove the speck from your brother's eye.'"

➡ **7. Read Matthew 7:3–5 in the margin. Underline Jesus' instructions for what you're to do before you can help correct your brother.**

When God has adopted us into His family, His continued acceptance is not based on our sinlessness but on His faithfulness. As a Father, He disciplines us to correct and train us in righteousness. We need to remember that our acceptance of other Christians likewise doesn't need to depend on their perfect living. God may want to use us to correct or reprove. Jesus warned us, however, to be careful and examine ourselves before trying to correct others.

Jesus Accepted Others

Jesus often accepted people whom others, including religious leaders, thought He shouldn't accept. Zacchaeus was one of those.

➡ **8. Read the story of Jesus and Zacchaeus below, and underline what people thought about Jesus' acceptance of Zacchaeus.**

Jesus and Zacchaeus

> *Jesus entered Jericho. . . . A man was there by the name of Zacchaeus; he was a chief tax collector and was wealthy. He wanted to see who Jesus was. . . . So he ran ahead and climbed a sycamore-fig tree to see*

him, since Jesus was coming that way.

When Jesus reached the spot, he looked up and said to him, "Zacchaeus, come down immediately. I must stay at your house today." So he came down at once and welcomed him gladly.

All the people saw this and began to mutter, "He has gone to be the guest of a 'sinner.' "

But Zacchaeus stood up and said to the Lord, "Look, Lord! Here and now I give half of my possessions to the poor, and if I have cheated anybody out of anything, I will pay back four times the amount."

Jesus said to him, "Today salvation has come to this house. . . . For the Son of Man came to seek and to save what was lost" (Luke 19:1–10).

The people thought Jesus should have stayed away from sinners like Zacchaeus, who worked for the hated Roman government and so was seen as a traitor to the Jews. Tax collectors also had a tendency to collect more than was due, so they were considered thieves as well as traitors. But Jesus saw that the Father was working with Zacchaeus, since he was seeking Jesus with such intensity. Jesus focused on what Zacchaeus could become; He saw His mission as seeking those who—like Zacchaeus—were lost and bringing them to salvation.

➡ **9. What lesson do you think we might learn from Jesus' example with Zacchaeus? Check one or write your own.**

❏ a. I should accept those who are honestly seeking after the Lord, even when they haven't yet straightened out their sinful lives.

❏ b. I should accept those with whom God wants me to work, knowing that He can change their lives.

❏ c. Other: _____

_____

Others whom Jesus accepted who failed Him (through denial or doubt) or who would not have been widely accepted by other Jews included:

- a Canaanite woman with a demon-possessed daughter (Matthew 15:21–28)
- a man with leprosy (Matthew 8:1–4)
- a Roman soldier (centurion) who had a sick servant (Luke 7:1–10)
- Nicodemus—a religious leader who sought Jesus out but was too afraid to be seen with Him in the daylight (John 3:1–21)
- Peter, even after he had denied Jesus three times (Mark 14:66–72; John 21:15–19)
- the Samaritan woman at the well who had been married five times and was living in adultery (John 4)
- the woman caught in the act of adultery (John 8:1–11)
- Thomas, even after he had doubted the resurrection (John 20:24–29)

Acts 10:34–35

"I now realize how true it is that God does not show favoritism but accepts men from every nation who fear him and do what is right."

Romans 15:1–2

"We who are strong ought to bear with the failings of the weak and not to please ourselves. Each of us should please his neighbor for his good, to build him up."

Instructions on Accepting Others

Earlier you read a statement from Peter in Acts 10:34 in which he acknowledged that God accepted people from all nations who feared Him and sought to do what's right. Paul wrote specific instructions to the Christians in Rome concerning their relationship with other Christians (see Romans 15:1–2). In the list below (under #11), you'll find some guidelines for God-honoring relationships with brothers and sisters in Christ. These should help you learn to accept others as Christ has accepted us.

➡ **10. Review the people groups you may have numbered in activity #2 at the beginning of this lesson. Write the ones you numbered below:**

① _____ ② _____ ③ _____

➥ Pause for a moment of prayer. Ask God to help you learn to accept others who are genuine brothers and sisters in Christ in the same way as Christ has accepted you.

❖ ❖ ❖

➥ 11. As you read the following list of instructions, check those that you realize God wants you to apply in relationships to other believers. You may want to read the verses from Romans 14:1–22 in your Bible.

❑ a. Accept those from every nation, culture, and ethnic or social background who fear God and seek to do what's right and pleasing to Him (Acts 10:34).

❑ b. Accept those whose faith is weak (Romans 14:1).

❑ c. Don't pass judgment on others because of disputable matters (Romans 14:1).

❑ d. Don't look down on those who are more strict in their rules for living (Romans 14:3).

❑ e. Don't condemn those who are less strict in their rules for living (Romans 14:3).

❑ f. Don't stand in judgment or look down on those who are the Lord's servants and your brothers and sisters (Romans 14:4, 10).

❑ g. Don't place any stumbling block in your brother's way or do anything in his presence that causes him to fall (Romans 14:13, 20–21).

❑ h. Do what leads to peace and mutual edification (Romans 14:19).

❑ i. Don't cause others to stumble in their weak faith by practicing your liberty (Romans 14:21).

❑ j. Keep disputable matters between you and the Lord (Romans 14:22).

❑ k. Stand alongside and help those who are weak (Romans 15:1).

➥ What, if anything, do you sense God has said to you through today's lesson? Write *one* of the most meaningful things He has said below.

_____

_____

➥ Conclude today's lesson by praying about the way you accept other Christians.

• Ask God to forgive you for the times you've been judgmental, critical, or unaccepting of other Christians.

• Ask Him to give you specific opportunities to show your repentance by accepting others who are different from you.

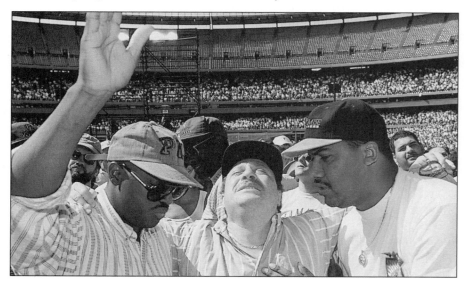

LESSON 5 LOVING ONE ANOTHER

Scripture for Meditation

"A new command I give you: Love one another. As I have loved you, so you must love one another. By this all men will know that you are my disciples, if you love one another" (John 13:34–35).

A Beginning Prayer

Father, You have shown Your great love by sending Jesus to die for me. You protect me and provide for my needs. I want to experience even greater dimensions of Your love. I realize that one of the ways I will experience that love is through the body of Christ as believers love each other. Teach me to love others the way You've loved me. Put a deep compassion in my heart for all believers—both those who are like me and those who are very different. Amen.

PRINCIPLE 2
Commitment to Relationship: Loved by God and adopted into His family, we are called to committed love relationships with our brothers.

The standard for our love is God's love for us.

➡ **Read and think about the Scripture for Meditation in the left margin. Since verse 34 is also your Scripture memory verse for this week, spend a minute or two making sure you have it committed to memory. Then begin the lesson with prayer.**

❖ ❖ ❖

Acceptance is just a beginning point for committed relationships between Christians. Following Christ's model and command, you must go on to love others as Jesus has loved you. Our focus in principle 2 is committed *love* relationships. God's love for us is the model.

➡ **Review the statement of principle 2 in the margin.**

In March 1996, a Christian group from the United States went to the Ukraine to provide discipleship training for 300 Christian leaders from various republics of the Commonwealth of Independent States. Vera (secretary to the mayor of Illeria, Ukraine) observed this group during its two-week stay. She made this comment to one of the local missionaries:

> "I've never seen people who seemed to be so close to one another. I couldn't understand anything they said, but I could just feel their love. All we know is how to be angry with each other. I want to be a part of a group like that. I want someone to care about me the way they seem to care about each other. . . . When are you going to start an adult Bible study? I want to know what it is that makes those people like that."

The way Christians love each other is the best way to tell if they're disciples (followers) of Jesus Christ. Thus far, you've learned that we're called to accept and forgive one another as God has accepted and forgiven us. Now we move to a deeper level of God-honoring relationships where we're called to *love* one another. This love isn't just a feeling or thought toward another. *Love* is a verb. It calls for action. The standard for our love is God's love for us. Jesus said, *"God so loved the world that he* gave *his one and only Son, that whoever believes in him shall not perish but have eternal life"* (John 3:16).

Loved by God

On the night before His crucifixion, Jesus ate a final supper with His twelve disciples. He was well aware of what would take place in the hours to come. This was an intimate time with the men He had trained to carry the gospel to the world. It was also a farewell meal when He gave some significant teachings to His disciples. John tells us, *"Having loved his own who were in the world, he now showed them the full extent of his love"* (John 13:1).

➡ **Pause for a moment of reflection. Think about Jesus on the cross—beaten, bruised, bleeding, and dying. He was there to pay for your sins and provide a way for you to be forgiven and adopted into God's family. Imagine Jesus speaking to you from the cross, saying, "I love you this much." That's how much He loved you. Spend a few moments in prayer, thanking Him for loving you enough to die for you.**

❖ ❖ ❖

God's love for us is a perfect love. It's not based on changing circumstances. It's trustworthy and safe. Nothing can separate us from the love of Christ.

➡ **1. Read Romans 8:35–39 below, and underline the words that describe the things that *can't* separate us from God's love. We've underlined one for you.**

Romans 8:35–39: *Who shall separate us from the love of Christ? Shall <u>trouble</u> or hardship or persecution or famine or nakedness or danger or sword? As it is written: "For your sake we face death all day long; we are considered as sheep to be slaughtered." No, in all these things we are more than conquerors through him who loved us. For I am convinced that neither death nor life, neither angels nor demons, neither the present nor the future, nor any powers, neither height nor depth, nor anything else in all creation, will be able to separate us from the love of God that is in Christ Jesus our Lord.*

God's love for you is unshakable, strong, true, and lasting. It doesn't change in the face of trouble, hardship, persecution, famine, nakedness, danger, or war. No being in all creation is able to separate us from His love—not even angels or demons. God's love is not conditional. It doesn't dependent on our always pleasing Him. Even if we sin, God disciplines us because of His love (Hebrews 12:6).

Hebrews 12:6
"The Lord disciplines those he loves."

How Are You to Love Others?

➡ **2. Your Scripture memory verse for this unit describes how you're to love other believers. Review it one more time, and see if you can write it here from memory.**

John 13:34: _____

_____

_____

_____

Many Scriptures describe the kind of Godlike love we're to demonstrate. Let's take a look at some of these qualities.

➡ **3. Read each of the following Scriptures, and underline the words or phrases that describe what love should be like or should do. We've underlined one for you. Write in the margin some of the things that love does *not* do. We've written two for you. You'll discuss your findings in your small-group session.**

Romans 12:9–10, 13: *Love must <u>be sincere</u>. Hate what is evil; cling to what is good. Be devoted to one another in brotherly love. Honor one another above yourselves. . . . Share with God's people who are in need. Practice hospitality.*

1 Corinthians 13:4–8: *Love is patient, love is kind. It does not envy, it does not boast, it is not proud. It is not rude, it is not self-seeking, it is not easily angered, it keeps no record of wrongs. Love does not delight in evil but rejoices with the truth. It always protects, always trusts, always hopes, always perseveres. Love never fails.*

Colossians 3:12–14: *Clothe yourselves with compassion, kindness, humility, gentleness and patience. Bear with each other and forgive whatever grievances you may have against one another. . . . And over all these virtues put on love, which binds them all together in perfect unity.*

Hebrews 13:1–3: *Keep on loving each other as brothers. Do not forget to entertain strangers, for by so doing some people have entertained angels without knowing it. Remember those in prison as if you were their fellow prisoners, and those who are mistreated as if you yourselves were suffering.*

Love Does Not . . .

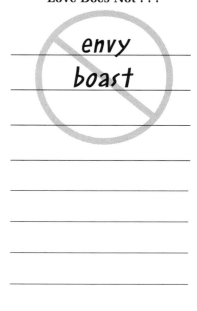

Love Does Not . . .

_____

_____

_____

_____

_____

_____

_____

_____

Luke 10:27
"'Love the Lord your God with all your heart and with all your soul and with all your strength and with all your mind'; and, 'Love your neighbor as yourself.'"

Meeting needs of Christian brothers and sisters is one way for healing to come to the body of Christ.

The walls of racism and sectarianism are disappearing as Christians reach out in love to brothers and sisters in Christ.

James 2:14–17: *What good is it, my brothers, if a man claims to have faith but has no deeds? Can such faith save him? Suppose a brother or sister is without clothes and daily food. If one of you says to him, "Go, I wish you well; keep warm and well fed," but does nothing about his physical needs, what good is it?*

Galatians 5:13–15: *Do not use your freedom to indulge the sinful nature; rather, serve one another in love. The entire law is summed up in a single command: "Love your neighbor as yourself." If you keep on biting and devouring each other, watch out or you will be destroyed by each other.*

Ephesians 4:15–16: *Speaking the truth in love, we will in all things grow up into him who is the Head, that is, Christ. From him the whole body, joined and held together by every supporting ligament, grows and builds itself up in love, as each part does its work.*

1 Timothy 1:3–5: *Command certain men not to teach false doctrines any longer nor to devote themselves to myths and endless genealogies. These promote controversies rather than God's work—which is by faith. The goal of this command is love, which comes from a pure heart and a good conscience and a sincere faith.*

Love Is Meeting Needs
The Law of the Old Testament can be summed up as loving God with all your being and loving your neighbor as yourself (see Luke 10:27). A person asked Jesus to clarify, *"Who is my neighbor?"* (Luke 10:29). In response, Jesus told the story of a man who was robbed, beaten, and left for dead. Both a priest and a Levite (religious leaders) saw the needy man and passed by. A despised Samaritan saw him and stopped to help meet his needs. Then Jesus asked:

> *"Which of these three do you think was a neighbor to the man who fell into the hands of robbers?"*
> *The expert in the law replied, "The one who had mercy on him."*
> *Jesus told him, "Go and do likewise"* (Luke 10:36–37).

A simple way to explain what it means to love others is this: When you see a person or group with a need, the way to demonstrate love is to help meet that need. And meeting needs of Christian brothers and sisters is one way for healing to come to the body of Christ, and for that body to become God's trophy.

Further, this demonstration of love must come through relationships. Just meeting needs but not wanting to have anything to do with the person or group is called paternalism. Meeting needs and a love relationship go together.

At the time we're writing this course, many churches are being burned by arsonists. God is calling forth an outpouring of love and support for those needy churches. Offerings are being given to pay for rebuilding. Volunteer teams are providing free labor to help with construction. Whites are seeing the wickedness of racism and saying, "That's enough!" The walls of racism and sectarianism are disappearing as Christians reach out in love to brothers and sisters in Christ. Even the secular media are reporting on a spirit of unity that's developing in communities. This is what God calls us to do in love for one another.

➡ **4. Suppose you knew fellow Christians who had the needs listed in the left column on the next page. How could you demonstrate your love by meeting those needs? Match each need on the left with a way to meet the need on the right. Write a letter beside each numbered need.**

Need	Possible Way to Meet the Need
___ 1. lonely	a. find/provide shelter
___ 2. grieving a death	b. baby-sit the children
___ 3. without a job	c. spend time talking/visiting
___ 4. hungry	d. network him with an employer needing his skills
___ 5. single parent	e. teach literacy class or tutor
___ 6. homeless	f. provide food
___ 7. can't read	g. comfort, help her talk about good memories

Ways to meet a need may vary depending on the circumstances. If God wants you to help meet the need, spend enough time with the needy person or group to see how to help effectively. Keep in mind that love will be costly and may require sacrifice. Prayer should also be a major part of your seeking directions on ways to help. (Answers: 1-c; 2-g; 3-d; 4-f; 5-b; 6-a; 7-e)

➡ **5. Read through the following list prayerfully. Ask the Lord to help you begin to recognize His invitations to show love to other believers or to people in need. Check items that you sense may be specifically meaningful to you. Write names or situations in the margin if any specific needs come to mind.**
- ❏ Build up and encourage your brother. Help him to grow strong (1 Corinthians 8:1).
- ❏ By the love of the Spirit working through you, pray for others (Romans 15:30).
- ❏ Demonstrate love by meeting needs (model of the Good Samaritan in Luke 10:25–37).
- ❏ Love your brother in the easy times, and keep on loving during the trials and troubles of life.
- ❏ Offer hospitality to visitors, aliens, strangers, and to one another (Hebrews 13:2; 1 Peter 4:9).
- ❏ Share your material and financial resources with those in need.
- ❏ Show mercy to those who need your help (Luke 10:37).
- ❏ Show your love to others, even while they're still sinners (Romans 5:8).
- ❏ Take a stand for those who can't speak up for themselves.
- ❏ Under God's direction, be willing to lay down your own life or reputation for a brother (John 15:13).

➡ **What, if anything, do you sense God has said to you through today's lesson? Write *one* of the most meaningful things He has said below.**

_____

_____

1. What do You want me to do in my personal relationship with You?
2. What do You want me to do in relationship to other people in my church or denomination?
3. What do You want me to do in relationship to Christians in other denominations or Christian traditions?
4. What do You want me to do in relationship to Christians of other races or ethnic backgrounds?

➡ **For each lesson this week, you've been recording what you sense God has said to you. Review the final activity for each of the previous lessons on pages 76, 78, 80, and 84. What's the major emphasis of what you sense God wants you to do in response to this unit's lessons? Pray and ask Him what He wants you to do. Then write notes in the margin or in a separate notebook. You might use the questions in the margin in your prayer.**

➡ **Conclude today's lesson by praying for the Lord to enlarge your ability to demonstrate love through committed relationships.**
- Ask Him to open your eyes to see needs and to give you wisdom in how to meet those needs.
- Ask Him to show you specific ways you may show your love to those in your small group.
- Pray for your group members by name.

UNIT 5 INTENTIONALITY

Scripture Memory Verse
"Make every effort to keep the unity of the Spirit through the bond of peace."
—Ephesians 4:3

Unit Learning Goal
You will understand the principle of intentionality, and you'll demonstrate determination in following the Lord's directions in a ministry of reconciliation.

Overview of Unit 5
Lesson 1: Making Every Effort to Maintain Unity
Lesson 2: God-Centered Intentionality
Lesson 3: The Principle of Intentionality
Lesson 4: Breaking Down Walls Intentionally
Lesson 5: Becoming Intentional

PRINCIPLE 3
Intentionality: Experiencing a committed relationship with my brothers requires purposeful, positive, and planned activities that facilitate reconciliation.

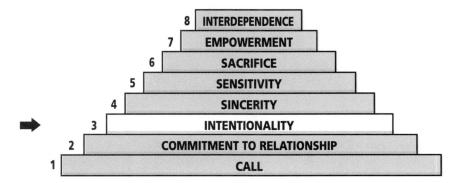

8	INTERDEPENDENCE
7	EMPOWERMENT
6	SACRIFICE
5	SENSITIVITY
4	SINCERITY
3	INTENTIONALITY
2	COMMITMENT TO RELATIONSHIP
1	CALL

Key Summary Statements from Unit 5
- Developing a committed relationship with someone of a different race or denomination in the body of Christ does not happen by accident.
- Intentionality keeps committed relationships growing toward maturity.
- For intentionality to be fruitful as God intends, it must be God-centered.
- If we'll take the time in relationship to the Lord to hear His directions and then obey them, the end result will be far more fruitful, and God will be glorified.
- Our role is to carry out His purposes in His ways and on His timetable.
- As salt, we can expect to feel rejection, but we can also help to restore a society threatened with rot.
- As Christ's ambassadors, we follow His purposes and directions.
- We don't need our plans; we need God's plans.
- We have the right and authority to break down our walls.
- We can enter another person's life and have a far greater impact if we do it by invitation rather than by trying to force entry and compliance on the other person.

The Body of Christ

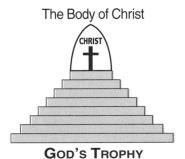

GOD'S TROPHY

FROM HOMELESS TO "GRANDPA CLYDE"

by Glen Kehrein

Both the Kehreins and the Washingtons have had numerous people live in our homes. When Clyde Dooley—an older black man—came to live in the white Kehrein home, it was an exercise in intentionality. Besides having spent decades in a homosexual lifestyle, Clyde had also been a heroin addict for twenty years. Now, as a new Christian, his life had miraculously changed. Clyde had lost his small apartment because a new owner was charging more than he could afford. Clyde was on disability and couldn't afford another apartment. He was homeless; we had an extra room. But accepting him might require extended lodging. Were we prepared to have him for a long time? Yes, Lonni and I decided. Intentionality requires risk.

Several of our children were not excited by the possibility. They didn't make Clyde feel welcome—quite the opposite. Tension built; the road was rocky. But intentionality means you don't throw in the towel when things get rough.

"Brother Glen, I think the children don't feel comfortable with an old man in the house," Clyde said after a week. "I think I need to just stay in my room until I can find someplace else. I don't want to cause any trouble."

"That's not the right solution," I told him firmly. When people who are different from us come into our space, it's natural to feel discomfort at first. Our kids were reacting. I encouraged Clyde to hang in there. Lonni and I spoke to the kids more intentionally about why we felt God had given us this opportunity. We reminded them how the innkeepers had turned away Mary and Joseph when they were looking for a place to stay in Bethlehem. In effect, they were turning away Jesus, the Messiah, who was born homeless, in a stable. What was our family going to do when a homeless, poor person needed a place to stay? They finally agreed to give Clyde a chance.

As the days went by, Clyde won the kids over (especially when he did their turn at the dishes). Dinner-table talks included Clyde reminiscing about moving many times as he was growing up. Perhaps the most touching moment came at Christmas. Our tradition is a fondue meal and warm family time on Christmas Eve, concluding with a time around the tree. We limit gifts to only one per person. This Christmas, however, each of the children had bought Clyde a gift.

It seemed like a touching scene out of a Christmas movie when Clyde opened his gifts. Here was a sixty-nine-year-old man, frail, his life almost spent. He said with tears streaming, "I've never had a real Christmas before. Never a real family like this. Never had a tree. I remember as a boy seeing Christmas trees in other folks' houses and dreaming about what it must be like. Now I know. This is wonderful." It was as if Christ himself—not old Saint Nick—was peeking in our window.

God continues to grace our lives with "Grampa Clyde," as the kids call him. After six months, I was able to get Clyde a newly rehabbed, subsidized apartment just blocks from Circle Urban Ministries. He calls us his family, and we still spend holidays together when we can. Our lives have been deeply enriched by being intentional about crossing these kinds of barriers.

LESSON 1 MAKING EVERY EFFORT TO MAINTAIN UNITY

Scripture for Meditation
"Make every effort to keep the unity of the Spirit through the bond of peace" (Ephesians 4:3).

A Beginning Prayer
Father, thank You for providing the potential for unity through the Spirit of Christ and the work of Christ. Already, I'm realizing that reconciled and committed relationships require effort. Give me the strength and determination to stay in relationships with brothers in Christ so we can experience Your unity together. Amen.

Intentionality keeps committed relationships growing toward maturity.

Ephesians 4:1–3
"I urge you to live a life worthy of the calling you have received. Be completely humble and <u>gentle</u>; be patient, bearing with one another in love. Make every effort to keep the unity of the Spirit through the bond of peace."

➡ **Ephesians 4:3 (in the margin) is your Scripture memory verse for this unit. Remove the perforated card from the back of your book, and begin memorizing it. Then start the lesson with prayer.**

❖ ❖ ❖

God has called all of us to be ambassadors of Christ, carrying the message of reconciliation to others across human barriers. The foundation for reconciliation is a committed relationship—first to Christ and then to members God has added to His body. Developing a committed relationship with someone of a different race or denomination in the body of Christ does not happen by accident.

➡ **1. Read Ephesians 4:1–3 in the lower left margin. Underline the words that describe ways you're to live in relationship to others in the body of Christ. We've underlined one.**

➡ **2. According to Paul in Ephesians 4:3, what are you to do to keep the unity the Holy Spirit of Christ has made possible?**

Christians are to *"make every effort"* to maintain unity in the body of Christ. Gentleness, humility, patience, and love are ways we can live a worthy life in relationship to others in the body. The "cement" for this unity is peace (a fruit of the Spirit—Galatians 5:22). If reconciliation and unity were a train, intentionality would be the engine. The train would go nowhere without it. Intentionality keeps committed relationships growing toward maturity.

➡ **Read the following illustration in which Raleigh Washington experienced a relationship with friends that required effort and love from them.**

I was a second lieutenant in the army in 1960. I was attending a training course in Indiana with fifty-nine men of the lighter hue. I had three very good friends, and we decided to go out to eat on Friday night. Jim, Bob, Lou, and I walked into a diner in Lawrence, Indiana. People were busy eating and enjoying conversation until I walked in, and then a hush came over the place. I knew why, but my friends didn't. We waited about ten minutes and got no service. Finally Lou talked to the manager. He came back and said, "Raleigh, let's get out of this place and go somewhere else."

When we got to the car, I explained what was going on and suggested that I go back to the barracks so they could go out and have a good time. Lou said, "Raleigh, shut up and stay in the car. We're going to eat together if we have to try every restaurant between Lawrence and Indianapolis."

To save me from embarrassment, Lou left me in the car and went into the second restaurant—no luck. He tried a third restaurant with no luck. Finally, at the fourth restaurant we could eat together. It was a swanky French restaurant with red carpet on the floors, red velvet chairs, and red velvet around the menus. I opened the menu and saw dollar signs everywhere. I'd never seen prices like that in all my life. I was looking it over, trying to find something I could handle. Then I called the waitress over and said I was ready to order. She said, "Sir, your meal has already been ordered."

They brought me out a platter of chateaubriand (a tenderloin steak). I had chocolate eclairs for dessert. I dined sufficiently that night! Then I remembered. That was the most expensive meal on the menu. I sucked in my gut, got up my courage, and asked the waitress for my bill. She said, "Sir, your bill has already been paid."

Lou, my white friend, wouldn't eat that night unless we ate together. Lou, my white friend, took us to probably the best restaurant in the area. Lou, my white friend, ordered for me the most expensive meal on the menu. And Lou, my white friend, paid the bill! That night the alienation I could have felt because of racism was destroyed by the love of one man who wouldn't let that night happen that way. Lou taught me what love could look like. He showed me how intentionality could affect a relationship.

During the coming lessons, we're going to study ways God may lead you to be intentional in building reconciled relationships.

➥ **What, if anything, do you sense God has said to you through today's lesson? Write *one* of the most meaningful things He has said below.**

_____

_____

➥ **Conclude today's lesson by praying. Ask the Lord to teach you the kind of efforts required to keep the unity of the Spirit. Pray for each of your small-group members by name.**

LESSON 2 GOD-CENTERED INTENTIONALITY

Scripture for Meditation

"I am the vine; you are the branches. If a man remains in me and I in him, he will bear much fruit; apart from me you can do nothing. . . . This is to my Father's glory, that you bear much fruit, showing yourselves to be my disciples" (John 15:5, 8).

A Beginning Prayer

Father, I know that unity and reconciliation don't just happen. I know You call us to love and unity, and I have to respond to Your call. Teach me today how I can join You in what You're doing and obey all You ask me to do. Direct my steps, and I will be intentional in my obedience to You. Amen.

➥ **Read and think about the Scripture for Meditation in the left margin, and begin the lesson with prayer.**

❖   ❖   ❖

➥ **1. Based on Jesus' statements in your Scripture for Meditation, how much can you accomplish of kingdom value apart from Him?**

_____

➥ **2. Who gets the glory when Jesus bears fruit through your life?**

_____

In tomorrow's lesson, you're going to learn about the principle of intentionality. But before you misunderstand your role, let's draw a line between God-centered and human-centered intentionality. Many people may try to be intentional about relationships. But in their human strength and wisdom, they won't accomplish lasting, Godlike results. Unless you stay related to Jesus so He can work through you, you'll be able to accomplish nothing of kingdom value. For intentionality to be fruitful as God intends, it must be God-centered. Then God the Father gets the glory for what results.

➥ **3. On the next page are descriptions of how two different individuals became intentional about crossing denominational lines. See if you can notice the difference between the God-centered approach and the human-centered approach. Write "God-centered" or "human-centered"** beside each description.

_____ Charlie: I heard about this emphasis on experiencing unity across denominational barriers. I thought it sounded like a good idea. I got to thinking how nice it would be to set up a joint relationship with a church of a different denomination. I could write an article about what we're doing and get our picture in the *Community News Journal*. While I was thinking about who to approach, the name of a city council member came to mind. He's a member at a church of another denomination. If I could get him involved, it would really make this project more newsworthy. I talked with him, and he agreed it would provide good publicity for our churches. We got our pastors involved and held a joint worship service. We pulled it off with excellence!

_____ Tyrone: I was attending a citywide concert of prayer and met a believer from a church of another denomination. As we prayed, I realized this brother and his church were very discouraged and experiencing severe financial difficulties. As I prayed for him and his church, the Lord brought a Scripture to mind:

> *Suppose a brother or sister is without clothes and daily food. If one of you says to him, "Go, I wish you well; keep warm and well fed," but does nothing about his physical needs, what good is it? In the same way, faith by itself, if it is not accompanied by action, is dead* (James 2:15–17).

I realized God wanted me to do more than pray for him. I discussed the situation with three of my church friends. We invited this brother and two of his church friends to meet weekly for prayer and encouragement on Sunday afternoons. God allowed us to encourage them and lift them up during this trying time. We also collected $1,000 between us and gave it to the church to help with the bills.

Human-Centered Intentionality

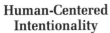

God-Centered Intentionality

Did you notice Charlie didn't acknowledge that God had anything to do with his project? Though God could have directed him, Charlie made his own plans, thought his own thoughts, and "pulled it off" in his own strength. God might have directed Charlie to do some of the same things he did, but only God has a right to direct His kingdom work.

Tyrone, on the other hand, recognized God's activity. The Spirit spoke to Him through prayer and the Scriptures. With directions from the Lord, Tyrone didn't just sit around and wait. He was intentional in doing what the Lord was inviting him to do.

➥ **4. In each pair of statements below, check the one that is God-centered rather than human-centered.**
  ❑ a1. If I really apply myself, I can make things happen that will accomplish reconciliation and unity.
  ❑ a2. As Christ works in and through my life, He can accomplish reconciliation and produce unity that bring His Father glory.

  ❑ b1. As I spend time in God's Word and prayer, He will reveal what I'm to do to join Him in His work. Then I must obey.
  ❑ b2. Spending much time in God's Word and prayer isn't practical if I want to see changes take place. I've got to get out there and make things happen.

We can work hard in our own wisdom and strength, and we may make things happen. But we're servants of King Jesus. He's the one who has a

If we'll take the time in relationship to the Lord to hear His directions and then obey them, the end result will be far more fruitful, and God will be glorified.

right to direct our actions. He says we can accomplish nothing lasting of kingdom value without Him. If we'll take the time in relationship to the Lord to hear His directions and then obey them, the end result will be far more fruitful, and God will be glorified. (Answers: a-2, b-1)

➡ **What, if anything, do you sense God has said to you through today's lesson? Write *one* of the most meaningful things He has said below.**

_____

_____

➡ **Conclude today's lesson by praying.**
- Ask the Lord to reorient your mind to be like the mind of Christ.
- Ask Him to teach you how to remain in Him so you can be fruitful.
- Ask the Lord to help you know when He has given you directions so you can obey Him.
- Ask Him to convict you any time you keep waiting when you should be obeying what He has already directed you to do.

LESSON 3 THE PRINCIPLE OF INTENTIONALITY

Scripture for Meditation
"If anyone would come after me, he must deny himself and take up his cross daily and follow me. For whoever wants to save his life will lose it, but whoever loses his life for me will save it" (Luke 9:23–24).

A Beginning Prayer
Father, taking up a cross and following Christ won't be easy. It may involve difficulty, rejection, and pain, as the cross did for Jesus. Give me strength to deny myself and follow Christ so I can experience the fullness of life You have intended for me. I yield my life in order to experience the real life You have planned for me. Amen.

PRINCIPLE 3
Intentionality: Experiencing a committed relationship with my brothers requires purposeful, positive, and planned activities that facilitate reconciliation.

➡ **Read and think about the Scripture for Meditation in the left margin, and begin the lesson with prayer.**

❖ ❖ ❖

➡ **Using the memory card from the back of your book, read Principle 3: Intentionality two or three times. In the margin to the left, you'll see the same text. Memorize the three words beginning with "p" that describe the kind of activities that facilitate reconciliation. Write those three words below.**
Intentionality requires: P_____,

P_____, and P_____ activities.

Intentionality Requires Purposeful Activities
God is working to reconcile the world to Himself through Christ. He's working through Christ to reconcile men to one another. He has a good purpose in mind. But He has chosen you to be His ambassador. An ambassador doesn't speak or act on his own. He speaks and does what he's instructed to say or do on behalf of the one who sent him. As you pray, read the Scriptures, and talk with other believers, God will begin to give you direction, concern, or a burden regarding your role in reconciliation and unity. Your responsibility is to carry out His purposes in His ways and on His timetable.

➡ **1. What's one kind of intentional activity required for reconciliation?**

_____ activity

➡ **2. As Christ's ambassador, whose purposes are you supposed to carry out? Check one.**
❑ a. I let other people tell me what my purposes should be.
❑ b. I look to God in the Scriptures and prayer for His purposes.
❑ c. I use my own wisdom and best thinking to decide what my purposes should be.

Romans 15:5
"May the God who gives endurance and encouragement give you a spirit of unity among yourselves as you follow Christ Jesus."

Matthew 5:13–14
"You are the salt of the earth. . . . You are the light of the world."

As salt, we can expect to feel rejection, but we can also help to restore a society threatened with rot.

Intentionality requires purposeful activities. But God is the one whose purposes are always right and best. In yesterday's lesson, Tyrone and his friends did several purposeful activities. They met together to "encourage." That was their God-given purpose, for God is the God of all encouragement (Romans 15:5).

Intentionality Requires Positive Activities
Jesus told us to be salt and light in the world (Matthew 5:13–14). As salt, we're the preserving agent of society so it doesn't get rotten. As light, we shine God's truth on our relationships; we open up our lives, cutting through the darkness. Even God the Father was intentional as He planned for our reconciliation by sending Christ to earth. God sought to rebuild the relationship with us that had been broken by sin. To do that, Jesus suffered agonizing pain and rejection. But that's what it takes for reconciliation. As salt, we can expect to feel rejection, but we can also help to restore a society threatened with rot.

➡ **3. What's the second kind of intentional activity needed to facilitate reconciliation? Write it below:**

_____ activity

Through purposeful and positive activities, we can help society have a flavor that's pleasing and productive. God sets the purposes and gives the positive directions. We must be intentional in obeying Him. Unless we are, reconciliation is not going to happen. "Whew!" you're saying. "That's really above and beyond the call of duty." Is it? Jesus told us to take up our cross and follow Him (Luke 9:23–24). The cross is going to mean rejection; it's going to mean pain. We can't just talk about it. We can't just sing about it. We have to live it! But on the other side of the cross, there's reconciliation and resurrection glory!

➡ **4. When you deny self, whose directions must you follow?**

_____

Luke 9:23–24
"If anyone would come after me, he must deny himself and take up his cross daily and follow me. For whoever wants to save his life will lose it, but whoever loses his life for me will save it."

As Christ's ambassador, you follow His purposes and directions.

As Christ's ambassador, you follow His purposes and directions. Positive actions will be far more powerful than negative ones. Do you remember the story of Jesus with the woman at the well in Samaria? He could have focused on negative issues like her adulterous relationships or her ignorant worship practices. Instead He focused on the positive "living water" to which He wanted to introduce her. Yesterday, Tyrone and his friends didn't give a lecture about financial responsibility. They took up an offering. That's a positive and loving response. Not only were Tyrone and his friends God-centered, but they also followed godly purposes in positive ways.

Intentionality Requires Planned Activities
Intentionality also calls for planning. Planning will help make the difference between a poor or haphazard response and a healthy and effective response. Seeking God's guidance (by following Christ) will help you keep your planning on track. You don't need *your* plans; you need God's plans. The best news about that is that God accomplishes what He plans and purposes!

You don't need *your* plans; you need God's plans.

➡ **5. What's a third kind of intentional activity needed to facilitate reconciliation? Write it below:**

_____ activity

Intentional actions of reconciliation require us to leave our "comfort zone." But why do that? To leave our comfort zone to be ambassadors of reconciliation is to take on the mind of Christ. Paul said, *"Your attitude should* be the same as that of Christ Jesus: Who, being in very nature God, did not consider equality with God something to be grasped, but made himself nothing, taking the very nature of a servant, being made in human likeness" (Philippians 2:5–7).

Have you ever been in a group setting where you were the minority? Maybe you were in the racial minority, or perhaps you were the only person who knew no one else. It was uncomfortable to stand around with no one to talk to. But when a stranger, sensitive to your discomfort, initiated a conversation, immediately you were put at ease. This intentional act required your new acquaintance to leave his comfort zone (his friends) and initiate a conversation with a stranger. It did a lot to make you feel a part of things.

The momentum of separation has long been established through past church culture, societal actions, and laws of separatism. For our separation to continue, we just need to do nothing. For reconciliation to be lived out, we must become intentional and responsive to God's initiatives through purposeful, positive, and planned activities.

➥ **What, if anything, do you sense God has said to you through today's lesson? Write *one* of the most meaningful things He has said below.**

_____

_____

➥ **Conclude today's lesson by praying. Focus on the small group God has placed you with for this study.**
  • Ask Him to help you be a positive influence rather than becoming negative and depressing.
  • Ask the Holy Spirit to empower your intentionality so you can experience reconciliation and unity in His ways.
  • Ask the Lord to help you keep your eyes on Christ, your ears open to His voice, and your heart responsive to the needs of the world around you.

> For reconciliation to be lived out, we must become intentional and responsive to God's initiatives through purposeful, positive, and planned activities.

LESSON 4   BREAKING DOWN WALLS INTENTIONALLY

Scripture for Meditation
"Anyone, then, who knows the good he ought to do and doesn't do it, sins" (James 4:17).

A Beginning Prayer
Father, I'm learning that I must be intentional in the ministry of reconciliation to which You call me. I don't want to just do something from my own human motives. I want to do what You desire. I want to obey You. Please guide me to be intentional out of love for and obedience to You. Amen.

➥ **Read and think about the Scripture for Meditation in the left margin, and begin the lesson with prayer.**

❖ ❖ ❖

By now, you probably realize you're already being intentional about reconciliation and unity. This course of study is an act of intentionality, isn't it? Your meeting with a small group to build and experience reconciled relationships is also an act of intentionality. But God may want you to begin doing other things that will contribute to reconciliation.

Our course title implies some intentionality as well. Walls of separation and alienation come down through intentional committed relationships. "Wall busting" can be good, but it can also be harmful. As you become more intentional in breaking down walls, you need to understand what actions are appropriate and which ones may do more harm than good.

In ancient times, walls were built around a city to protect the inhabitants from enemy attack. They were for defensive purposes. Great care was given to maintain a strong wall against outsiders. Gates were placed in the wall to allow people to come and go. But the gate was guarded to keep the wrong people from coming inside the city.

Emotional and psychological walls are built to protect and defend us personally. We build walls to keep from getting hurt by others. Racial and religious walls are built because of prejudices or past hurtful experiences.

➡ **1. Why do we build racial or religious walls? Write a brief explanation below.**

_____

_____

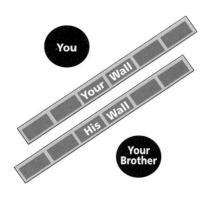

Often there are two walls of separation between you and others who aren't like you. One is a wall you've erected to "protect" yourself or to isolate yourself from the other person or group. The other is one the other person (or group) has erected to "protect" himself or isolate himself from you or your group. In breaking down walls, you need to understand which ones you're dealing with. You need to know the right approach to relate to the person on the other side of these walls. The goal is for both walls to come down between those who are brothers in Christ.

➡ **2. If someone came along and tried to break down your wall without your permission, how would you respond? Check the response that comes closest.**
 ❑ a. I would calmly stand by and encourage him.
 ❑ b. I would call 911 for help.
 ❑ c. I would get angry or upset and do what I could to stop him.

Probably most of us would check *c*. That's a natural response to actions that seem threatening. Keep this in mind as you break down walls of racism and sectarianism. Respect your brother, and start with your own wall(s).

Dealing with Your Wall

You have the right and authority to break down your wall. As you study the Scriptures and pray, the Lord can help you understand which walls need to come down. Some walls need to remain. For instance, we're instructed to come out and be separate from the sinful world and its influences (2 Corinthians 6:17). We're told not to be yoked to an unbeliever (2 Corinthians 6:14). We're instructed to flee from false teachers (1 Timothy 6:3–5, 11). These are some walls that should remain to protect us.

➡ **3. Name at least two walls that ought to remain up to protect a believer.**

_____

_____

However, walls that separate brothers and sisters in Christ need to come down. We're to be one body in Him. Christ has already broken down the wall of hostility between us, making our unity possible. But we've built walls between us that don't belong. You can tear down the walls you've erected. If you have difficulty, you have a right to invite someone else to come through the gate and help you tear down the wall on your side. Our prayer is that this is taking place in your small-group sessions.

Dealing with Someone Else's Wall

Walls that belong to someone else are a different matter. Since they were built for defensive purposes, an attack by an outsider will only cause the

2 Corinthians 6:17
"Therefore come out from them and be separate, says the Lord. Touch no unclean thing, and I will receive you."

2 Corinthians 6:14
"Do not be yoked together with unbelievers. For what do righteousness and wickedness have in common? Or what fellowship can light have with darkness?"

1 Timothy 6:3–5, 11
"If anyone teaches false doctrines and does not agree to the sound instruction of our Lord Jesus Christ and to godly teaching, he is conceited and understands nothing. He has an unhealthy interest in controversies and quarrels about words that result in envy, strife, malicious talk, evil suspicions and constant friction between men of corrupt mind, who have been robbed of the truth and who think that godliness is a means to financial gain. . . .

"But you, man of God, flee from all this, and pursue righteousness, godliness, faith, love, endurance and gentleness."

other person to become more defensive. The more fierce the attack, the more effort he will give to fortify his defenses. If another man breaks down the wall, it will probably be rebuilt in time.

However, when a person is a believer, God is working on the other side of the wall. He's the one who can convince the other person to break down his wall. When God does the convincing, the wall can come down quickly and permanently. What's your role? First, God may want you to talk to the "watchman" on the wall and speak truth from God's Word. It's the Holy Spirit's job to convince the other person that this is the truth. If you try to play the role of the Spirit, you get in the way of His work in the other person's life. As God works on the other side with the other person, He'll bring the person to a change of heart when that person is ready to respond. Then the other person may invite you through his gate to help him break down his wall. You can enter another individual's life and have a far greater impact if you do it by invitation rather than by trying to force entry and compliance on the other person.

➡ **4. After you've broken down your own wall, what's the best approach to getting your brother's wall down? Check the best response.**
- ❏ a. Talk to my brother, share the truth of God's Word with him, pray for him, and give the Holy Spirit time to convince him to tear down his wall. I can help by invitation from my brother.
- ❏ b. Get a battering ram, friends, and a fierce attitude, and tear that wall down. I should keep fighting until my brother gives up the battle.
- ❏ c. I should sit around and do nothing until he decides on his own that the wall should come down.

Waiting around and doing nothing will probably accomplish nothing. If no one helps your brother know that the wall needs to come down, he'll never break it down himself. God can use the Scriptures and other people to reveal that to your brother, but He may want to use you to be the messenger. When you explain the truth in a loving way and wait on the Lord, the Holy Spirit can bring conviction. When God does the convincing, the results will be greater and longer lasting. On the other hand, if you come in rage, anger, or fierceness to break down the wall from the outside, your brother will resist, and the wall may grow bigger than it was. *A* is the best response for lasting and God-directed results. A summary of the basic instructions is in the box in the margin.

➡ **What, if anything, do you sense God has said to you through today's lesson? Write *one* of the most meaningful things He has said below.**

_____

_____

➡ **Conclude today's lesson by praying.**
- Pray for brothers who may still have walls up that separate them from other believers.
- Pray that God will accomplish all He desires in the lives of the members of your small group.
- Ask the Lord if there are remaining walls in your own life that need to come down.

You can enter another individual's life and have a far greater impact if you do it by invitation rather than by trying to force entry and compliance on the other person.

Breaking Down Walls Intentionally

1. Under God's direction, break down your own walls.
2. If you need help, you may invite others to help you break down your walls.
3. Don't attack another person's wall or you'll only strengthen the resistance.
4. Under God's direction, speak the truth to others in love and submission.
5. Trust the Holy Spirit to bring about the conviction needed for the other person to choose to break down his own wall.
6. When invited to do so, you may help another person break down his wall.
7. Make prayer a major part of your strategy. God will work in you and then invite you to join Him in His work with others. What God purposes to do, He brings to pass, and He gets the glory.

LESSON 5 BECOMING INTENTIONAL

Scripture for Meditation
"Whatever you do, whether in word or deed, do it all in the name of the Lord Jesus, giving thanks to God the Father through him" (Colossians 3:17).

A Beginning Prayer
Father, I want to obey You and be intentional so that walls will come down to Your glory. I don't want to lag behind You, but I don't want to run ahead of You, either. Please reveal to me what I'm to do. Then enable me to do it with all Your power, for Your glory, in Jesus' name. Amen.

➡ **Read and think about the Scripture for Meditation in the left margin, and begin the lesson with prayer.**

❖ ❖ ❖

You've just reached the halfway point in this course. Before we complete our study of intentionality, let's take a few minutes for review. See if you can answer the following questions from memory. If you can't, look back through the previous units to help you review.

➡ **1. Why did Jesus pray that His followers would have complete unity?**

So that the world would believe _____

➡ **2. Which of the following is the basis for our unity?**
❑ a. Belonging to the same denomination or church.
❑ b. Agreeing on all our doctrines.
❑ c. Having a common relationship to Jesus Christ.
❑ d. Covering up our differences so the world won't see them.

➡ **3. Which of these root sins is the basis for racism and sectarianism?**
❑ unbelief   ❑ rebellion   ❑ pride

➡ **4. Name *two or more* biblical illustrations of our unity as God's people.**

_____

➡ **5. List the first three principles of reconciliation and unity.**

Principle 1: _____

Principle 2: _____

Principle 3: _____

➡ **6. See if you can quote your Scripture memory verses from memory. If you have trouble, use your cards, and keep reviewing them regularly.**
• John 17:23: *"I in them . . ."*   • Ephesians 2:14: *"He himself . . ."*
• 2 Corinthians 5:19: *"God was . . ."*   • John 13:34: *"A new . . ."*
• Ephesians 4:3: *"Make every . . ."*

Provided your leader and your group agree, we recommend you take a break during the coming week so everyone can catch up on homework and review before you begin the final half of the course. You'll still have a small-group session, but you won't have additional homework assignments. We also suggest you take at least one opportunity to be intentional about relationships this next week. The following are suggestions for you to pray about. Choose one, or follow the Lord's leadership in another purposeful, positive, and planned activity. Make your plans soon so you can give a report on your experience in next week's small-group session. If you have to plan further in advance, at least be prepared to describe your plans to your group.

Ideas for Intentionality
➡ **7. As you read through the following list, check ideas that might be**

possibilities. Though this may seem a little trivial to pray about, it's not. The Lord cares about every aspect of your life. Ask Him to guide you to just the right activity with just the right person or group. We recommend you be intentional in choosing a person of another race, ethnic group, or denominational background. The Christian brother does not have to be in your small group; move into new territory (not just with an old friend who's just like you).

❑ Get together with a brother for breakfast, lunch, or dinner during the week, with no agenda but to get to know each other better.

❑ If jobs permit, visit your brother at his workplace this week, and let him show you around. (Lunch too?)

❑ Ask a brother to take you to church with him so you can experience worship together. Take your family, too. Line up substitutes if you have teaching or other responsibilities at your home church.

❑ As an alternative and to develop sensitivity, go to a worship service where you're in the minority and you don't know anyone. See how it feels to be a minority. Join in the worship experience that may be very different from that to which you're accustomed.

❑ Invite a brother to bring his family (or wife or girlfriend) to your house (with your wife's permission) for a meal and time to get acquainted.

❑ If time and funds permit, plan an overnight trip for two or more couples. Focus on time together, and don't worry about a detailed agenda. You don't have to go far; just have a good time.

❑ If you're aware of some needs, plan a joint work day (or evening) to accomplish a project (fixing a car, painting, etc.).

❑ Go hunting, fishing, golfing, or bowling with your brother(s). If you prefer, take your sons along. If you're not the outdoor type, go to a ball game instead. (You could plan a dads and daughters trip instead.)

❑ Introduce your brother to your hobby. Show him your collection, or participate together (depending on your hobby, of course).

You get the idea. Don't hesitate to come up with an even better plan!

➡ **8. Once you make your plan, write down it down, and list the person or persons who will be involved.**

Activity: _____

Person(s): _____

➡ **What, if anything, do you sense God has said to you through today's lesson? Write *one* of the most meaningful things He has said below.**

_____

_____

1. What do You want me to do in my personal relationship with You?

2. What do You want me to do in relationship to other people in my church or denomination?

3. What do You want me to do in relationship to Christians in other denominations or Christian traditions?

4. What do You want me to do in relationship to Christians of other races or ethnic backgrounds?

➡ **For each lesson this week, you've been recording what you sense God has said to you. Review the final activity for each of the previous lessons on pages 92, 94, 96, and 98. What's the major emphasis of what you sense God wants you to do in response to this unit's lessons? Pray and ask Him what He wants you to do. Then write notes in the margin or in a separate notebook. You might use the questions in the margin in your prayer.**

➡ **Conclude today's lesson by praying for your upcoming intentional activity. Pray for your small-group members, too.**

UNIT 6 SINCERITY AND SENSITIVITY

Scripture Memory Verse
"Speaking the truth in love, we will in all things grow up into him who is the Head, that is, Christ."

—Ephesians 4:15

PRINCIPLE 4
Sincerity: We must be willing to be vulnerable and express our feelings, attitudes, differences, and perceptions with the goal of resolution and building trust.

PRINCIPLE 5
Sensitivity: We must seek knowledge about our brothers in order to relate empathetically to people from different denominations, traditions, races, social standings, or cultures.

The Body of Christ

GOD'S TROPHY

Unit Learning Goal
You will understand the principles of sincerity and sensitivity, and you'll demonstrate openness and honesty in relationship with your brothers in Christ.

Overview of Unit 6
Lesson 1: The Need for Sincerity
Lesson 2: The Principle of Sincerity
Lesson 3: Developing Your Sincerity
Lesson 4: The Need for Sensitivity
Lesson 5: The Principle of Sensitivity

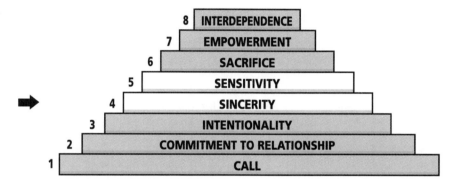

8	INTERDEPENDENCE
7	EMPOWERMENT
6	SACRIFICE
5	SENSITIVITY
4	SINCERITY
3	INTENTIONALITY
2	COMMITMENT TO RELATIONSHIP
1	CALL

Key Summary Statements from Unit 6
- Trust is built in a relationship with another person or group.
- When we only talk with people like us about others who aren't like us, we'll usually come up with negative stereotypes about them.
- We must create an environment in which we can share with each other our feelings, attitudes, differences, and perceptions.
- Our goal is to hear, understand, and build a foundation of trust.
- Sincerity disarms tension and distrust.
- As we express our feelings, we must do so in a way that will not offend or hurt our brothers.
- When believers who are surrendered to the lordship of Christ pray for unity in a spirit of sincerity, God works to bring about resolution.
- Sincerity says, "I really want to hear what you feel and think."
- The principle of sensitivity brings your head (knowledge and understanding) into your relationships.
- When one member is allowed to suffer without the support of the other members, the whole body suffers greater harm.
- We aren't given the option of not caring or not being concerned.
- If we don't know a person's background or life experiences, we . . . won't know or understand his pain and suffering, and the body of Christ will lack the health it could have.
- Master using the request: Would you help me understand?

FROM APATHY TO LOVE

by John Alan Jones

In November 1995, I became involved in what was to be a successful bone marrow drive to save the life of the eight-month-old daughter of some close church friends. God moved through me, and I found myself speaking to church congregations, on television and radio, and to other large groups.

During the drive, I was contacted by a wonderful African-American lady whose best friend's daughter had just been diagnosed with leukemia. I told her how to get a life-saving drive set up and offered my help if she needed it. Several weeks later, she contacted me and asked if my offer to help was still good. I kept my word and became involved as one of the coordinators. I had the organizational and promotional experience needed to help try to save this woman's life.

In the bone marrow drive, I got involved personally and emotionally in the fight for the little girl. Her parents were my close friends. This drive for an African-American woman lacked personal feelings, but I knew it was the right thing to do. God, however, used this opportunity to "open my eyes and make me see."

Soon after I became involved, I started seeing African Americans in a different light. I found myself genuinely caring for them as I would for members of my own family. The real impact on me came when the lady with leukemia took a turn for the worse and ultimately died. She left a husband and three lovely children behind. On her deathbed, she asked that the drive continue so others could be helped even though her fight was nearing an end.

I looked at the tears of her husband and placed myself in his situation. Suddenly I realized the tears he was crying were the same tears as mine. I looked at the children and realized their tears were the same as my children would be crying if it were their mother. From this shared pain, Eddie Josie (the husband) and I became brothers in the truest sense of the word.

Through this experience, God brought me into the black community. He let me see it from the inside. He let me see and feel the pain. He showed me that, in Christ, we're the same. We may be black, white, red, or yellow on the outside; but we cry the same tears and bleed the same blood. Most importantly, we are *all* washed in the same blood of Jesus Christ, our Lord and Savior. We're all brothers and sisters in God's family. God took away my apathy and replaced it with love—His love!

LESSON 1 THE NEED FOR SINCERITY

Scripture for Meditation

"Speaking the truth in love, we will in all things grow up into him who is the Head, that is, Christ" (Ephesians 4:15).

A Beginning Prayer

Father, I want to grow up into Christ, the Head of the church. I know I can't do it alone. I'm learning that the body is much bigger and more diverse than I had ever realized. Help me learn to speak Your truth in love to my brothers. I also ask that You help me listen when my brothers speak truth to me. Fill me with Yourself in such a way that I will always bear love as the fruit of the Spirit in me, especially in my speech. Amen.

> Trust is built in a relationship with another person or group.

➡ **Ephesians 4:15 (in the left margin) is your Scripture memory verse for this unit. Remove the perforated card from the back of your book, and begin memorizing it. Read and think about the verse, and start the lesson with prayer.**

❖ ❖ ❖

Separation from people who are different develops and even encourages distrust. Human beings have a tendency not to trust across ethnic, social, national, and denominational lines. We don't trust people we don't know. We've heard from others everything we know about these different people. The lack of authentic, meaningful relationships means we talk mainly with others like us, who reinforce our negative preconceptions and limited understanding.

➡ **Mark the following statements as either True (T) or False (F).**

_____ 1. We tend to trust people we don't know personally.

_____ 2. Separation and isolation can encourage and maintain a lack of trust.

_____ 3. The best way to learn about people who are different from me is to talk to others who are just like me.

Trust is built in a relationship with another person or group. The best way to get to know another person or group is to talk with them directly. (Answers: 1 and 3 are false; 2 is true.)

We tend to interpret the actions of others based on our own life experiences. Without knowledge of the other person's life, we may jump to incorrect or unfair conclusions. Prejudice can develop and be encouraged by this lack of truth. If we base our opinions of others only on the statements of those who are like us, we're liable to get a biased viewpoint. We've summarized this truth in the "Kehrein-Washington Law of Racial Dynamics," or "The WWB/BBW Dynamic."

WWB

BBW

> **Kehrein-Washington Law of Racial Dynamics**
> Whites know how to talk to whites about blacks (WWB).
> The result is negative and stereotypical.
> This communication widens divisions and deepens distrust.
> and
> Blacks know how to talk to blacks about whites (BBW).
> The result is negative and stereotypical.
> This communication widens divisions and deepens distrust.

> When we talk only with people like us about others who aren't like us, we'll usually come up with negative stereotypes about them.

This same principle can be applied to any racial combination. It could be the HHB and BBH Dynamic for Hispanics and blacks. It could be the KKC and CCK for Koreans and Chinese. Whatever the groupings, when we talk only with people like us about others who aren't like us, we'll usually come up with negative stereotypes about them.

The principle can apply to denominations as well. Fundamentalists talking to other fundamentalists about charismatics will likely have some negative stereotypes. But the same would be true for charismatics talking to charismatics about fundamentalists. In such sessions, we share our common fears, frustrations, and ignorance about "why they act like that."

We must create an environment in which we can share with each other our feelings, attitudes, differences, and perceptions.

Our goal is to hear, understand, and build a foundation of trust.

Separate life experiences contribute to our lack of trust, because we interpret the actions of others as we would our own. The only way beyond such barriers is sincerity in face-to-face relationships. We must create an environment in which we can share with each other our feelings, attitudes, differences, and perceptions. Our goal is to hear, understand, and build a foundation of trust. What a rural person might perceive as a "chip on his shoulder" might actually be a city person's survival technique. When we open up and discuss life experiences, we begin to understand, and trust grows.

➡ **3. What groups of people do you probably have the strongest negative and stereotypical feelings about? Think about the categories below, and write the name of one group in each that you have strong opinions about. For instance, you might write "whites" for the ethnic group and "Pentecostals" for the denomination/Christian tradition group.**

Ethnic group: _____

Denomination/Christian tradition: _____

➡ **4. For each of those groups, write one statement about them that would be commonly heard among those like you. For instance, you might write about whites, "They're arrogant and always want to be in control."**

Ethnic group: _____

_____

Denomination/Christian tradition: _____

_____

These stereotypes are one reason for the principle of sincerity. In tomorrow's lesson, we'll study that principle and how to apply it to our relationships.

➡ **What, if anything, do you sense God has said to you through today's lesson? Write *one* of the most meaningful things He has said on the following lines.**

_____

_____

➡ **Conclude today's lesson by praying. Ask the Lord to open your mind and heart to seek understanding in your relationships, and to do so with honesty and sincerity.**

LESSON 2   THE PRINCIPLE OF SINCERITY

Scripture for Meditation

"'I no longer call you servants, because a servant does not know his master's business. Instead, I have called you friends, for everything that I learned from my Father I have made known to you'" (John 15:15).

A Beginning Prayer

Father, thank You that You have adopted me into Your family. I want to be more than a servant of Yours. I want to be Your friend. I also want to learn to have that same kind of relationship with my brothers in Christ. I want to be friends so we can share openly and sincerely with each other as we go about doing Your business. Help me learn to be a friend of Yours and of my brothers in Christ. Amen.

PRINCIPLE 4

Sincerity: We must be willing to be vulnerable and express our <u>feelings</u>, <u>attitudes</u>, <u>differences</u>, and <u>perceptions</u>, with the goal of resolution and building trust.

---

feelings
attitudes
differences
perceptions

➡ Read and think about the Scripture for Meditation in the left margin, and begin the lesson with prayer.

❖   ❖   ❖

➡ Using the memory card for the fourth principle, read the text for sincerity two or three times. In the margin to the left, you'll see the same text. Memorize the four words that describe the things we share with others in order to resolve differences and build trust.

➡ 1. What can you express in a committed relationship that will resolve differences and build trust? Write the four words you've learned.

F_____, A_____,

D_____, and P_____

Casual relationships with Christians across racial or denominational lines are a good beginning. But members of the body of Christ must move beyond casual relationships to loving, caring, trusting friendships that last.

The principle of sincerity says we must talk to each other and honestly disclose our thoughts. This takes us back to the previous principles, because such efforts will not happen without intentionality or outside committed relationships. Talking about those things that divide us, especially racial issues, can be very threatening. We fear even using the "r" words (*racism* or *racist*). We may believe that discussing them would be asking for trouble or conflict. Such fear entraps us in our isolation. Paul told us, *"God did not give us a spirit of timidity, but a spirit of power, of love and of self-discipline"* (2 Timothy 1:7). In practice, the revealing of ourselves brings understanding, which leads to resolution of differences.

➡ 2. By this time in your small group, you probably have already experienced sincerity. Think back over your group experiences thus far. What has been done or said that indicates a person was being sincere? Briefly describe what happened when a person openly expressed feelings, attitudes, differences, or perceptions. (You might write something like this: "Jim told us about the hatred he felt when his nephew was shot by a gang.")

_____

_____

Fudge Ripple Meetings

We've found that sometimes the pump of discussion needs to be primed in a safe atmosphere. At Rock Church, we hold what we call "Chocolate/Vanilla and Fudge Ripple Meetings." Separate meetings of blacks (chocolate) and whites (vanilla) help raise questions and discuss feelings that usually aren't revealed in a mixed setting. This is an "All you wanted to know (or say) about black/white people but were afraid to voice" session. We ask people to write down questions anonymously. The leaders take time to guide expression of feelings and concerns. Then both groups are brought together for our fudge ripple meeting. The issues raised in the separate meetings are discussed in an atmosphere of honesty and love. These sessions help us all understand how very differently we see the world around us. They're vital to our multicultural church, helping us avoid problems or resolve them before they grow.

Another benefit, however, is that individuals and small groups learn to practice sincerity on a personal level. We've made it okay to talk about the "forbidden" racial topics. We've found that the world doesn't explode into uncontrollable chaos when we do. In fact, quite the opposite is true; sincerity disarms tension and distrust.

Sincerity disarms tension and distrust.

Satan has sold us the lie that if we raise a sensitive issue, people will get hurt. In reality, covering up issues is the greater danger. Suppressed feelings, fermenting in misperceptions and ignorance, eventually erupt in passion. Unfortunately, suppression is the norm for racial communication, and we don't talk about concerns until they can no longer be contained. As in any interpersonal setting, this is a formula for disaster. But prevention—that is, the exercising of sincerity—is worth many times the cure.

➥ **3. When is the best time to discuss issues, concerns, misunderstandings, and hurt feelings with people who are different? Check your response.**
   ❑ a. It's best not to discuss these matters. Keep quiet and the problems will go away.
   ❑ b. It's best to discuss these concerns when they arise. Then they can be dealt with, and trust can be developed and maintained.
   ❑ c. It's best to wait as long as possible. If the problem doesn't go away, then you can deal with it when it blows up into a big problem.

1 John 1:7
"If we walk in the light, as he is in the light, we have fellowship with one another, and the blood of Jesus, his Son, purifies us from all sin."

Timing and Manner of Sharing
The best time to discuss these concerns is when they arise (*b*). Scripture calls this *"walking in the light"* (see 1 John 1:7). We must be willing to expose our feelings to the light of God's truth. God's Word is our measuring rod. As we express our feelings, we do so in a way that won't offend or hurt our brothers. Turning to the Lord in prayer, we can get the help we need to speak in a way that will be right. This sharing with each other can provide the answer or resolution to our differences. When believers who are surrendered to the lordship of Christ pray for unity in a spirit of sincerity, God works to bring about resolution.

As we express our feelings, we do so in a way that won't offend or hurt our brothers.

When believers who are surrendered to the lordship of Christ pray for unity in a spirit of sincerity, God works to bring about resolution.

➥ **4. Which of the following would be the *better* way to express feelings, attitudes, differences, or perceptions? Think about how the listener would respond. Check one.**
   ❑ a. In anger and with a harsh spirit of accusation and condemnation.
   ❑ b. In honesty and with a spirit of love and a desire to resolve differences.

Sincerity calls for the revealing of our feelings, attitudes, differences, and perceptions. Often, feelings control how we speak. If we talk harshly and with a spirit of accusation or condemnation, our listeners will likely become defensive. That doesn't lead to resolving differences. We can, however, express anger or hurt with a desire to see differences resolved. Stating truth in love will receive a much better response from our listeners.

Sincerity says, "I really want to hear what you feel and think."

When this sharing is done by one person, the other person may respond defensively by describing "the facts." Of course, "the facts" are themselves really only the facts "as I see them." Sincerity says, "I really want to hear what you feel and think." Our perceptions and feelings drive our actions far more than the facts. When we take the risk to speak across racial lines, distrust begins to give way to understanding.

➥ **What, if anything, do you sense God has said to you through today's lesson? Write *one* of the most meaningful things He has said below.**

_____

_____

➡ **Conclude today's lesson by praying.**
- Ask the Lord to give you a commitment to walk in the light of His truth.
- Ask Him to give you a spirit of love even though you may have experienced great pain or hurt. Ask Him to help you speak in sincerity so your brothers can help bring His healing to that hurt.
- Ask the Lord to help you learn to listen to the sharing of others without becoming defensive, even if they speak in anger, harshness, or condemnation.

LESSON 3 DEVELOPING YOUR SINCERITY

Scripture for Meditation

"Encourage the young men to be self-controlled. In everything set them an example by doing what is good. In your teaching show integrity, seriousness and soundness of speech that cannot be condemned, so that those who oppose you may be ashamed because they have nothing bad to say about us" (Titus 2:6–8).

A Beginning Prayer

Father, teach me to be self-controlled—especially in my speech. Help me to only speak truth about others so that no one will have a reason to say anything bad about You because of my words or actions. Amen.

➡ **Read and think about the Scripture for Meditation in the left margin, and begin the lesson with prayer.**

❖ ❖ ❖

Expressing yourself in sincerity requires you to be humble and risk vulnerability. It also requires an act of faith. You may ask yourself, *If I say this, will God take care of me?* Inevitably someone will say, "I revealed myself like that once, and they really hurt me. I won't do that again." Such a response to rejection is understandable, but it closes the door on reconciliation in the name of self-protection. When we conform to the likeness of Christ, we can expect to suffer for His sake at times. If you should experience rejection or hurt because you took the risk of sharing, God can take those experiences and use them to help you grow into maturity:

Consider it pure joy, my brothers, whenever you face trials of many kinds, because you know that the testing of your faith develops perseverance. Perseverance must finish its work so that you may be mature and complete, not lacking anything (James 1:2–4).

As we enter into a relationship of sincerity, God deepens our dependence on Him and equips us to be ambassadors of reconciliation. Let's look a little deeper at what sincerity is:

> **Sincerity**
> 1. Sincerity means investing time in the relationship.
> 2. Sincerity means taking the initiative to share my own life.
> 3. Sincerity means being open and honest.
> 4. Sincerity means a willingness to be vulnerable.
> 5. Sincerity means withholding judgment long enough to understand.
> 6. Sincerity means being willing to trust.

➡ **1. Think about your own responses in your small-group sessions. Using the list in the box above for evaluation, how much are you practicing sincerity? On a scale of 1 (poorly) to 10 (perfectly), rate yourself on your sincerity in your small group. Circle a number.**

poorly 1 2 3 4 5 6 7 8 9 10 perfectly

➡ **2. Using the list in the box again, what's your greatest weakness or area you need to work on to practice sincerity? Describe one or more areas in the left margin.**

_____

_____

_____

➡ **3. What do you want (or need) to discuss with your small group to deepen your relationships and resolve differences or avoid misunderstandings? Using the list below, write down several items or topics that you believe would be helpful for your group to hear or discuss. Today's lesson is a little shorter than usual so you can give more time to thinking through this question. Take some time to work on it.**

Feelings: _____

_____

_____

_____

Attitudes: _____

_____

_____

_____

Differences: _____

_____

_____

_____

Perceptions: _____

_____

_____

_____

➡ **What, if anything, do you sense God has said to you through today's lesson? Write *one* of the most meaningful things He has said below.**

_____

_____

➡ **Conclude today's lesson by praying for a spirit of sincerity.**
  • Ask the Lord to help you be open to sharing with others to develop trust and understanding.
  • Pray for courage, transparency, perseverance, and maturity.

LESSON 4 THE NEED FOR SENSITIVITY

Scripture for Meditation
"If I have the gift of prophecy and can fathom all mysteries and all knowledge, and if I have a faith that can move mountains, but have not love, I am nothing" (1 Corinthians 13:2).

A Beginning Prayer
Father, I'm learning that I need knowledge about my brothers in order to relate to them with understanding and compassion. If I don't have love, my knowledge will be worthless. Help me to develop sensitivity toward my brothers and to do so with love. Amen.

PRINCIPLE 5
Sensitivity: We must seek knowledge about our brothers in order to relate empathetically to people from different denominations, traditions, races, social standings, or cultures.

The principle of sensitivity brings your head (knowledge and understanding) into your relationships.

➥ Read and think about the Scripture for Meditation in the left margin, and begin the lesson with prayer.

❖ ❖ ❖

➥ Remove the memory card for sensitivity from the back of your book. Read the text two or three times. In the margin you'll find the same text. Circle one key word that describes what you seek in order to relate with understanding to people who are different.

❖ ❖ ❖

➥ 1. Based on the principle of sensitivity, what do you seek in order to relate empathetically (with compassion and understanding) to your brothers?

_____

Suppose you see a man walk into the mini-market with three preschool children. The children are rowdy and out of control. The father seems not to notice or care. He walks around the aisles collecting a few groceries while the kids terrorize the rest of the customers. While you're trying to pay for your gas, one of the older boys runs by you and nearly knocks you down.

➥ 2. What would you think about this father? Check your opinion.
❏ a. This is an irresponsible father. He should keep his children under control.
❏ b. This father is a poor disciplinarian. Why hasn't he taught these kids to behave?
❏ c. Other: _____

Then suppose the man apologizes to you: "I'm sorry. My wife—their mother—died yesterday," he explains. "I'm still dazed by it all, and the kids seem to be more hyperactive than usual. I don't think they really understand why their mother isn't around."

Does that change your feelings and opinions toward him? Sure it does. Instead of wanting to lecture him or turn him in to social services for negligent parenting, you wish there were some way you could help. That bit of knowledge about his wife caused you to empathize with him. Suddenly you felt some of his pain and loss. Now you can understand why he may have been slow to discipline the children.

The principle of *sincerity* brings your heart and emotions into your relationships. You begin genuinely to care about others. The principle of *sensitivity* brings your head (knowledge and understanding) into your relationships.

➥ 3. Match the principle on the left with the aspect of your being (on the right) that the principle brings into your relationships. Write a letter by the principle.
___ 1. The principle of sincerity   a. head (knowledge and understanding)
___ 2. The principle of sensitivity   b. heart and emotions

(Answers:1-b; 2-a.)

Racism and Discrimination Are Not Dead
An investigative television news show in 1995 broadcast a stunning destruction of the myth that discrimination is now rare. Two investigators were similar in every way—except that one was white and the other was black. The plan was simple: Both men would do everyday activities in a white community (it happened to be St. Louis) and see if they were treated differently. In a dozen instances—buying

shoes or a car, applying for a job or an apartment—the young men were treated in nearly opposite ways. While the white man was welcomed, the black man was ignored or insulted. Such covert racism is seldom, if ever, experienced by whites, who sometimes view blacks as being "overly sensitive" about racism.

➤ **4. If you were ignored, mistreated, or insulted regularly, how do you think you would feel about the group that treated you that way? Check a response or write one of your own.**
❑ a. loving and understanding
❑ b. angry and hateful
❑ c. envious
❑ d. Other: _____

Without becoming sensitive to the experiences of another person, we can't possibly know how we might respond in similar circumstances. Being ignored and mistreated or insulted *once* is a matter that can be overlooked. Experiencing that *daily* could easily lead to anger and even hate. Racism is painful. Constantly experiencing it can have a profound effect on a person, family, or group.

➤ **5. Have you ever experienced racism or discrimination because of your skin color, accent, clothes, or because of some other difference?** ❑ yes ❑ no

➤ **6. If you answered yes, briefly describe one situation in the margin. Also describe how you felt.**

➤ **7. How frequently would you say you face racism or discrimination from others? Check one.**

❑ a. Almost every day	❑ d. Seldom (a few times in my life)
❑ b. Regularly (twice or more weekly)	❑ e. Only once that I can remember
❑ c. Occasionally (a few times a year)	❑ f. Never

In 1992, following the Los Angeles riots, a paraphrase of Rodney King's plea became a coined phrase: "Why can't we all just get along?" It's a poignant question, and it's even more crucial when asked about the body of Christ. It's one matter when a sinful world can't get along, but it's much more serious when brothers and sisters in Christ can't get along. Some Christians might think, *If I'm doing okay, why should I worry or care about other Christians?* The answer is found in 1 Corinthians 12:21–26.

➤ **Read 1 Corinthians 12:21–22, 24–26 in the margin. As you read, look for reasons you should be concerned about other Christians.**

➤ **8. Why should you be concerned about how other Christians are treated? Check one.**
❑ a. Each member of the body of Christ needs all the others to be complete.
❑ b. God wants us to have equal concern for one another.
❑ c. If another member of the body of Christ suffers, the whole body suffers.
❑ d. All of the above.

➤ **9. Suppose that we decide not to be concerned about other members of the body and the suffering, hurt, or rejection they must endure. Based on 1 Corinthians 12:21–22, 24–26, what could be said about us? Check one.**
❑ a. We're acting contrary to the Scriptures by saying with our actions, "We don't need you."
❑ b. We contribute to divisions in the body of Christ by not caring and by doing nothing.
❑ c. By not caring for the suffering, we contribute to the harm done to the body of Christ, because those who suffer don't receive the help and healing they need.
❑ d. All of the above.

1 Corinthians 12:21–22, 24–26
"The eye cannot say to the hand, 'I don't need you!' And the head cannot say to the feet, 'I don't need you!' On the contrary, those parts of the body that seem to be weaker are indispensable. . . . God has combined the members of the body . . . so that there should be no division in the body, but that its parts should have equal concern for each other. If one part suffers, every part suffers with it; if one part is honored, every part rejoices with it."

Did you check *d* for both questions? Those are the correct answers. God has put the body of Christ together in such a way that every member is to have concern for every other member. When one member is allowed to suffer without the support of the others, the whole body suffers greater harm.

When one member is allowed to suffer without the support of the others, the whole body suffers greater harm.

➡ **10. If God were to evaluate your life based on the concern you have for other members of the body of Christ—particularly those who aren't like you— what kind of grade do you think He would give you? Check your opinion.**
❑ A – Superior concern; just what pleases the Father.
❑ F – Failing to measure up to God's standards.

Are you wondering what happened to the B, C, and D grades? God isn't interested in comparing you to other Christians. You're either obeying Him and following His guidelines for living in the body of Christ or you aren't. This is more like a pass or fail grade. You could be average compared to other Christians, but the average Christian may be functioning at a failing level in caring for other members of the body.

> **We aren't given the option of not being concerned.**

Lack of Knowledge Limits Understanding

The cultural isolation in which most of us live places us in different worlds. We may practice the out-of-sight-out-of-mind approach to caring about the body of Christ. If we can remain ignorant, we suppose, then maybe God won't hold us accountable. Another response could be a failure to recognize that we have separate histories, environments, and life experiences. The common expression that "we're all Americans" assumes we all experience life in more or less the same ways. We do not. A Christian who grew up in south-central Los Angeles will have had experiences very different from those of one who grew up on a Nebraska farm. We must be intentional in developing a sensitivity to the needs of other members of the body.

We must be intentional in developing a sensitivity to the needs of other members of the body.

The moral revolution and the deterioration of family values in our world often tempt us to wish for the "good old days." Family life seemed so healthy back then—to some, but not to all. Those were also the days of Jim Crow laws that dehumanized people and enforced racial segregation—in churches as well as in the rest of society. Those were the days of the Ku Klux Klan that terrorized African Americans and others. Those were the days of sharecropping, where landowners often got rich at the expense of those who worked the farms. To return to those days would be a nightmare from that standpoint.

For Americans of European background, Ellis Island evokes warm feelings of ancestors from the "old country." But it seems different to Hispanic immigrants who are struggling today for the same entrance to American citizenship. If we don't know a person's background or experiences, we won't understand his attitudes, actions, and beliefs. We won't know his pain and suffering, and the body of Christ will lack the health it could have.

➡ **11. Think back on your family's history. In the margin, write words and phrases that describe what life was like for your forefathers one or two generations ago.**

➡ **12. How have their experiences influenced your own life? Think about ways their choices, living conditions, education, job opportunities, and other situations have had an influence on you and your family. Write in the margin some words or phrases that describe some of those influences.**

➡ **What, if anything, do you sense God has said to you through today's lesson?**

Write *one* of the most meaningful things He has said below.

_____

_____

➡ **Conclude today's lesson by praying. Talk to your heavenly Father about your thoughts and feelings after studying this lesson.**
  • Are you feeling wounded and hurting? Tell Him all about your feelings.
  • Are you feeling you have fallen short of His expectations? Tell Him, and seek His forgiveness.
  • Are you wondering why you don't care, even after reading about why you should be concerned for other members of the body? Tell the Lord, and ask Him to examine and change your heart and mind.

LESSON 5 THE PRINCIPLE OF SENSITIVITY

Scripture for Meditation
"Speaking the truth in love, we will in all things grow up into him who is the Head, that is, Christ. From him the whole body, joined and held together by every supporting ligament, grows and builds itself up in love, as each part does its work" (Ephesians 4:15–16).

A Beginning Prayer
Father, You have placed me in the body of Christ. I submit to Christ as Head of the body, and I surrender to His will. I want to do my part in seeing the body grow and gain support from every part. I want to learn to speak the truth in love. Guard my tongue. Bring conviction every time I don't speak the truth or when I don't speak in love. Teach me to be sensitive to those around me so that we may grow up into Christ together. Amen.

PRINCIPLE 5
Sensitivity: We must seek knowledge about our brothers in order to relate empathetically to people from different denominations, traditions, races, social standings, or cultures.

➡ **Read and think about the Scripture for Meditation in the left margin, and begin the lesson with prayer.**

❖ ❖ ❖

➡ **Read again the statements of the last four principles on the perforated cards. Read "Principle 5: Sensitivity" two or three times. Review the first four principles on the cards.**

❖ ❖ ❖

I (Glen) was trying to teach my daughter to swim, but she was afraid of the water. She said she wanted to learn, but she resisted even getting into the pool. I tried all methods to encourage and even embarrass her into jumping in. "You're being silly; get in here," I said. Finally she told me a story I'd never heard before. A few years ago, she was in a wading pool. Several boys harassed her, dunked her in the water, and made her feel as if she would drown. She had been terrified of pools and bodies of water ever since.

With that knowledge, I could understand why she was struggling. I was sensitive to her feelings. I wouldn't call her feelings "silly" anymore, because I knew they were real. I couldn't change that past experience. But with my newfound sensitivity, I could approach my teaching job with a new love and understanding. I would be much more patient with her in the future.

Jesus Learned Sensitivity to the Human Condition
When God sought to reconcile us to Himself, He became one of us in the person of Jesus. Jesus grew from a baby to adulthood and experienced what it's like to be a man. He was able to empathize with us because of His knowledge of our experiences.

Who, being in very nature God, did not consider equality with God something to be grasped, but made himself nothing, taking the very nature of a servant, being made in human likeness (Philippians 2:6–7).

We do not have a high priest who is unable to sympathize with our weaknesses, but we have one who has been tempted in every way, just as we are— yet was without sin (Hebrews 4:15).

➡ **1. Based on these two scriptures, which of the following statements is true? Check it.**

❑ a. Jesus didn't really have to live the way most people do. After all, He was God and didn't have to put up with the same problems we face. He couldn't really understand what we've been through.

❑ b. Jesus was God in the flesh, but He had to live through the same kind of experiences and problems other people face. He so identified with all people that He can understand what we've been through, and He stands ready to help us through every difficulty.

While the ultimate purpose for Jesus' body was to be a sacrifice for our sins, Jesus also became flesh to identify with us. As a human being, He experienced the pain, struggles, and temptations of a man—yet without sin. He can identify with everything we face. We can feel the love of a God who is sensitive to our feelings and who has identified with our experiences.

We can feel the love of a God who is sensitive to our feelings and who has identified with our experiences.

Jesus modeled for us the principle of sensitivity. He became a friend of sinners and tax collectors. He chose to go through Samaria to meet the woman at the well. He took time to get to know people. Sometimes He even showed that He, too, felt their pain.

➡ **2. Read again the principle of sensitivity in the margin. What do you need to seek about your brothers in Christ if you're to be able to empathize with and understand them?**

_____

> **PRINCIPLE 5**
> **Sensitivity:** We must seek knowledge about our brothers in order to relate empathetically to people from different denominations, traditions, races, social standings, or cultures.

Developing Sensitivity

Sensitivity requires that you enter into the experience of your brothers and sisters in Christ. If they're different from you, you need knowledge to empathize and understand. The following are some ways you can begin developing sensitivity.

Read literature.

I. Read literature about and by other ethnic groups or denominations, or view video movies and/or documentaries. Reading a book or magazine article about and/or by people who are different will help you get inside the mind-set of others. Reading is one of the best nonthreatening ways to build sensitivity. Another nonthreatening way is to view a movie or documentary that helps you understand situations faced by persons of other ethnic backgrounds or denominations.

View a movie or documentary.

It's nearly impossible to read *Bury My Heart at Wounded Knee* or learn of the Cherokee Trail of Tears without being powerfully moved and sensitized to the pain of the Native American. The video *Eyes on the Prize* graphically depicts the heroic civil rights struggle and grips a viewer's heart with empathy. And minorities might be surprised at how much they could identify with the poverty, struggle, and prejudices experienced by many European immigrant groups by reading a book or watching a documentary about that era.

➡ **3. What's one way to develop sensitivity?**

_____

➡ **4. Have you ever watched a movie, seen a documentary, or read a book that gave you a sensitivity to the mistreatment or pain of others? If you have, check the people groups below that you learned about. Check all that apply, or list others in the margin.**

❑ Japanese Americans during World War II   ❑ migrant workers
❑ Jews during the Holocaust   ❑ Hispanic immigrants
❑ mixed races living in the inner cities   ❑ black slaves on a plantation
❑ Native Americans on reservations   ❑ poor whites in Appalachia

➡ **5. Turn to page 189 in the appendix. Read through the titles of books and resources listed. Based on the brief descriptions, which one of those resources do you think you would most want to read or view? Write it below:**

_____

Special Note: Those resources aren't necessarily religious works and may be written by non-Christians. We couldn't possibly endorse all that you might read or view in them. But they can give you a better understanding of other people and what they or their forefathers have been through. You may want to consider securing one of these resources from your library, a bookstore, or a video rental store for developing sensitivity. Your librarian may be able to point out other resources that could help you become sensitive to a particular people group.

Would you help me understand?

II. Master use of the request: "Would you help me understand . . . ?" We might like to believe we're completely free agents. We may believe the "American Dream"—that if you work hard enough, you can be anything you want to be. It's true that we can all make choices of how we respond to our surroundings. But we also are deeply influenced by our ethnic history and the models we've seen in those who have gone before us. Many have experienced pain as the result of sectarian strife. We can say, "The past is the past. Forget it and move on." But when we do, we're closing the door to understanding and sensitivity. Even though we might "feel" that others are living in the past, we can't understand without talking about experiences. Sensitivity—the gaining of knowledge to relate with empathy—requires that we reach out for understanding by asking, "Would you help me understand . . . ?"

They do want someone to hear their personal story and try to understand.

Most people want to be understood. Few believe the past can be changed or repaired by present actions. But they do want someone to hear their personal story and try to understand.

➡ **6. What's a second way to develop sensitivity in conversation with others?**

Master using the request: "_____"

➡ **What, if anything, do you sense God has said to you through today's lesson? Write *one* of the most meaningful things He has said below.**

_____

_____

1. What do You want me to do in my personal relationship with You?
2. What do You want me to do in relationship to other people in my church or denomination?
3. What do You want me to do in relationship to Christians in other denominations or Christian traditions?
4. What do You want me to do in relationship to Christians of other races or ethnic backgrounds?

➡ **For each lesson this week, you've been recording what you sense God has said to you. Review the final activity for each of the previous lessons on pages 104, 106, 108, 112. What's the major emphasis of what you sense God wants you to do in response to this unit's lessons? Pray and ask Him what He wants you to do. Then write notes in the margin or in a separate notebook. You might use the questions in the margin in your prayer.**

➡ **Conclude today's lesson by praying.**
   • Ask the Lord to guide you in learning to be sensitive to others in the body of Christ.
   • Ask Him to begin preparing and equipping you to help the body of Christ grow toward health as we become sensitive to one another.

UNIT 7   DEVELOPING SENSITIVITY

Scripture Memory Verse
"In everything, do to others what you would have them do to you, for this sums up the Law and the Prophets."
—Matthew 7:12

Unit Learning Goals
You will understand some ways of developing sensitivity, and you'll demonstrate your intentionality by starting to develop sensitivity to at least one people group different from yours.

Overview of Unit 7
Lesson 1: Developing Ethnic Sensitivity
Lesson 2: Help Me Understand
Lesson 3: Sensitivity Building
Lesson 4: Developing Denominational Sensitivity
Lesson 5: Treating Brothers as Brothers

PRINCIPLE 5
Sensitivity: We must seek knowledge about our brothers in order to relate empathetically to people from different denominations, traditions, races, social standings, or cultures.

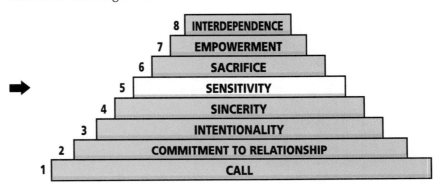

8 INTERDEPENDENCE
7 EMPOWERMENT
6 SACRIFICE
5 SENSITIVITY
4 SINCERITY
3 INTENTIONALITY
2 COMMITMENT TO RELATIONSHIP
1 CALL

Key Summary Statements from Unit 7
- Nothing beats an intentional and personal relationship of openness and sincerity to begin developing sensitivity.
- When we let ignorance divide us into camps, we've given Satan a victory he doesn't deserve.
- We must acknowledge that God's chosen people come in many different varieties. In fact, God has created much of the diversity for His redemptive purposes.
- As we all function in God's kingdom according to the assignment He has given us, His kingdom advances, and the body of Christ functions in a healthy way.
- Sometimes people can claim to know the truth and then deny it by their actions.

The Body of Christ

CHRIST

GOD'S TROPHY

I GOT IN TOUCH WITH THEIR PAIN[1]

By Bill McCartney

It happened in the mid-1980s. I had been the football coach at Colorado University for a few years when a black Denver attorney by the name of Teddy Woods died at the age of forty. In his college days, Teddy had excelled as a student-athlete at CU. Although he didn't play for me, I had met him and knew of his prowess and influence in the Denver area.

I arrived early for the funeral and found a seat in the front of the church. By the time the service began, the auditorium was full. Now, bear in mind that I didn't know the other people and had only met Teddy in passing. I was there to pay my respects because he had played football for CU, and I was the current coach.

What happened to me that day changed my life. It may be hard for you to understand, but when I sat down and started listening to the music, I was deeply affected. The mournful singing of the mostly black congregation expressed a level of pain I hadn't seen or felt before. As I looked from side to side across the crowd, I realized their grief over the loss of Teddy Woods was bringing to the surface an even deeper hurt. This wasn't just a funeral; it was also a gathering of wounded, long-suffering believers.

In response, I began to weep uncontrollably. I tried to cover my tears, fearing someone would see me and recognize that I barely knew Teddy Woods. I thought they might accuse me of grandstanding to gain acceptance and approval in the inner city as a recruiting ploy. Yet I couldn't hold back the tears. The grieving and groaning exceeded anything I had ever experienced. I have never been the same since then.

I had come in touch, for the first time, with the pain, struggle, despair, and anguish of black people. Stunned by that experience, I felt a great desire to understand what I had observed. I also wanted to pursue what I had felt in my spirit. Although Boulder, the city where I live, is 98 percent white, I worked with black families during recruiting season every year. And I had a sense that God was calling me to a deeper understanding of their lives that would greatly influence me both personally and in my role as a leader of Promise Keepers.

So I began to question black people I had known for years. It amazed me that despite wide differences in their ages and the places where they had grown up, they all identified directly with the pain I had felt in the church that day. They told stories about dramatic experiences and everyday examples of the injustices they face as black Americans.

[1]Adapted from "A Call to Unity," by Bill McCartney in *Seven Promises of a Promise Keeper* (Colorado Springs: Focus on the Family, 1994), pp. 157-58.

LESSON 1 — DEVELOPING ETHNIC SENSITIVITY

Scripture for Meditation

"In everything, do to others what you would have them do to you, for this sums up the Law and the Prophets" (Matthew 7:12).

A Beginning Prayer

Father, just as I want people to be sensitive to my feelings and needs, so I want to be sensitive toward theirs. Help me to be sensitive to the feelings of others. Help me to live out the Golden Rule by treating others the way I want to be treated—regardless of whether they're red, yellow, black, white, or brown. Amen.

PRINCIPLE 5
Sensitivity: We must seek knowledge about our brothers in order to relate empathetically to people from different denominations, traditions, races, social standings, or cultures.

Jack and Jenny

➡ **Matthew 7:12 (the Golden Rule) in the margin is your Scripture memory verse for this unit. Remove the perforated card from the back of your book for unit 7, and begin memorizing this verse. Read and think about this verse, and start the lesson with prayer.**

❖ ❖ ❖

➡ **Read again the statement of the principle of sensitivity in the margin. Then answer the following questions.**

➡ **1. What do you seek in order to develop sensitivity?**

_____

➡ **2. Why is sensitivity needed? (fill in the blank)**

In order to r_____ empathetically to people from different denominations, traditions, races, social standings, or cultures.

To develop sensitivity, you need knowledge in order to relate with understanding and compassion. Sensitivity will help you build committed relationships. It won't happen, however, without intentionality.

➡ **3. Are you willing to begin developing sensitivity toward people who are different from you, especially brothers and sisters in Christ? Check your response.**
❑ a. Yes, I'm willing and ready to become more sensitive by seeking knowledge.
❑ b. Almost. I'm moving in the direction of willingness, but tell me what I must do before I make any commitments.
❑ c. No, I'm not ready to make any commitments to developing sensitivity. I'm content where I am.

We doubt that many of you would check *b* or *c* by this stage. In fact, if you've been studying your lessons, you probably are already developing sensitivity. In this lesson, we want you to take a next step.

One Couple's Experience

Jack and Jenny live in a community just north of Chicago that prides itself on being ethnically diverse and racially sensitive. They were shocked to discover, however, that their next-door neighbors—the only black family on the block—had recently received several anonymous "hate letters" enumerating various complaints and telling them to get out of the neighborhood. Suspicions and accusations regarding who had sent the letters broke apart the fragile racial peace of that city block. Up to this point, except for "Hi" across the fence, there had been little relationship between the black family and the white neighbors. Most of the whites gave as their reason certain irritations, such as late-night noise, as well as the hostility of the black grandmother, who wouldn't even say hello.

What the letter-writers didn't know was that the grandmother had seen her own brother lynched by the Klan when she was a child. When Jack, Jenny, and some other neighbors started trying to get to know the family, they began to understand them. A glimmer of empathy broke through some of the judgmental attitudes in the neighborhood. Without knowing who had written the letters, Jack and Jenny wrote (and signed!) a letter inviting all the neighbors to use the incident as an opportunity to build relationships between black and white and work out problems person to person. They didn't want isolation and ignorance to breed further distrust and alienation. That letter was only a step—but it was a step in the right direction. Jack and Jenny were developing sensitivity by seeking out knowledge.

➡ **4. What did Jack and Jenny do to begin developing sensitivity? Check one.**
    ❑ a. They asked their white neighbors about the black family.
    ❑ b. They watched television and made assumptions based on stereotypes of black families.
    ❑ c. They began talking with the black family and got to know them personally.

> Nothing beats an intentional and personal relationship of openness and sincerity to begin developing sensitivity.

Nothing beats an intentional and personal relationship of openness and sincerity to begin developing sensitivity. Jumping to conclusions based on prejudices or stereotypes doesn't help. Talking to people just like you doesn't help unless they've already begun developing sensitivity themselves. Building a personal relationship like Jack and Jenny is the better choice. They took the time to ask, "Help me understand . . ."

We Need Sensitivity Toward Others

White people in the church in the United States need to understand that minorities normally know far more about them than they do about minorities. This is not an accusation but a fact of life. Why? Because the United States is based on the culture of the white majority. Our standards are white middle-class standards. Business, political life, and the educational system run on white middle-class cultural values. To compete in this world requires a minority person to try to assimilate into that standard by learning and living by the rules of another culture. The minority person's views of whites, however, may be tainted because of the poor models of white people he has seen, known, or heard about.

> If we're going to learn how to get along with each other in the body of Christ, we need to become sensitized to the other members of the body.

The majority whites normally have little motivation to learn the cultures of minorities. They just aren't "relevant" to them. If we're going to learn how to get along with each other in the body of Christ, however, we need to become sensitized to the other members of the body. The love of Christ and the need for unity in His body should cause us to want to know about our brothers and sisters.

At the same time, minorities must avoid the assumption that only whites can be prejudiced. Having to survive in the white world can cause a person to be angry. Past hurts and painful family stories can build resentment. Small and sometimes innocent indiscretions can reinforce stereotypes that build walls. They can prevent well-meaning gestures of friendship. Asking for help in understanding why a particular thing happened or why a person responded in a particular way will begin to break down walls built by our own prejudice.

No one would deny that there can be great differences in our various ethnic and church cultures. But we're all created in God's image. From His viewpoint, we're all His creations. Our enemy, Satan, would trick us into believing that "those people" are very different—and therefore we should keep separate from them. When sensitivity gives us understanding of how or why we might approach things differently, however, we soon come to understand our goals are the same. As Christians, the bottom line is the same: to glorify

When we let ignorance divide us into camps, we've given Satan a victory he doesn't deserve.

God and see a lost world come to know the Savior. When we let ignorance divide us into camps, we've given Satan a victory he doesn't deserve.

➥ **5. Which of the following words describe things sensitivity tries to remove? Check all that apply.**
  ❑ a. ignorance   ❑ c. misunderstanding   ❑ e. prejudice
  ❑ b. isolation   ❑ d. false stereotypes

Did you check all the words? Good! That's the purpose of developing sensitivity.

What If I Say or Do the Wrong Thing?

First apply the Golden Rule toward others: *"Do to others what you would have them do to you"* (Matthew 7:12).

More than likely you've been racially or denominationally insensitive at some time or another. As you build relationships, you'll say and do some wrong things in the process. Realize that those you're building relationships with may say or do some wrong things, too. First apply the Golden Rule toward others: *"Do to others what you would have them do to you"* (Matthew 7:12). When you're the offended one:
- Be ready to forgive even without being asked.
- Give the benefit of the doubt, and don't jump to conclusions about motives.
- Lovingly and privately talk about any insensitivities or offenses so the offender can learn to avoid similar actions or words in the future.

➥ **6. Have you been offended by someone who did or said the wrong thing? If so, do you need to do one of the things listed above? If you do, draw a star beside it, or write a note to yourself in the margin.**

When You're the Offender:

Don't dismiss racial or denominational insensitivity just because it was unintentional.

- Seek to understand what you said or did that was insensitive.
- Don't dismiss racial or denominational insensitivity just because it was unintentional. It can still hurt.
- Learn from the experience; find out what the appropriate response or words would have been.
- Apologize for insensitivity, and ask for forgiveness.
- If some sort of restitution or retraction is needed, do what's right so your conscience can remain clear before the Lord.
- Ask the Lord to help you become more sensitive in the future.

➥ **7. Have you been the offender by saying or doing the wrong thing? If so, do you need to do one of the things listed above? If you do, draw a star beside it, or write a note to yourself in the margin.**

➥ **What, if anything, do you sense God has said to you through today's lesson? Write *one* of the most meaningful things He has said below.**

_____

_____

➥ **Conclude today's lesson by praying for increased sensitivity toward others.**
  - Ask the Lord to reveal any insensitivities you may have committed. Invite Him to reveal them through others. Ask Him to help you receive the information in a positive and constructive way rather than a defensive way.
  - Ask the Lord to help you know when and how you should speak to others about insensitivities for their sake.

LESSON 2 HELP ME UNDERSTAND

Scripture for Meditation

"Blessed is the man who finds wisdom, the man who gains understanding, for she is more profitable than silver and yields better returns than gold. She is more precious than rubies; nothing you desire can compare with her. Long life is in her right hand; in her left hand are riches and honor. Her ways are pleasant ways, and all her paths are peace" (Proverbs 3:13–17).

A Beginning Prayer

Father, I know You are the ultimate source for understanding. I ask You to give me a spirit of understanding toward other ethnic peoples and people of other denominations or Christian traditions so I can have meaningful relationships with those You bring into my life. Guide me as I seek understanding. Amen.

➡ **Read and think about the Scripture for Meditation in the left margin, and begin the lesson with prayer.**

❖ ❖ ❖

Already we've learned that an easy way to begin developing sensitivity is to make the request, "Help me understand . . ." This introduction to seeking knowledge and understanding is not threatening to others. Few will be unwilling to help you understand. Below are some things you may want to seek understanding on. "Would you help me understand . . .

- what I may say or do that's hurtful, offensive, or just insensitive?"
- what common ways people intentionally or unintentionally express insensitivity toward your race or ethnic group?"
- what pain and frustration is felt by your denomination or Christian tradition because of its history?"
- some of the ways you personally have experienced racism or sectarianism that have been painful?"

➡ **1. If you were entering into a cross-cultural relationship, what topics would you tend to avoid because of feelings of guilt, shame, inadequacy, or fear? Check all that you would tend to avoid.**

❑ place and type of work ❑ family relationships
❑ family history/heritage ❑ personal feelings
❑ educational background ❑ personal experiences
❑ religious knowledge

➡ **2. Using the same list, what topics would you feel most comfortable with because of feelings of pride, accomplishment, or success? Circle them.**

➡ **3. Suppose you were interviewing a person for a job. What stereotypes have you been taught about people of other backgrounds that might influence your thinking before you even asked the first question? Write two or three ideas beside each ethnic group listed below.**

A. If the person were black? _____

_____

B. If the person were white? _____

_____

C. If the person were Asian? _____

_____

D. If the person were Hispanic? _____

_____

E. If the person were Native American? _____

_____

➡ 4. Choose a group of people who are different from you ethnically, socially, or denominationally. If you're in a small group with people who are different, select a group from which one of your small-group members comes. Describe the group on the following line:

_____

➡ 5. What are some things about this group of people that you don't understand? Write at least three questions to which you would like to know answers. A sample question might be, "Would you help me understand why so many young African-American males express so much anger and violence?" Use *who, what, when, where, why,* and *how* kinds of questions.
Would you help me understand . . .

_____

_____

_____

➡ What, if anything, do you sense God has said to you through today's lesson? Write *one* of the most meaningful things He has said below.

_____

_____

➡ Conclude today's lesson by praying for understanding of at least one group of people who are different from you.

LESSON 3 SENSITIVITY BUILDING

Scripture for Meditation
"Be careful to do what is right in the eyes of everybody. If it is possible, as far as it depends on you, live at peace with everyone" (Romans 12:17–18).

A Beginning Prayer
Father, I want to do what's right, and I want to live at peace with others—especially those who are my brothers and sisters in Christ. Help me to understand what's right in the eyes of people of other races and ethnic groups so I won't offend them intentionally or unintentionally. Amen.

➡ Read and think about the Scripture for Meditation in the left margin, and begin the lesson with prayer.

❖ ❖ ❖

Today's lesson is going to be different from any others you've studied. In the appendix, we have included some sensitivity-building articles for you. We asked men from different ethnic backgrounds to help us better understand men from their ethnic group. We've called these articles sensitivity builders because we pray they will help you develop sensitivity and build relationships across racial and ethnic barriers. You'll focus on one ethnic group today.

➡ 1. Choose one of the following articles for today's lesson. You may want to choose one that will help you best to build relationships in your small group. The choice is yours. Check your choice.
❏ Sensitivity Builders: A Hispanic Perspective (p. 178)
❏ Sensitivity Builders: An African-American Perspective (p. 179)
❏ Sensitivity Builders: An Asian-American Perspective (p. 181)
❏ Sensitivity Builders: A Native-American Perspective (p. 183)
❏ Sensitivity Builders: A White Perspective (p. 185)

➡ Read the following questions. Then turn to the article of your choice on the page indicated above and read it. Next, answer the questions.

Write your answers below or in the margin.

➡ 2. What's one of the most important things you just learned that you didn't know or understand in the past?

_____

_____

➡ 3. What's one idea you've received that should help you build a more meaningful relationship with a person from this background?

_____

_____

➡ 4. What's one thing you probably should avoid as you try to build a relationship with a person of this background?

_____

_____

➡ 5. If you could ask this author one question about his ethnic group, what would you ask?

_____

_____

➡ What, if anything, do you sense God has said to you or taught you through today's lesson? Write *one* of the most meaningful things He has said below.

_____

_____

Ephesians 3:16–19

"I pray that out of his glorious riches he may strengthen you with power through his Spirit in your inner being, so that Christ may dwell in your hearts through faith. And I pray that you, being rooted and established in love, may have power, together with all the saints, to grasp how wide and long and high and deep is the love of Christ, and to know this love that surpasses knowledge—that you may be filled to the measure of all the fullness of God."

➡ **Conclude today's lesson by praying for the ethnic group you've studied.**
• Ask the Lord to work mightily in the lives of believers in that ethnic group to lift up Christ. Use Paul's prayer from Ephesians 3:16–19 in the margin to pray for this group.
• Ask the Lord to bind up any brokenness and remove the hurt of past experiences.
• Ask the Lord to bring down the barriers that may keep them separated from the rest of the body of Christ.
• Ask the Lord what He might want you to do to build relationships with this group or one person within this group.

LESSON 4 DEVELOPING DENOMINATIONAL SENSITIVITY

Scripture for Meditation

"He [Jesus] replied to him, 'Who is my mother, and who are my brothers?' Pointing to his disciples, he said, 'Here are my mother and my brothers. For whoever does the will of my Father in heaven is my brother and sister and mother'" (Matthew 12:48–50).

A Beginning Prayer

Father, You have adopted children into Your spiritual family. I want to treat my brothers and sisters as I should. Give me sensitivity to those who really are my brothers and sisters in Christ. Amen.

As we all function in God's kingdom according to the assignment He has given us, His kingdom advances and the body of Christ functions in a healthy way.

➡ **Read and think about the Scripture for Meditation in the left margin, and begin the lesson with prayer.**

❖ ❖ ❖

This lesson deals with one of the most sensitive areas that limits experiencing unity in the body of Christ. People have learned to hold on to their doctrines and faith with conviction and without compromise. God certainly wants truth to prevail. He hates heresy and false teaching. However, we've allowed our doctrinal differences and church practices to keep us isolated from other parts of the body.

➡ **For further study, you may want to read the Promise Keepers statement "Biblical Unity and Biblical Truth" beginning on page 173.**

We must acknowledge that God's chosen people come in many varieties. In fact, God has created much of the diversity for His redemptive purposes. Some denominational groups may be able to reach one kind of person best, while another denomination is far more effective in reaching another type. One may be strong in worship and intercession, while another's strength is in ministry and missions. As we all function in God's kingdom according to the assignment He has given us, His kingdom advances, and the body of Christ functions in a healthy way.

For today's lesson, we're going to study a parable to learn a valuable spiritual lesson. The following parable about Christian unity was presented by Max Lucado, well-known pastor and author, during the Promise Keepers Clergy Conference in Atlanta, Georgia, on February 14, 1996. As you read the parable, we'll pause occasionally for a learning activity to gain understanding and make application. You'll find the parable was intended to be humorous at points to help us deal more freely with a serious need in the body of Christ. Don't let the wording offend you. As believers, we're all in this boat together!

LIFE ABOARD THE FELLOW-SHIP [1]
By Max Lucado

God has enlisted us in his navy and placed us on his ship. The boat has one purpose—to carry us safely to the other shore.

This is no cruise ship; it's a battleship. We aren't called to a life of leisure; we are called to a life of service. Each of us has a different task. Some, concerned with those who are drowning, are snatching people from the water. Others are occupied with the enemy, so they man the cannons of prayer and worship. Still others devote themselves to the crew, feeding and training the crew members.

➡ **1. In this parable of the boat (or battleship), the boat represents what spiritual reality? Check your opinion below.**
  ❑ a. The boat represents a denomination.
  ❑ b. The boat represents a nation.
  ❑ c. The boat represents all believers in the church universal—the body of Christ.
  ❑ d. The boat represents the World Council of Churches.

Lucado is comparing the body of Christ to a battleship and a navy (c).

> "Each can tell of a personal encounter with the captain, for each has received a personal call."

Though different, we are the same. Each can tell of a personal encounter with the captain, for each has received a personal call. He found us among the shanties of the seaport and invited us to follow him. Our faith was born at the sight of his fondness, and so we went.

We each followed him across the gangplank of his grace onto the same boat. There is one captain and one destination. Though the battle is fierce, the boat is safe, for our captain is God. The ship will not sink. For that, there is no concern.

My Personal Encounter with Jesus

_____

_____

_____

_____

_____

_____

➡ **2. Think about your personal encounter with Jesus Christ. When and how did you come to know and trust Him as your Savior and Lord? Write a few notes about your "personal encounter with the Captain" in the margin.**

Perhaps even at this point in the study, you realize you've never had that kind of personal encounter with Jesus Christ. If that's the case, stop and turn to "How to Be Reconciled to God" on page 170, and consider this as God's invitation for you to turn to Christ for salvation. Call a pastor or Christian friend if you need counsel or help.

There is concern, however, regarding the disharmony of the crew. When we first boarded we assumed the crew was made up of others like us. But as we've wandered these decks, we've encountered curious converts with curious appearances. Some wear uniforms we've never seen, sporting styles we've never witnessed. "Why do you look the way you do?" we ask them.

"Funny," they reply. "We were about to ask the same of you."

The variety of dress is not nearly as disturbing as the plethora of opinions. There is a group, for example, who clusters every morning for serious study. They promote rigid discipline and somber expressions. "Serving the captain is serious business," they explain. It's no coincidence that they tend to congregate around the stern.

There is another regiment deeply devoted to prayer. Not only do they believe in prayer, they believe in prayer by kneeling. For that reason you always know where to locate them; they are at the bow of the ship.

And then there are a few who staunchly believe real wine should be used in the Lord's Supper. You'll find them on the port side.

Still another group has positioned themselves near the engine. They spend hours examining the nuts and bolts of the boat. They've been known to go below deck and not come up for days. They are occasionally criticized by those who linger on the top deck, feeling the wind in their hair and the sun on their face. "It's not what you learn," those topside argue. "It's what you feel that matters."

And, oh, how we tend to cluster.

➡ **3. As you think about your own denomination, association, or tradition, which of the following seems to be the stronger emphasis? Check your opinion below, on the following page, or write your own.**
❏ a. Bible study and gaining knowledge of the Bible
❏ b. Prayer and the deeper devotional life
❏ c. Tradition, liturgy, and solemnity of worship
❏ d. Spontaneity, feelings, emotion, and free expression in worship

❑ e. Ministry, evangelism, and missions

❑ Other? _____

Some think once you're on the boat, you can't get off. Others say you'd be foolish to go overboard, but the choice is yours.

Some believe you volunteer for service; others believe you were destined for the service before the ship was even built.

Some predict a storm of great tribulation will strike before we dock; others say it won't hit until we are safely ashore.

There are those who speak to the captain in a personal language. There are those who think such languages are extinct.

There are those who think the officers should wear robes, there are those who think there should be no officers at all, and there are those who think we are all officers and should all wear robes.

And, oh, how we tend to cluster.

➡ **4. As you read through the following paragraph, notice the contrasts in worship styles. For each contrast, underline the emphasis given in your church. For instance, if your church is more quiet and formal, you would probably underline *quiet* and *ritual*.**

And then there is the issue of the weekly meeting at which the captain is thanked and his words are read. All agree on its importance, but few agree on its nature. Some want it loud, others quiet. Some want ritual, others spontaneity. Some want to celebrate so they can meditate; others meditate so they can celebrate. Some want a meeting for those who've gone overboard. Others want to reach those overboard but without going overboard and neglecting those on board.

And, oh, how we tend to cluster.

The consequence is a rocky boat. There is trouble on deck. Fights have broken out. Sailors have refused to speak to each other. There have even been times when one group refused to acknowledge the presence of others on the ship. Most tragically, some adrift at sea have chosen not to board the boat because of the quarreling of the sailors.

➡ **5. Have you ever known a person who has chosen not to turn to Christ or join a church because "Christians are hypocrites" or because "they can't even get along with each other"? ❑ yes ❑ no**

"What do we do?" we'd like to ask the captain. "How can there be harmony on the ship?" We don't have to go far to find the answer.

On the last night of his life Jesus prayed a prayer that stands as a citadel for all Christians:

I pray for these followers, but I am also praying for all those who will believe in me because of their teaching. Father, I pray that they can be one. As you are in me and I am in you, I pray that they can also be one in us. Then the world will believe that you sent me. (John 17:20) [2]

[2]*Holy Bible, New Century Version,* copyright 1987, 1988, 1991 by Word Publishing, Dallas, Texas 75039. Used by permission.

➡ **6. Since Jesus saw unity as a priority concern for His followers, which of the following do you believe best describes how we should relate to other Christians who are different? Check your opinion.**

❏ a. Christians ought to stay in their own groups, do their own thing, and pretend that nobody else matters—"We don't need them."

❏ b. Christians ought to join together and compromise everything necessary until we're all just alike in our doctrine and practice. Everything we can't agree on should be dropped as unimportant.

❏ c. Christians ought to relate to brothers and sisters in Christ in love and respect. We should be patient with those who differ and try to help each other grow into Christlikeness.

❏ d. As Christians, we ought to fight with each other, condemn each other, and criticize and ridicule each other in the hopes that those groups who are wrong will get straightened out and become just like us.

❏ e. Other: _____

_____

How precious are these words. Jesus, knowing the end is near, prays one final time for his followers. Striking, isn't it, that he prayed not for their success, their safety, or their happiness.

He prayed for their unity. He prayed that they would love each other.

As he prayed for them, he also prayed for "those who will believe because of their teaching." That means us! In his last prayer Jesus prayed that you and I be one.

Of all the lessons we can draw from this verse, don't miss the most important: Unity matters to God. The Father does not want his kids to squabble. Disunity disturbs him. Why? Because "all people will know that you are my followers if you love each other" (John 13:35). Unity creates belief How will the world believe that Jesus was sent by God? Not if we agree with each other. Not if we solve every controversy. Not if we are unanimous on each vote. Not if we never make a doctrinal error. But if we love one another.

➡ **What, if anything, do you sense God has said to you through today's lesson? Write *one* of the most meaningful things He has said below.**

_____

_____

➡ **Conclude today's lesson with prayer. Pray for your own church and denomination or Christian tradition.**

• Ask the Lord to help you love and accept other brothers and sisters in Christ in a way that will honor and please Him.

• Thank Him for people and groups from other traditions or denominations who have contributed to your spiritual growth. Make a list in the margin of some people from other Christian backgrounds who have influenced your own walk with the Lord.

• Tell the Lord about any struggles you may have with relating to Christians from other denominations. Ask Him to help you know how to respond in a way that will please Him.

LESSON 5 TREATING BROTHERS AS BROTHERS

Scripture for Meditation
"We ought therefore to show hospitality to such men so that we may work together for the truth" (3 John 8).

A Beginning Prayer
Father, I sometimes don't know how to respond or relate to people who hold different beliefs. Would You give me a spirit of discernment to know those who are my brothers in Christ? Then guide us to relate to each other in a way that would bring glory to Christ. Amen.

Gaius
"It gave me great joy to have some brothers come and tell about your faithfulness to the truth and how you continue to walk in the truth. I have no greater joy than to hear that my children are walking in the truth.

"Dear friend, you are faithful in what you are doing for the brothers, even though they are strangers to you. They have told the church about your love. You will do well to send them on their way in a manner worthy of God. It was for the sake of the Name that they went out, receiving no help from the pagans. We ought therefore to show hospitality to such men so that we may work together for the truth" (3 John 3–8).

Diotrephes
"I wrote to the church, but Diotrephes, who loves to be first, will have nothing to do with us. So if I come, I will call attention to what he is doing, gossiping maliciously about us. Not satisfied with that, he refuses to welcome the brothers. He also stops those who want to do so and puts them out of the church" (3 John 9–10).

➥ **Read and think about the Scripture for Meditation in the left margin, and begin the lesson with prayer.**

❖ ❖ ❖

How are we to relate to brothers and sisters in Christ, especially those from different denominations or Christian traditions? In Third John, the apostle John commended his friend Gaius for the way he treated some brothers in Christ. He then contrasted this response with the actions of Diotrephes, who was more exclusive. As you read about the ways of these two men, see which one is more like you.

➥ **1. Read about Gaius in the margin. Underline ways he treated brothers.**

Gaius was faithful to the truth. He evidently didn't compromise it, but he demonstrated it by the way he related to brothers in Christ. Sometimes people can claim to know the truth and then deny it by their actions. Not Gaius. His life reflected Christlikeness. Gaius demonstrated love, acceptance, and support for the brothers even though they were *"strangers."* The brothers were serving Christ (*"the Name"*) and didn't depend on pagans for their help. Gaius showed hospitality toward them so they could work together to advance the cause of Christ.

➥ **2. Now read about Diotrephes in the margin. Underline ways he treated brothers.**

Diotrephes allowed pride to keep him separated from brothers in Christ, men like John the apostle. He didn't want to have anything to do with others. He gossiped and talked maliciously about those who were different. He refused to welcome brothers in Christ into fellowship or relationship. He showed no hospitality toward the outsiders. He even put out of the church believers who wanted to act more like Gaius by loving, accepting, and encouraging other believers.

➥ **3. In what ways do you seem to be like Gaius or Diotrephes in the way you relate to Christian brothers? In each pair below, check the one that's more like you. If neither seems to apply, check neither.**

❑ A1. I tend to be accepting toward believers who are different and enjoy opportunities to fellowship with them.
❑ A2. I tend to avoid believers who are different and don't want to have anything to do with them if at all possible.
❑ Neither A1 nor A2

❑ B1. I tend to encourage and watch for ways to support others as they seek to serve the Lord.
❑ B2. I tend to criticize, condemn, and gossip about those who are different because they're not serving the Lord the way I do.
❑ Neither B1 nor B2

❑ C1. If people differ from me, I tend to pray for them and see how God might want to use me to help them grow. Or I seek the Lord to see if I'm the one who needs to make some changes.
❑ C2. If people differ from me, I'm ready to kick them out of the church. I'm ready to break off fellowship. That is the easiest way to deal with troublemakers—get rid of them.
❑ Neither C1 nor C2

The Parable of the Weeds

"Jesus told them another parable: 'The kingdom of heaven is like a man who sowed good seed in his field. But while everyone was sleeping, his enemy came and sowed weeds among the wheat, and went away. When the wheat sprouted and formed heads, then the weeds also appeared.

"'The owner's servants came to him and said, "Sir, didn't you sow good seed in your field? Where then did the weeds come from?"

"'"An enemy did this," he replied.

"'The servants asked him, "Do you want us to go and pull them up?"

"'"No," he answered, "because while you are pulling the weeds, you may root up the wheat with them. Let both grow together until the harvest. At that time I will tell the harvesters: First collect the weeds and tie them in bundles to be burned; then gather the wheat and bring it into my barn"'" (Matthew 13:24–30).

"Then he left the crowd and went into the house. His disciples came to him and said, 'Explain to us the parable of the weeds in the field.'

"He answered, 'The one who sowed the good seed is the Son of Man. The field is the world, and the good seed stands for the sons of the kingdom. The weeds are the sons of the evil one, and the enemy who sows them is the devil. The harvest is the end of the age, and the harvesters are angels.

"'As the weeds are pulled up and burned in the fire, so it will be at the end of the age. The Son of Man will send out his angels, and they will weed out of his kingdom everything that causes sin and all who do evil. They will throw them into the fiery furnace, where there will be weeping and gnashing of teeth. Then the righteous will shine like the sun in the kingdom of their Father'" (Matthew 13:36–43).

Did you find that you're more like the first statement in each pair, like Gaius? Or do you tend to act more like Diotrephes (the second statement)? Ask the Lord to help you act more like Gaius in relating to your brothers in Christ!

➡ **4. Read the parable of the weeds in the margin, and be prepared to discuss with your small group the instructions from this parable that might relate to our relationship with others who claim to be "wheat." Write notes to yourself below.**

_____

_____

_____

_____

_____

➡ **What, if anything, do you sense God has said to you through today's lesson? Write *one* of the most meaningful things He has said below.**

_____

_____

➡ **For each lesson in this unit, you've been recording what you sense God has said to you. Review the final activity for each of the previous lessons on pages 120, 122, 123, and 127. What's the major emphasis of what you sense God wants you to do in response to this unit's lessons? Pray and ask Him what He wants you to do. Then write notes in the margin or in a separate notebook. You might use these questions in your prayer:**

1. What do You want me to do in my personal relationship with You?
2. What do You want me to do in relationship to other people in my church or denomination?
3. What do You want me to do in relationship to Christians in other denominations or Christian traditions?
4. What do You want me to do in relationship to Christians of other races or ethnic backgrounds?

➡ **Conclude today's lesson by praying.**
- Ask the Lord to give you a spirit of discernment to stand for truth and demonstrate love the way Gaius did.
- Ask Him to guide you to be patient with others who claim the name of Christian but may look different. Ask Him to help you know how to draw appropriate lines between those who are Christian and those who are more like a cult.
- Pray for increased sensitivity toward people from other denominations and Christian traditions.

UNIT 8 SACRIFICE

PRINCIPLE 6
Sacrifice: We must be willing to give up an established status or position and accept a lesser position in order to facilitate reconciling relationships.

Unit Learning Goals
You will understand the principle of sacrifice and demonstrate your willingness to lay down your status, position, or rights as God may direct you for the sake of reconciliation.

Overview of Unit 8
Lesson 1: Jesus and Sacrifice
Lesson 2: The Principle of Sacrifice
Lesson 3: Learning Sacrifice
Lesson 4: Jesus Calls for Servanthood
Lesson 5: Instructions for Sacrificial Service

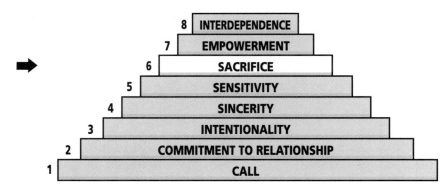

8 INTERDEPENDENCE
7 EMPOWERMENT
6 SACRIFICE
5 SENSITIVITY
4 SINCERITY
3 INTENTIONALITY
2 COMMITMENT TO RELATIONSHIP
1 CALL

Key Summary Statements from Unit 8
- Sacrifice is always necessary for reconciliation.
- If we're to follow Jesus as our model, we, too, must be prepared to sacrifice for reconciliation.
- As Christians, we must not get so caught up in seeking political or social solutions that we miss what God would have us do personally.
- Sacrifice will require that we trust God to care for us.
- Interdependence is possible only if we're willing to sacrifice.
- We can't trust our human wisdom to make right choices.
- God alone can correctly guide you to make the sacrifices that will accomplish His kingdom purposes.
- Being an ambassador of reconciliation is to lay down your "rights" at the foot of the cross.
- Jesus served others by meeting needs.
- Jesus wanted His disciples to get rid of their pride and learn to serve others from a position of lowliness and humility.

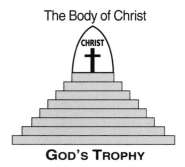

The Body of Christ
CHRIST
GOD'S TROPHY

FERNANDO, AN UNLIKELY MESSENGER[1]

by John Avant

Fernando was a former drug addict, had been in jail, and had done nearly everything a person could do. He overdosed on drugs and almost died. On one occasion his wife had told him, "Fernando, look in the mirror. What you see is not a man, because a man takes care of his wife and children." Through the love of his mother and his wife, he accepted Jesus. God completely changed his life, and he moved to our town in central Texas.

After his conversion, Fernando became convinced God had a plan and purpose for him. When he came to town, he became a dishwasher at a restaurant. One day I went into the restaurant, and I left a little witnessing card on the table. The waiter took it back to Fernando. He saw it and said, "God, maybe this is the person I need to talk to." So he stuck the card on a mirror over where he washed dishes so he could pray about his ministry.

One day a church member brought Fernando to see me and said, "I want you to meet Fernando. He has a ministry." God laid it on my heart that we were to support him as a church. I brought the issue to our church and said, "Folks, I just want you to see something." Fernando paraded in some gang kids with whom he had been working.

Our city has had a Hispanic gang problem, but these kids had been completely changed by the power of God after being helped by Fernando. The young men trembled with fear standing before the large congregation. They shared simple testimonies like, "I was a drug addict, living on the street, and Jesus changed my life." Seeing lives so changed by the gospel made quite an impact. Our church unanimously voted to join in this mission effort. What makes this venture unique is that it's a joint project between a Baptist church and a charismatic church! And guess what we found out — that we can work together even though we disagree on some doctrinal points. God began to work. Pretty soon we started baptizing kids from the gangs. In early fall 1995, we had baptized thirty kids from his ministry.

One day the junior high principal contacted Fernando, who has about an eighth-grade education and no GED. The principal had noticed that kids who were flunking out of school were now making passing grades. He said, "Fernando, I have so many problems! Would you come and talk to our kids?"

Fernando said, "The only thing I know to tell them is Jesus."

The principal replied, "If that will help, then go ahead."

The principal brought the whole school into the auditorium for an assembly and turned it over to a man who had been in jail and who could hardly read. Fernando said, "Let me just tell you about my life, and let me tell you what changed it." He told them about Jesus. Later the principal said, "I am going to set up an office for you here. You can do anything you want. Before school, after school, or during school, whatever you want."

The high school principal called and said, "Listen, will you come and have an office at the high school, too, and be a counselor at our high school?" Fernando never attended high school! God has taken this unbelievably desperate life and changed it forever!

We began to witness God's mighty power when the charismatic church found out we didn't hate them, and we discovered they didn't hate us. We started having a prayer group together. Soon it included Nazarene, Methodist, Baptist, Pentecostal, Church of Christ, and Assembly of God people. The pastors started to pray, "God, we don't care about our differences. We just want to see Jesus bring revival into this community."

God began to unify our churches, and a small-group discipleship course called *Experiencing God* began to sweep across denominational lines. People who had nothing to do with Baptist life began going through this course. Once the charismatic pastor said, "John, you must know this. We have many people going through *Experiencing God* in our church, and it has changed our lives. We have a group right now that is led by a Presbyterian, meeting in a charismatic church full of charismatics, with a Church of Christ pastor in it, and it is Baptist material. It has got to be revival!"

---

[1] Adapted from *Revival! The Story of the Current Awakening in Brownwood, Ft. Worth, Wheaton, and Beyond* by John Avant, Malcolm McDow, and Alvin Reid (Nashville: Broadman & Holman, 1996), pp 7-9.

LESSON 1   JESUS AND SACRIFICE

Scripture for Meditation

"Do nothing out of selfish ambition or vain conceit, but in humility consider others better than yourselves. Each of you should look not only to your own interests, but also to the interests of others" (Philippians 2:3–4).

A Beginning Prayer

Father, I confess that I probably focus on myself and my needs more than I show concern for the needs and interests of others. I also confess that I sometimes think and act as though I'm better than others. Forgive me. Teach me to live and act like Christ, with a willingness to sacrifice for the sake of others. I do want to see the whole body of Christ become a healthy body for Your glory. Amen.

Sacrifice is always necessary for reconciliation.

➥ Philippians 2:3–4 (in the margin) is your Scripture memory verse for this unit. Remove the perforated card from the back of your book, and begin memorizing it. Read and think about this verse, and start the lesson with prayer.

❖   ❖   ❖

➥ Take a few minutes to review your other Scripture memory verses. Check the ones you can quote by memory already.
- ❑ John 17:23
- ❑ 2 Corinthians 5:19
- ❑ Ephesians 4:3
- ❑ Matthew 7:12
- ❑ Ephesians 2:14
- ❑ John 13:34
- ❑ Ephesians 4:15

➥ Using your memory cards, read again the first five principles of reconciliation and unity. Check them after you've reviewed them.
- ❑ Principle 1: Call
- ❑ Principle 2: Commitment to Relationship
- ❑ Principle 3: Intentionality
- ❑ Principle 4: Sincerity
- ❑ Principle 5: Sensitivity

In this unit, we'll begin to focus on the sixth principle of sacrifice. First let's look at the example Jesus left for us to follow.

Jesus did not come only to identify with us. He didn't come only to teach us—or to love us. Ultimately, God's plan to reconcile us to Himself required Jesus to be a sacrifice. Sacrifice is always necessary for reconciliation. Your memory verse for this unit is followed by a description of what Jesus did for us.

➥ **Read the following Scripture, and answer the questions that follow.**

Your attitude should be the same as that of Christ Jesus: Who, being in very nature God, did not consider equality with God something to be grasped, but made himself nothing, taking the very nature of a servant, being made in human likeness. And being found in appearance as a man, he humbled himself and became obedient to death—even death on a cross! Therefore God exalted him to the highest place and gave him the name that is above every name, that at the name of Jesus every knee should bow, in heaven and on earth and under the earth, and every tongue confess that Jesus Christ is Lord, to the glory of God the Father (Philippians 2:5–11).

➥ 1. Whose attitude (or mind-set) should become yours? _____

➥ 2. What are some of the things Jesus sacrificed for us to be reconciled to God? Check all that apply.
- ❑ a. He sacrificed His high position in heaven to become a man on earth.
- ❑ b. He sacrificed His reputation by accepting the ridicule and false accusations of the religious leaders.
- ❑ c. He sacrificed His life when He died on the cross.
- ❑ d. He sacrificed personal pride and humbled Himself as a servant.

➡ **3. What were the rewards the Father gave Jesus after Jesus made the sacrifice of His life?**

_____

_____

We're commanded to have the same attitude, or mind-set, that Jesus had. He's our model for living as Christians (Christlike ones). Jesus did all the things listed in the second question. He gave up His position in heaven to become "nothing." He gave up His reputation to accept the ridicule and rejection the religious leaders gave Him. He humbled Himself and became a servant. As a servant, He obeyed His Father and died on the cross so we could be reconciled to God. Following His sacrifice, God the Father highly exalted Jesus for eternity.

If we're to follow Jesus as our model, we, too, must be prepared to sacrifice for reconciliation.

Sacrifice is the ultimate expression of love. *"'Greater love has no one than this, that he lay down his life for his friends'"* (John 15:13). Every believer lives with the eternal benefit of God's sacrifice on our behalf. If we're to follow Jesus as our model, we, too, must be prepared to sacrifice for reconciliation. We don't have to repeat Jesus' sacrifice. It was a once-for-all offering that provided for human redemption. But we will face opportunities where we'll be invited by God to give up things for the cause of His kingdom.

➡ **4. Which of the following are you willing to give up for the cause of reconciliation? Check the ones about which you're confident. If you have reservations, don't check them.**

❑ a. My position or status   ❑ d. My reputation
❑ b. My pride   ❑ e. My personal rights or expectations
❑ c. My material possessions   ❑ f. My life, if God requires it

Once Peter was concerned about the sacrifices he and the other disciples had made for the kingdom. He asked, *"We have left everything to follow you! What then will there be for us?"* (Matthew 19:27).

> *Jesus said to them, ". . . everyone who has left houses or brothers or sisters or father or mother or children or fields for my sake will receive a hundred times as much and will inherit eternal life. But many who are first will be last, and many who are last will be first"* (Matthew 19:28–30).

God is aware of the sacrifices we make and the ones He requires for His kingdom purposes. He does have a plan to reward those who make sacrifices for His kingdom.

➡ **What, if anything, do you sense God has said to you through today's lesson? Write *one* of the most meaningful things He has said below.**

_____

_____

➡ **Conclude today's lesson by praying.**
- Thank the Lord Jesus for the sacrifices He made for your reconciliation and redemption.
- Ask the Lord to work in you in such a way that you'll have His mind and attitudes.
- Ask the Lord to give you the willingness to humble yourself in order to become a faithful servant of His.

LESSON 2 — THE PRINCIPLE OF SACRIFICE

Scripture for Meditation

"I am the good shepherd; I know my sheep and my sheep know me—just as the Father knows me and I know the Father—and I lay down my life for the sheep" (John 10:14–15).

A Beginning Prayer

Father, I agree: Jesus is a Good Shepherd! Thank You for guiding my life and providing for my needs. I especially want to thank You for sending Jesus to die for me. Jesus, thank You for laying down Your life for me. I love You for that. Amen.

PRINCIPLE 6

Sacrifice: We must be willing to give up an established status or position and accept a lesser position in order to facilitate reconciling relationships.

As Christians, we must not get so caught up in seeking political solutions that we miss what God would have us do within the body of Christ.

➡ Read and think about the Scripture for Meditation in the left margin, and begin the lesson with prayer.

❖ ❖ ❖

➡ Remove the perforated card from the back of your book for principle 6: Sacrifice. Read it two or three times. In the margin to the left, you'll see the same text. Underline two things you must be willing to give up, and circle one thing you must be willing to accept.

➡ 1. Based on principle 6, what are two things you may need to give up to encourage and facilitate reconciling relationships?

_____ or _____

➡ 2. When you give up status or position, what must you be willing to accept to facilitate reconciling relationships?

_____

Frank Sinatra built an image of being a tough guy. This mind-set is heard in his popular song "My Way!" Sacrifice, an essential element in reconciliation, says, "I did it *God's* way." Sacrifice is the willingness to give up anything to see God's will in reconciliation happen.

To one degree or another, all the previous principles for reconciliation and unity might make some practical sense to the world. Sacrifice does not. Human pride and selfishness refuse to give up position, status, security, or personal rights for the sake of someone else. Applying the principle of sacrifice will require that you allow Christ and His Spirit to work in and through you. For the one who has Christ inside, sacrifice is possible—even if it requires your life someday.

Racism and sectarian strife have left terrible scars on many nations. Time has not and will not heal all the wounds. As Christians, we must not get so caught up in seeking political solutions that we miss what God would have us do within the body of Christ. Despite many well-intended political programs, the chasms between people seem only to get wider. If the heart of a man is not right with God and his fellow man, any actions—no matter how well-intended—will fail to bring reconciliation.

➡ 3. Which of the following do you believe has the greatest potential to bring about lasting change between races in the church?
   ❏ a. Bureaucratic programs to legislate fair treatment between the races.
   ❏ b. God's agenda to bring about right relationships with Him and others.

Christians don't need to ignore the procedural means that may help, but history has shown that those actions alone don't produce much lasting change. God has answers, but they will require costly sacrifice. While we think of sacrifice in the ultimate sense—literally giving up one's life—more often it means giving up other things.

Without sacrifice, meaningful relationship is doomed. The tighter we hold on to our own desires, the more we separate ourselves from others.

Sacrifice will require that we trust God to care for us.

Sacrifice is really giving in to God—yielding everything we have to His use. It will require that we trust God to care for us. We, in turn, will give our attention to caring for others.

➡ **4. In the Sermon on the Mount, Jesus gave some "impractical" instructions. As you read them below, check the one you think would be the most difficult for you to obey.**
- ❑ a. *"Do not resist an evil person. If someone strikes you on the right cheek, turn to him the other also"* (Matthew 5:39).
- ❑ b. *"If someone wants to sue you and take your tunic, let him have your cloak as well"* (Matthew 5:40).
- ❑ c. *"If someone forces you to go one mile, go with him two miles"* (Matthew 5:41).
- ❑ d. *"Give to the one who asks you, and do not turn away from the one who wants to borrow from you"* (Matthew 5:42).
- ❑ e. *"Love your enemies and pray for those who persecute you"* (Matthew 5:44).

When being a love ambassador is our goal, Jesus tells us to be willing to sacrifice our time, possessions, energy, and even safety. All too often, those are the very things about which we wonder, *Why should I do that? I've worked hard for what I've got.* When we resist obedience in these areas, however, we've lost sight of the goal: reconciliation. God calls on us to use things and love people, but the world presses us to love things and use people.

PRINCIPLE 6
Sacrifice: We must be willing to give up an established status or position and accept a lesser position in order to facilitate reconciling relationships.

➡ **5. Review the principle of sacrifice in the margin. Which of the following actions are examples of this principle? In each pair of actions below, check the appropriate one.**
- ❑ a1. Demanding that church leaders cater to my worship preferences all the time.
- ❑ a2. Accepting and learning to appreciate the different worship styles of others in our congregation.

- ❑ b1. For the sake of harmony, choosing to submit to and follow the leadership of a brother who's different.
- ❑ b2. Trying to take control from one who is different because "our kind" have a better understanding of how things need to be done.

- ❑ c1. Demanding that others adjust to my way of doing things if they want to have a relationship with me.
- ❑ c2. Adjusting my personal expectations so I can have a relationship with those who have a different opinion about how things ought to be done.

- ❑ d1. Encouraging my brother to assume a leadership role, and supporting him as he develops skills and gains experience in that position.
- ❑ d2. Automatically assuming the leadership role myself since I have more experience and I want the job done right the first time.

Sometimes we may become so task oriented in the body of Christ that we lose focus on the importance of relationships and growth. Occasionally we need to sacrifice for the sake of building up the body *"until we all reach unity in the faith and in the knowledge of the Son of God and become mature, attaining to the whole measure of the fullness of Christ"* (Ephesians 4:13). We need to encourage others to move into leadership positions so they can grow into experienced and mature leaders. We need to be willing to adjust our expectations and preferences, yield our rights or positions, and learn mutual submission to others in the body. (Answers: a-2, b-1, c-2, d-1)

➡ **What, if anything, do you sense God has said to you through today's lesson? Write *one* of the most meaningful things He has said below.**

_____

_____

➡ **Conclude today's lesson by praying.**
- Tell the Lord of your willingness to sacrifice for His kingdom.
- Ask the Lord to guide you to make any sacrifices that will more effectively facilitate reconciled relationships.

LESSON 3 LEARNING SACRIFICE

Scripture for Meditation
"My sheep listen to my voice; I know them, and they follow me. I give them eternal life, and they shall never perish; no one can snatch them out of my hand" (John 10:27–28).

A Beginning Prayer
Father, help me to know Christ Jesus and His voice so clearly that I will always obey and follow Him. I thank You that my relationship with You is secure. I know I can follow You in sacrifice and not endanger that relationship. Teach me the ways of sacrifice for Your kingdom's sake. Amen.

➡ **Read and think about the Scripture for Meditation in the left margin, and begin the lesson with prayer.**

❖ ❖ ❖

One of the "rites of passage" in our inner-city ministry is when a newcomer "donates" his car battery or radio to a local neighborhood thief. Not that we rejoice in this common occurrence, but we do remind the victim, "Welcome to the 'hood. Satan is alive and well here. Don't grow faint in doing good." Our commitment to follow Christ will be tested through sometimes costly sacrifice. If we believe it's too much to sacrifice a few earthly possessions for the sake of the gospel, our priorities need adjustment.

➡ **1. Which of the following is most important for the sake of the gospel of Christ? Check one.**
❑ a. Holding on to and protecting my earthly possessions because they are mine.
❑ b. Being willing to sacrifice earthly possessions if necessary so that Christ's kingdom will advance. After all, these possessions actually are His.

Sacrifice goes much deeper than: "If I come to the 'hood, will my car be safe?" God may require you to give up position or status to serve Him. The doctors in our medical clinic are the best family physicians you could find, but they have little status among their peers. The world says only those who can't cut it elsewhere serve in the inner city. What well-trained doctor would choose to work with the poor, where it's tough and the pay is poor? But these physicians have sacrificed such status for a much higher calling as ambassadors of reconciliation for the King!

The principle of sacrifice is late in our list of principles because you need to have a good handle on the others first. Through intentionality, sincerity, and sensitivity, you begin building relationships that are meaningful. You're aiming toward an interdependence with the rest of the body of Christ in which each member is important and needed. But interdependence is possible only if you're willing to sacrifice.

Interdependence is possible only if you're willing to sacrifice.

If you were to study streams around the world, you would find that all streams are not alike. Some have fresh, sparkling water and plush banks. Others are polluted and may run through filthy territory. Likewise, while "all men are created equal," their circumstances aren't always equal. Ambassadors of reconciliation are called to lift up their brothers by being willing to take a back seat when that's God's desire. The world says, "I've earned it. I've spent long hours in school (or whatever), and I have a right to this position. I deserve it!" But being an ambassador of reconciliation is to lay down your "rights" at the foot of the cross. There's no formula or set list of actions that will "correct the problem." The way of the cross is a faith journey that constantly asks God, "What would You have me do?"

Being an ambassador of reconciliation is to lay down your "rights" at the foot of the cross.

➥ **2. Which of the following should you do to see the body of Christ grow stronger through the application of this principle of sacrifice?**
  ❏ a. Constantly ask the Lord to guide me in my relationships and actions.
  ❏ b. Find a book with the best program for building strong relationships, and follow the instructions exactly.
  ❏ c. Follow my well-trained "gut feelings" every time I need to make a judgment call.

We can't trust our own wisdom to make right choices.

Because our sinful and self-centered human nature keeps trying to gain control of our lives, we can't trust our own wisdom to make right choices. Because every situation has different dynamics, no book (even this one) will have all the answers you need to see the body of Christ built into a strong and healthy spiritual body. God alone has the right instructions for you to follow. He is Lord of your life. You need to turn to Him constantly to receive directions for your actions. He alone can correctly guide you to make the sacrifices that will accomplish His kingdom purposes.

He alone can correctly guide you to make the sacrifices that will accomplish His kingdom purposes.

Justice

If believers follow that simple pattern, reconciliation would produce the fruit of justice. The world selfishly cries, "I want my fair share." God calls for justice:

For the LORD is righteous, he loves justice; upright men will see his face (Psalm 11:7).

The LORD loves righteousness and justice; the earth is full of his unfailing love (Psalm 33:5).

Yet the LORD longs to be gracious to you; he rises to show you compassion. For the LORD is a God of justice. Blessed are all who wait for him! (Isaiah 30:18).

The body of Christ can offer a clear witness to the power of the gospel if we're willing to sacrifice anything God asks for the sake of reconciliation!

The body of Christ can offer a clear witness to the power of the gospel if we're willing to sacrifice anything God asks for the sake of reconciliation! This demonstration begins in small ways when we commit to sacrifice in order to cross barriers and break down walls.

➥ **3. Can you remember a time when you had to make a sacrifice to facilitate a reconciled relationship? If so, briefly describe the sacrifice in the margin.**

➥ **What, if anything, do you sense God has said to you through today's lesson? Write *one* of the most meaningful things He has said below.**

_____

_____

➥ **Conclude today's lesson by praying for God's wisdom in your sacrifices.**

LESSON 4 JESUS CALLS FOR SERVANTHOOD

Scripture for Meditation

"Whoever wants to become great among you must be your servant . . . just as the Son of Man did not come to be served, but to serve, and to give his life as a ransom for many" (Matthew 20:26, 28).

A Beginning Prayer

Father, Jesus came as a Servant, and He set a wonderful example for me to follow. Would You please open my eyes to see the opportunities for serving others in Christ's name and Spirit? Help me be intentional in serving others out of love for Christ, love for my brothers, and with a spirit of sacrifice such as Jesus had. Amen.

➡ **Read and think about the Scripture for Meditation in the left margin, and begin the lesson with prayer.**

❖ ❖ ❖

On several occasions, Jesus had to deal with His disciples regarding their desire for greatness. It seems that a favorite topic of conversation for the twelve was: Which one of us is going to be the greatest in Christ's kingdom?

➡ **1. When you think of a person achieving greatness from the world's viewpoint, what thoughts do you have? Of the following achievements, which one best defines human greatness for you? Check one.**

❑ becoming a millionaire or billionaire
❑ becoming CEO of a Fortune 500 company
❑ being elected president of your country
❑ being inducted into a sports hall of fame
❑ being invited to the White House to receive an award
❑ being selected as *Time* magazine's man of the year
❑ being the highest paid rookie in the NFL or NBA
❑ being the movie star in this year's blockbuster movie
❑ discovering a cure for a major disease
❑ having authority to tell thousands of people what to do
❑ writing a best-selling book
❑ winning an Oscar or Emmy

Some people are willing to "do what it takes" to achieve this kind of success. They may give their whole lives to such goals and never make one of them. But these are not the measures of success for a child of God and a servant of Christ.

When Jesus spoke to the disciples, they were thinking greatness would be determined by their position in the court of Jesus' earthly kingdom. They weren't thinking of a heavenly kingdom and misunderstood godly greatness. They were thinking of greatness the worldly way. Jesus defined greatness differently:

"Whoever wants to become great among you must be your servant."

> *"You know that the rulers of the Gentiles lord it over them, and their high officials exercise authority over them. Not so with you. Instead, whoever wants to become great among you must be your servant, and whoever wants to be first must be your slave—just as the Son of Man did not come to be served, but to serve, and to give his life as a ransom for many"* (Matthew 20:25–28).

➡ **2. In your own words, how did Jesus say a person would achieve greatness in His kingdom?**

_____

The Gentiles (the world) saw greatness coming from position or personal authority and influence. They tried to accomplish things by "throwing their weight around." Jesus said He measured greatness by the service one gives. The greatest in the kingdom will be the one who serves others.

He served others by meeting needs.

Jesus didn't preach one thing and live another, either. He said, *"The Son of Man did not come to be served, but to serve, and to give his life as a ransom for many"* (Matthew 20:28). He served others by meeting needs. He healed the sick, fed the hungry, raised the dead, forgave sinners, and cast out demons. He didn't try to achieve a high-ranking religious or political position. He didn't try to win a popularity contest. At times His demands were so great that the crowds left Him disappointed because the cost of following Him was too great. On the night before going to the cross, Jesus gave the disciples a moving example of what He meant by being a servant.

➥ **Read the story of Jesus' servanthood on the night of the Last Supper (in the margin). Then try to sum up the principle Jesus was teaching.**

❖ ❖ ❖

➥ **3. Which of the following do you believe is the key principle Jesus was trying to teach His disciples? Check your opinion, or write your own.**
  ❑ a. When you come together for the Lord's Supper, wash each other's feet.
  ❑ b. Follow Jesus' example by serving each other with a humble spirit.
  ❑ c. Tell your pastor that he must follow Jesus' example and do all the lowly tasks that church members don't want to do.

  ❑ d. Other: _____

Some Christians do practice foot washing, and it can be a humbling and meaningful experience for the "washer" and the "washee." However, Jesus was giving the disciples a much deeper principle to follow. He had every right as Master and Teacher to be served by others. Yet He showed them what humility and a servant attitude looked like. He wanted His disciples to get rid of their pride and learn to serve others from a position of lowliness and humility (*b*). This was never intended to be a club with which church members could threaten their pastor. A Christlike pastor will want to be a servant to the flock of God entrusted to him. However, he'll also have the responsibility of teaching the members to be servants like Christ. He will be saying, like Paul, *"Follow my example, as I follow the example of Christ"* (1 Corinthians 11:1).

A quick review of history will reveal that Satan has used selfish ambition and greed to bring alienation. "Getting my piece of the pie" has often been at the expense of others. Native Americans, for example, lost their land through hundreds of treaties the white man didn't honor. African Americans toiled unjustly as slaves, and immigrant groups of all types were exploited as laborers. For these groups, selfish economic pursuits of past generations have created a legacy of alienation.

That's why sacrificial service is the opposite of the world's ways. Service and sacrifice are God's path toward reconciliation. Jesus, who came to be King, chose to be a servant to reconcile us to God. As agents of reconciliation, we also must serve rather than be served. Humble service offered in obedience to God and love for others is a powerful way for walls of alienation to be broken down.

➥ **4. Can you think of a time when someone else served you or met your needs in a way that was unexpected but very appreciated? If so, briefly describe one such time in the margin.**

➥ **5. How did that make you feel toward the person or group?**

➥ **6. Can you think of a time when you chose the role of a servant and served another person who had no right to expect you to serve him or her? If so, briefly describe one such time in the margin.**

➥ **What, if anything, do you sense God has said to you through today's lesson? Write *one* of the most meaningful things He has said below.**

Jesus Serves the Disciples

"Jesus knew that the Father had put all things under his power, and that he had come from God and was returning to God; so he got up from the meal, took off his outer clothing, and wrapped a towel around his waist. After that, he poured water into a basin and began to wash his disciples' feet, drying them with the towel that was wrapped around him. . . .

"When he had finished washing their feet, he put on his clothes and returned to his place. 'Do you understand what I have done for you?' he asked them. 'You call me "Teacher" and "Lord," and rightly so, for that is what I am. Now that I, your Lord and Teacher, have washed your feet, you also should wash one another's feet. I have set you an example that you should do as I have done for you. I tell you the truth, no servant is greater than his master, nor is a messenger greater than the one who sent him. Now that you know these things, you will be blessed if you do them'" (John 13:3–5,12–17).

He wanted His disciples to get rid of their pride and learn to serve others from a position of lowliness and humility.

_____

_____

_____

_____

_____

_____

➡ **Conclude today's lesson by praying.**
- Thank the Lord for those who have sacrificed and served you in some meaningful way.
- Talk to the Lord about your personal willingness to be a servant.
- Ask the Lord to reveal to you those brothers and sisters in Christ or others who are needy whom He wants you to serve.

LESSON 5 INSTRUCTIONS FOR SACRIFICIAL SERVICE

Scripture for Meditation

"'But you are not to be called "Rabbi," for you have only one Master and you are all brothers. And do not call anyone on earth "father," for you have one Father, and he is in heaven. Nor are you to be called "teacher," for you have one Teacher, the Christ. The greatest among you will be your servant. For whoever exalts himself will be humbled, and whoever humbles himself will be exalted'" (Matthew 23:8–12).

A Beginning Prayer

Father, Jesus commanded me not to assume the high positions, but to humble myself and be a servant. Teach me the ways to be a faithful servant in Your kingdom. Amen.

PRINCIPLE 6
Sacrifice: We must be willing to give up an established status or position and accept a lesser position in order to facilitate reconciling relationships.

➡ **Read and think about the Scripture for Meditation in the left margin, and begin the lesson with prayer.**

❖ ❖ ❖

➡ **1. Fill in the blanks in the statement of principle 6 below. If you need help, refer to the box in the lower left margin.**
We must be willing to give up an established s_____ or

p_____ and accept a lesser p_____ in order to facilitate reconciling relationships.

Giving up position and status and becoming a servant is God's way for His people. Many passages in the New Testament describe different aspects of service. Let's take a look at other instructions for sacrificial service.

➡ **Read the Scriptures below, and answer the questions that follow each one.**

Hebrews 9:14: *How much more, then, will the blood of Christ, who through the eternal Spirit offered himself unblemished to God, cleanse our consciences from acts that lead to death, so that we may serve the living God!*

➡ **2. What's required so you will be prepared to serve God? What must Christ do in your life?**

_____

➡ **3. Is your conscience clean and clear of all sinful acts?** ❑ yes ❑ no

Galatians 5:13: *You, my brothers, were called to be free. But do not use your freedom to indulge the sinful nature; rather, serve one another in love.*

➡ **4. Instead of indulging your sinful nature, how are you to serve others?**

_____

1 Peter 4:8–10: *Above all, love each other deeply, because love covers over a multitude of sins. Offer hospitality to one another without grumbling. Each one should use whatever gift he has received to serve others, faithfully administering God's grace in its various forms.*

➡ 5. What should you use in serving others?

_____

➡ 6. What's one example of service you can give to another believer?

_____

1 Timothy 6:17–19: *Command those who are rich in this present world not to be arrogant nor to put their hope in wealth, which is so uncertain, but to put their hope in God, who richly provides us with everything for our enjoyment. Command them to do good, to be rich in good deeds, and to be generous and willing to share. In this way they will lay up treasure for themselves as a firm foundation for the coming age, so that they may take hold of the life that is truly life.*

➡ 7. What does God command rich believers to do with their wealth? Read 1 Timothy 6:17–19 again, and underline the commands for the rich.

➡ 8. Now read Matthew 25:34–40 in the margin. Underline ways that believers can serve Christ by serving others. We've underlined one for you.

➡ 9. If Christ were to evaluate your service to Him based on the way you have ministered to the hungry, the thirsty, the stranger, the naked, the sick, and the prisoner, what would *He* probably say about you? Check your opinion, and be honest.
❏ a. You've been a good servant. Come enter your rest, faithful servant.
❏ b. You've done many good things, but you haven't served me. I'm disappointed.
❏ c. You've served me in some ways, but I'm not just middle class and suburban. You've really neglected the very needy people. I want you to pay attention to the needs of the poor as well.
❏ d. You've been so selfish and self-centered that you've only served yourself. He who tries to save his life, loses it.

➡ 10. In each pair of statements below, one represents the attitude of a servant; the other represents an opposite attitude. Read both statements in each pair, and check the servant attitude.
❏ 1a. I've done my part. Someone else ought to do that job and take care of my needs.
❏ 1b. Because I love her, I'm going to step in and do that job for her.

❏ 2a. If Jesus can wash feet to meet the needs of others, I can do this job and serve my brothers in Christ.
❏ 2b. People in my position don't have to do menial jobs like that. We hire others to do that kind of work.

❏ 3a. Lord, I know someone ought to do that, but that isn't my gift. You need to find someone else for the job.
❏ 3b. Lord, You are my master. At your command, I will gladly and joyfully do this work for Your people.

❏ 4a. This is an opportunity for me to help my pastor so he can give his time to more important matters. I'll be happy to take care of that job.
❏ 4b. No, I won't do that. This is what we pay the pastor for. Get him to do it.

Matthew 25:34–40

" 'Come, you who are blessed by my Father; take your inheritance, the kingdom prepared for you since the creation of the world. For I was hungry and <u>you gave me something to eat</u>, I was thirsty and you gave me something to drink, I was a stranger and you invited me in, I needed clothes and you clothed me, I was sick and you looked after me, I was in prison and you came to visit me.'

"Then the righteous will answer him, 'Lord, when did we see you hungry and feed you, or thirsty and give you something to drink? When did we see you a stranger and invite you in, or needing clothes and clothe you? When did we see you sick or in prison and go to visit you?'

"The King will reply, 'I tell you the truth, whatever you did for one of the least of these brothers of mine, you did for me.' "

Ephesians 6:5–8

"Slaves, obey your earthly masters with respect and fear, and with sincerity of heart, just as you would obey Christ. Obey them not only to win their favor when their eye is on you, but like slaves of Christ, doing the will of God from your heart. Serve wholeheartedly, as if you were serving the Lord, not men, because you know that the Lord will reward everyone for whatever good he does, whether he is slave or free."

Titus 2:9–10

"Teach slaves to be subject to their masters in everything, to try to please them, not to talk back to them, and not to steal from them, but to show that they can be fully trusted, so that in every way they will make the teaching about God our Savior attractive."

1 Peter 2:18–25

"Slaves, submit yourselves to your masters with all respect, not only to those who are good and considerate, but also to those who are harsh. For it is commendable if a man bears up under the pain of unjust suffering because he is conscious of God. But how is it to your credit if you receive a beating for doing wrong and endure it? But if you suffer for doing good and you endure it, this is commendable before God. To this you were called, because Christ suffered for you, leaving you an example, that you should follow in his steps. 'He committed no sin, and no deceit was found in his mouth.' When they hurled their insults at him, he did not retaliate; when he suffered, he made no threats. Instead, he entrusted himself to him who judges justly. He himself bore our sins in his body on the tree, so that we might die to sins and live for righteousness; by his wounds you have been healed. For you were like sheep going astray, but now you have returned to the Shepherd and Overseer of your souls."

❏ 5a. Let's see if we can get a government agency to take care of that so it won't cost us any money.

❏ 5b. We have a wonderful opportunity to show the love of Christ by doing something that people don't expect of us. Let's demonstrate God's love!

A servant is ready to help—even when the work belongs to someone else. A servant doesn't claim personal rights, ask for a waiver due to his high position, or try to use his influence to get someone else to do the job. One who serves because he belongs to Christ does so out of love and a desire to please and honor the Lord. Giving even a cup of cold water in Christ's name will bring a heavenly reward. The servant attitude is represented by statements *1b, 2a, 3b, 4a,* and *5b.*

➥ **Read the three teachings for servants and slaves in the margin. As you read, underline instructions that would help you know how to be a faithful servant of Christ and even a God-honoring employee.**

❖ ❖ ❖

➥ **11. If God were to evaluate your attitudes toward helping and serving others, what would He conclude? Check what you think God sees in you.**

❏ a. You love Me and give yourself unselfishly to serve the needs of others in the name of My Son. Well done, good and faithful servant!

❏ b. Every time I invite you to serve Me by serving others, you run from the task or try to pass it off to someone else. You don't really acknowledge Me as your master, do you?

❏ c. You're so busy serving your job and trying to earn money that you don't even listen when I ask you to serve a brother in need. You can't serve God and money. Do you think I should use poor health or a job loss to slow you down so you'll listen?

❏ d. You're so proud and arrogant that you think you're too good to do these lowly jobs I have for you. If you're not willing to do these things, how could I possibly trust you with a more important assignment?

❏ e. Other: _____

➥ **What, if anything, do you sense God has said to you through today's lesson? Write *one* of the most meaningful things He has said below.**

_____

_____

➥ **For each lesson this week, you've been recording what you sense God has said to you. Review the final activity for each of the previous lessons on pages 133, 136, 137, and 140. What's the major emphasis of what you sense God wants you to do in response to this unit's lessons? Pray and ask Him what He wants you to do. Then write notes in the margin or in a separate notebook.**

➥ **Conclude today's lesson by praying.**

• If He has convicted you of sin regarding pride or lack of service, ask His forgiveness, and pledge to serve Him faithfully in the days to come.

• Ask the Lord to continue to reveal times and ways you're to be a servant for Him and His glory.

UNIT 9 EMPOWERMENT

Scripture Memory Verse
"Bear with each other and forgive whatever grievances you may have against one another. Forgive as the Lord forgave you."
—Colossians 3:13

PRINCIPLE 7
Empowerment: Through prayer, personal brokenness, repentance, and forgiveness, we remove barriers and are freed to experience the power of the Holy Spirit in reconciling relationships.

Unit Learning Goals
You will understand the nature and importance of repentance and forgiveness, and you'll demonstrate your obedience by forgiving and bearing the fruits of repentance.

Overview of Unit 9
Lesson 1: The Principle of Empowerment I
Lesson 2: The Principle of Empowerment II
Lesson 3: Confession
Lesson 4: Repentance and Restoration
Lesson 5: Godlike Forgiveness

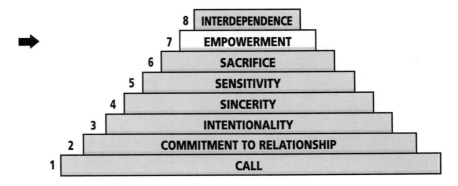

8 INTERDEPENDENCE
7 EMPOWERMENT
6 SACRIFICE
5 SENSITIVITY
4 SINCERITY
3 INTENTIONALITY
2 COMMITMENT TO RELATIONSHIP
1 CALL

Key Summary Statements from Unit 9
- Without empowerment, reconciled relationships won't happen.
- Prayer gets us in touch with God. From that relationship with Him, He guides and empowers us to do the right things.
- Reconcilers are broken people who recognize that the discipline of pain and struggle can yield godly fruit.
- When our hearts beat like God's, we'll be broken anytime brothers and sisters in God's family experience brokenness.
- "Let my heart be broken by the things that break the heart of God."
- Repentance is an essential turning point in reconciled relationships.
- Forgiveness can release a brother from a sense of unresolved guilt and restore in him a clear conscience. Forgiveness can complete the process of empowerment.
- When we confess the sins of our fathers, we're agreeing with God that what they did was wrong.
- God wants us, like the Good Samaritan, to take responsibility to be agents of healing by loving our neighbor as ourselves.
- If you don't forgive others when they sin against you, your heavenly Father won't forgive you.
- If we're to experience unity in the body of Christ, we must be reconciled to God and each other. We can't experience that without forgiving others.

The Body of Christ

CHRIST

GOD'S TROPHY

I'm Guilty; I Admit It [1]

by John Dawson

In New Zealand, in the summer of 1990, Sam stood at the front of the huge tent, held his guitar across his large chest, and talked about God the Father. His broad, brown face seemed to embody everything that's beautiful and redemptive about the Polynesian race. As he began to lead us in worship, we in the crowd started to feel as though we were wrapped in the arms of God. I counted it a special privilege to be Sam's friend, and I thanked God with a full heart.

He paused between songs and told us a story. He talked of a Polynesian childhood in a European culture. It had been confusing. He talked about wounds of rejection and feelings of inferiority. There was no bitterness in his voice. He just wanted to testify to God's grace. He wanted to tell us how God had healed his agonizing shyness and a debilitating speech impediment, a miracle that occurred the first time he was asked to share his faith in Jesus at a public meeting. *How could anybody hurt a beautiful person like Sam?* I thought. . . .

Sam introduced me, and an atmosphere of reverent expectation settled on the crowd. I looked over the faces of my beloved countrymen, and such depth of emotion welled up inside me that I could hardly speak.

I talked about New Zealand—the Polynesian roots and the coming of the missionary. . . . I talked about a people of destiny so full of potential, yet wounded and limping, confused and bound. God creates nations (see Acts 17), yet the beautiful dream in His heart for New Zealand was so far from coming true.

Wounds of rejection, fear of authority, rebellion and independence, loneliness and isolation, fear of intimacy, withdrawal, melancholy, inferiority, and addiction to false comforts—these were like livid scars marring our national face. How we had sinned against one another, race to race, management to labor, male to female, governor to governed, church to church!

As I spoke, a long-lost childhood memory began to haunt me. The crowd faded away, and I was in grade school again. A new kid came to our class. His skin was brown, and his school uniform was threadbare. He didn't fit in. We were white, middle-class, city kids, and he was a back-country Maori. We talked fast and knew our way around. He was lonely and confused. The kids picked on him; the teacher was impatient with him; he had no friend.

I was from a loving Christian home. My parents loved the Maori people; my unofficially adopted older brother was a Maori. All my compassion was aroused. I knew what to do. I should have offered him friendship, but I never moved across that room. I never joined him in the school yard. I seared my conscience. I just watched. Some of the kids mocked him because of his unusual name. His name was Wi. He soon left our school, and I never saw him again.

Now, standing in front of that huge crowd, the full force of remorse filled my chest. I couldn't speak. I began to weep. Just a few minutes before, I had wondered how anybody could have hurt Sam, yet I was no different from those who wounded him. Somewhere in New Zealand was a Maori man named Wi, just the same age as me, a man perhaps still deeply wounded by class and racial prejudice, a man whom God once tried to love through a Christian white boy named John, but I chose pride. I chose my peers. I did not choose love.

Through my tears, I confessed my actions. The Spirit of God was showing me that this was no small thing. I asked for forgiveness from every Maori present. I asked for God's forgiveness. I felt utterly ashamed.

Weeping began to spread through that huge crowd. Sam came up onto the platform and enveloped me in his huge arms. "Forgive me, brother," I said.

"I forgive you," Sam said. And we both wept as the great grieving heart of God was revealed in our emotions. It's as though the tears of many generations were poured out that day. There was no more preaching. Time didn't matter. The church of New Zealand was being held in the lap of the heavenly Father, and we wept like a grieving child until we had no more tears left to cry.

People streamed up to the microphone and unburdened their souls. Everybody was asking forgiveness of everybody. Painful things were brought into the open—the sins of our forefathers as well as the sins of today. The sins of men and women. Wounds between classes, races, and cultures were healed.

God moved among us for two days, all day and into the night. It was similar to what happened to the Israelites long ago when God healed their land. "The descendants of Israel separated themselves from all foreigners, and stood and confessed their sins and the iniquities of their fathers" (Nehemiah 9:2).

That summer in New Zealand, the prayers of the saints of many generations began to be answered. We saw an outpouring of grace for repentance in five of the main cities and heard that the same phenomenon was occurring in other cities throughout the land.

[1] John Dawson, *Healing America's Wounds* (Ventura, Cal.: Regal Books, 1994), pp. 25-28.

LESSON 1   THE PRINCIPLE OF EMPOWERMENT I

Scriptures for Meditation

"Bear with each other and forgive whatever grievances you may have against one another. Forgive as the Lord forgave you" (Colossians 3:13).

"If we confess our sins, he is faithful and just and will forgive us our sins and purify us from all unrighteousness" (1 John 1:9).

A Beginning Prayer

Father, I want to be cleansed of and forgiven for all my sins. I want to stay up to date with You. I also want to stand ready to forgive others who have sinned against me. Teach me how to relate to others in such a way that the body of Christ will know and experience Your mighty power working through us to bring our world to saving faith in Christ. Amen.

PRINCIPLE 7

Empowerment: Through prayer, personal brokenness, repentance, and forgiveness, we remove barriers and are freed to experience the power of the Holy Spirit in reconciling relationships.

Without empowerment, reconciled relationships won't happen.

➡ Read and think about the Scriptures for Meditation in the left margin. Colossians 3:13 is your Scripture memory verse for this unit. Remove the perforated card for unit 9 from the back of your book, and begin memorizing it. Then start the lesson with prayer.

❖ ❖ ❖

➡ Using the memory card, read "Principle 7: Empowerment" two or three times. In the margin to the lower left, you'll see the same text.

➡ 1. In the box for principle 7 in the margin, circle the four things through which we remove barriers and free ourselves to experience the power of the Holy Spirit. Now write them below:

_____

_____

The world uses the term *empowerment* as a process of enabling the poor and powerless to gain power. It's a man-centered attempt at achieving justice and equality. Almost exclusively, it involves worldly means with political and financial objectives. All too often, however, corruption prevents even political or economic empowerment from happening on a secular level.

As Christians, we must have a distinct and God-centered view of empowerment. Biblical empowerment is the use of prayer, personal brokenness, repentance, and forgiveness to bring about freedom from the bondage of bitterness, guilt, and alienation. Empowerment is not just for the other person. It's for you, too.

Empowerment is for the person guilty of sin and offenses toward others. But it's also for the person who may carry a grudge or bitterness toward the one who hurt him. Empowerment is for the person who may be broken and hurting because of another person's actions or lack of action. But it's also for the person who caused the brokenness.

➡ 2. **Which people need to apply the principle of empowerment? Check the correct response.**
❑ a. the offender   ❑ b. the offended   ❑ c. both a and b

➡ 3. **In the list of words below, check those that describe things you believe** *God could remove* **with the proper application of this principle of empowerment.**

❑ bitterness   ❑ guilt   ❑ grudges
❑ alienation   ❑ mental bondage   ❑ brokenness
❑ weakness   ❑ powerlessness   ❑ vindictiveness
❑ shame   ❑ regret   ❑ hatred
❑ resentment   ❑ blame   ❑ malice
❑ remorse   ❑ ill will   ❑ antagonism

Did you check all the words? You could have. When people have offended others, have been offended by others, or have the perception of an offense, these feelings can exist. God wants to remove every one and restore relationships. All the principles thus far have been leading up to this one. Without empowerment, reconciled relationships won't happen. Through prayer, personal brokenness, repentance, and forgiveness, God brings healing to broken relationships.

Prayer

Prayer is the vehicle to open the conduit of God's grace. Prayer is a relationship with God in which He guides us to know and do His will. We need to identify with the old gospel song: "I need to pray, sho' need to pray—pray every day." Without prayer, our efforts will only achieve what we can do. Only through communion with God will we gain the wisdom to navigate all the traps and snares Satan has set for us. Prayer emboldens us as God's Spirit empowers us. In prayer, we call upon the Spirit to fight our battles that we alone are not equipped to fight.

➡ **4. Why is prayer important to empowerment? Check one.**
   ❏ a. Prayer helps us psych ourselves up and get that power of positive thinking we need to do the right thing.
   ❏ b. Prayer is like magic words. When we say the right things, miracles happen.
   ❏ c. Prayer gets us in touch with God so we can know and do what He wants and receive the power of His Spirit to do it.

> *Prayer gets us in touch with God. From that relationship with Him, He guides and empowers us to do the right things.*

Prayer gets us in touch with God. From that relationship with Him, He guides and empowers us to do the right things (c). Notice that answers a and b focus on us and what we can do. Human efforts will never accomplish what God wants to do through reconciled relationships. A prayer relationship with God is essential.

Probably the most dramatic examples of interdenominational unity in the U. S. today are the prayer meetings taking place across the country. Pastors from all "tribes" meet to pray for their cities. Citywide concerts of prayer unite believers from nearly every Christian tradition. Unity and agreement in prayer are bringing great power and blessing into communities everywhere.

Personal Brokenness

> *Reconcilers are broken people who recognize that the discipline of pain and struggle can yield godly fruit.*

The old phase remains true, "God bruises whom He chooses." Reconcilers are broken people who recognize that the discipline of pain and struggle can yield godly fruit. In His great wisdom, God uses difficulties and trials to chip away things in our lives that don't belong there. He chips away self so the Spirit and character of Christ can shine through. Often, the ones God can use most powerfully are those who have allowed their brokenness to shape them to look and act like Christ.

> *God uses brokenness to challenge our pride and develop a spirit of humility.*

Arrogance and pride, on the other hand, are major construction elements in our walls of separation. God uses brokenness to challenge our pride and develop a spirit of humility. When we're broken, God can fill us with Himself and the power for reconciliation. Broken people tend to be humble, merciful, caring, and compassionate toward others.

> *When our hearts beat like God's, we'll be broken anytime brothers and sisters in God's family experience brokenness.*

God may develop this sense of brokenness in one of two ways. He may use personal experiences of hurt or trial, or He may give us such a heart for others that we feel empathy and experience brokenness when we hear of their brokenness. When our hearts beat like God's, we'll be broken anytime brothers and sisters in God's family experience brokenness. As Bob Pierce (who established World Vision and Samaritan's Purse) prayed, "Let my heart be broken by the things that break the heart of God."

➡ **5. Have you personally experienced brokenness in the area of racism or sectarianism?** ❏ yes ❏ no ❏ I'm not sure

➡ **6. If you checked yes, write a brief description in the margin of one experience where you were broken.**

➡ **What, if anything, do you sense God has said to you through today's lesson?**

Write *one* of the most meaningful things He has said below.

_____

_____

➡ **Conclude today's lesson by praying. Are you willing to let God give you His heart for the brokenness of others? If so, pray the prayer of Bob Pierce in the margin, and talk to the Lord about your willingness.**
   • Ask the Lord to deepen and strengthen your prayer life.
   • Ask the Lord to give you His heart for the interests and concerns of others. Invite Him to reveal the brokenness in the lives of others so you can pray for them and watch for ways to be involved in their healing and empowerment.

LESSON 2 THE PRINCIPLE OF EMPOWERMENT II

Scripture for Meditation
"You will receive power when the Holy Spirit comes on you; and you will be my witnesses in Jerusalem, and in all Judea and Samaria, and to the ends of the earth" (Acts 1:8).

A Beginning Prayer
Father, I want to know the fullness and power of Your Holy Spirit. I pray that You will empower me. Teach me to pray. Use personal brokenness in my life to accomplish Your purposes in me. Guide me to practice repentance and forgiveness so that nothing stands in the way of reconciled relationships for Your glory. Then use me as a witness of Your grace to bring others to Christ! Amen.

PRINCIPLE 7
Empowerment: Through prayer, personal brokenness, repentance, and forgiveness, we remove barriers and are freed to experience the power of the Holy Spirit in reconciling relationships.

➡ **Read and think about the Scripture for Meditation in the left margin, and begin the lesson with prayer.**

❖ ❖ ❖

➡ **1. Based on the last lesson, what are two things through which we remove barriers to reconciled relationships? Fill in the blanks below.**

Through p_____, personal b_____, repentance, and forgiveness, we remove barriers and are freed to experience the power of the Holy Spirit in reconciling relationships.

In today's lesson, we'll look at two more things we must use to experience empowerment in reconciled relationships, repentance and forgiveness.

Repentance
God is grieved by the lack of responsibility taken by His saints in the areas of racism and sectarianism. Because of pride, we can refuse to acknowledge our own contributions to the problems around us. We may think we've never done anything to hurt others and fail to realize that we've sinned by the things we *haven't* done. We can sin by doing the wrong things, but we can also sin by failing to do the right things.

For instance, we may be able to claim that we didn't own slaves, massacre Native Americans, or discriminate against Hispanics. But have we taken advantage of others for personal greed or economic gain? Have we failed to take a stand for the oppressed? Have we condemned other denominations because their worship styles are different from ours? Have we passed by opportunities to lift up a brother who is hurting and nurture him back to health? If God is convicting you of any sin, repentance is required.

➡ **2. As you have studied *Break Down the Walls* and participated in a small-group study, has the Lord convicted you of ways you've sinned regarding racism or sectarianism? If so, what has He dealt with you about?**

_____

_____

To see the body of Christ come to health, we need to repent of our personal sins. Racism and sectarianism are the two giants that must come down. That will begin to happen when individuals turn from (repent of) their sins and live in God-honoring relationships with others. Repentance is an essential turning point in reconciled relationships. We must take this issue very seriously.

> *Repentance is an essential turning point in reconciled relationships.*

➡ **3. Pause to pray and ask the Lord to help you understand the need for, and the ways of, confession and repentance. Ask Him to convict you of any sin of action or neglect of which you need to repent. As He brings conviction, agree with Him and choose to turn from the sin.**

❖ ❖ ❖

Forgiveness

Forgiveness is an act in which you release a person from an offense. You deliver the person from the penalty due him or her. You remove consideration of the cause of the offense. You decide you won't allow that offense to affect the way you relate to the person. Forgiveness can release a brother from a sense of unresolved guilt and restore in him a clear conscience. Forgiveness can complete the process of empowerment.

> *Forgiveness can release a brother from a sense of unresolved guilt and restore in him a clear conscience. Forgiveness can complete the process of empowerment.*

But forgiveness is *not* condoning the sin as being okay, acceptable, or good. It's *not* saying you don't care. It's *not* a confession that you weren't hurt. Nor is it a granting of permission to do the same thing again. Forgiveness is a mental choice you make to no longer hold an offense against another person or group.

> *Forgiveness is a mental choice you make to no longer hold an offense against another person or group.*

➡ **4. Try to write a definition of *forgiveness* in your own words:**

Forgiveness is _____

_____

➡ **5. Are there any people who have offended or hurt you that you've been unwilling to forgive? Perhaps you've been waiting for an apology or you think you've been hurt too badly to forgive. In the list below, check those that you may still need to forgive. If you think of others not listed, write their names (or initials) in the margin or on the lines provided.**

❑ my spouse   ❑ my child(ren)   ❑ my father
❑ my mother   ❑ my brother   ❑ my sister
❑ an ex-spouse   ❑ an in-law   ❑ a stepparent

❑ other relatives: _____

❑ pastor   ❑ teacher   ❑ deacon or elder
❑ neighbor   ❑ friend   ❑ coworker
❑ members who caused a split in our church

❑ other church members: _____

❏ charismatics who tried to force members to speak in tongues
❏ traditionalists who quenched the freedom of the Spirit in worship
❏ liberals/moderates/conservatives/fundamentalists who have corrupted or hurt our denomination (circle those that apply)
❏ prominent religious figures whose gross sin has been made public

❏ other Christians or Christian groups: _____

_____

❏ whites who . . .   ❏ blacks who . . .
❏ Japanese who . . .   ❏ Germans who . . .
❏ Chinese who . . .   ❏ Koreans who . . .
❏ Vietnamese who . . .   ❏ Italians who . . .
❏ Cubans who . . .   ❏ Mexicans who . . .
❏ Puerto Ricans who . . .   ❏ American Indians who . . .

❏ other nationalities or ethnic groups: _____

_____

❏ poor person who took advantage of my (our) generosity
❏ rich person who took advantage of me (us) for personal profit
❏ person who cheated or stole from me
❏ person who lied to or about me
❏ person who spread gossip or slander about me
❏ person who blamed me for something I didn't do
❏ person who physically or psychologically hurt me
❏ person who hurt a member of my family

❏ others: _____

_____

➡ **6. Look back over the ones you checked in the previous list. If you can remember specific events when you were offended or sinned against, write a note to yourself in the margin.**

We'll study what Godlike forgiveness is in lesson 5. Begin now to be sensitive to ways the Lord may prompt you to forgive others.

➡ **What, if anything, do you sense God has said to you through today's lesson? Write *one* of the most meaningful things He has said below.**

_____

_____

➡ **Conclude today's lesson by praying.**
  • Ask the Lord to convict you of anything you need to repent of regarding racism and/or sectarianism.
  • Ask the Lord to enable you to forgive all those who may have sinned or committed an offense against you.

LESSON 3 CONFESSION

Scripture for Meditation
"He who conceals his sins does not prosper, but whoever confesses and renounces them finds mercy" (Proverbs 28:13).

A Beginning Prayer
Father, I know that repentance is an important part of getting right with You. Sometimes I have concerns and questions about how to respond in the areas of racism and sectarianism. Please teach me Your ways today. Amen.

➡ **Read and think about the Scripture for Meditation in the left margin and begin the lesson with prayer.**

❖ ❖ ❖

Identifying the Sins of Our Fathers
In Jesus' day, the teachers of the Law and the Pharisees didn't realize they were continuing the sins of their forefathers. Jesus condemned them and announced, *"Look, your house is left to you desolate"* (Matthew 23:38). They needed to understand the sins of their fathers and depend on the Lord to keep them from going the same way, from committing the same sins.

➡ **Read Matthew 23:29–36 below. Then answer the question that follows.**

Matthew 23:29–36: *"Woe to you, teachers of the law and Pharisees, you hypocrites! You build tombs for the prophets and decorate the graves of the righteous. And you say, 'If we had lived in the days of our forefathers, we would not have taken part with them in shedding the blood of the prophets.' So you testify against yourselves that you are the descendants of those who murdered the prophets. Fill up, then, the measure of the sin of your forefathers!*

"You snakes! You brood of vipers! How will you escape being condemned to hell? Therefore I am sending you prophets and wise men and teachers. Some of them you will kill and crucify; others you will flog in your synagogues and pursue from town to town. And so upon you will come all the righteous blood that has been shed on earth, from the blood of righteous Abel to the blood of Zechariah son of Berekiah, whom you murdered between the temple and the altar. I tell you the truth, all this will come upon this generation."

➡ **1. Which of the following was true of the leaders Jesus described above?**
   ❏ a. They were righteous and would never treat God's messengers the way their forefathers had treated the prophets of their day.
   ❏ b. They would respond the same way their forefathers had, and they would kill and crucify the messengers God would send to them.

The religious leaders said they would not have sinned against the prophets like their fathers had they lived in the past. However, because they didn't understand and identify those sins, they continued to sin in the same way. Jesus said that this generation (first century) would suffer God's judgment because of the shedding of innocent blood. This was the very group that killed God's Son.

Is it possible that we could claim we would not have owned slaves or massacred Native Americans and yet continue to sin in a similar way? Many of our forefathers in the church failed to take a stand against sin and injustice in their day. We could claim that we would have taken a stand for the oppressed and would not have permitted the injustices. But is it possible that we could make those claims and still sin in similar ways? Yes, that's just as possible for us as it was for the religious leaders in Jesus' day. We all have been affected by the way we have been reared. What we value and how we act are often patterned after our fathers, grandfathers, and others who have gone before us. How can we avoid following that pattern? We would do well to try to identify what our forefathers did that was wrong and ask the Lord to reveal anything in us that may be a similar sin.

The place to begin is with identifying our forefathers' sins. We must invite God to cause us to be broken over the sins of previous generations. This godly sorrow can lead to live a different way, a right way. Without this process, we could wind up being just like the Pharisees of Jesus' day. We can continue to propagate the sins of racism and sectarianism.

➡ **2. Think about the previous generations of your own people (ethnic and denominational). What are some of the ways they may have sinned through racism or sectarianism? Check those that you think apply or write your own.**

❑ took advantage of others for ecconomic gain
❑ practiced hatred, carried bitterness, and refused to forgive
❑ failed to take a stand against injustice and oppression
❑ murdered, killed, or physically abused others
❑ showed arrogance and held a judgmental spirit toward others
❑ slandered, gossipped, or spoke evil about others
❑ refused to have fellowship with other Christians because they were different
❑ cheated or stole from others
❑ lied to others or lied about them
❑ failed to love others as Christ commanded them
❑ treated other human beings as less than human or as second-class citizens

❑ others: _____

_____

➡ **3. Have you sinned in similar ways? Have you sinned against other people because they are racially or culturally different? Have you sinned against other Christians because they did not believe or practice their faith the way you believe and practice yours? Ask the Lord to convict you of any sins you have committed toward others either by your actions or by your neglect.**

Confessing Your Sin

When God's Holy Spirit brings conviction of sin, you need to respond to Him. You begin by confessing your sin. "To confess" means "to agree with" or "to say the same thing." When you confess sin, you are agreeing with God that what you have done or failed to do was wrong. When you agree with God about your sin, you take a step to break the continuity of that sin. Not only must you change your mind by agreeing that the action (or attitude or neglect) was wrong, but you must also change your hearts. You need to realize how much your sin hurts your heavenly Father. God will use that godly sorrow to help you repent (turn away) and begin to live in a way that is pleasing to Him. Confession and repentance set the stage for you to experience the empowerment of God's Holy Spirit in your life and in your relationships.

> "To confess" means "to agree with" or "to say the same thing."

➡ **Read Proverbs 28:13 in the margin. If you're willing, confess any sins God has revealed to you. Agree with God that you were wrong. Ask the Lord to enable and empower you to live in a way that pleases Him.**

> **Proverbs 28:13**
> *"He who conceals his sins does not prosper, but whoever confesses and renounces them finds mercy."*

➡ **What, if anything, do you sense God has said to you through today's lesson? Write *one* of the most meaningful things He has said below.**

_____

_____

➡ **Conclude today's lesson by reading Proverbs 28:13 (left) and praying.**
• Ask God to reveal any sin that needs to be confessed.
• Talk to the Lord about any remaining questions you may have concerning confession and repentance. Ask the Lord to continue to teach and instruct you in His ways.

LESSON 4 REPENTANCE AND RESTORATION

Scripture for Meditation

"If my people, who are called by my name, will humble themselves and pray and seek my face and turn from their wicked ways, then will I hear from heaven and will forgive their sin and will heal their land" (2 Chronicles 7:14).

A Beginning Prayer

Father, these matters of confession and repentance aren't very comfortable. But I know they're important to You. I know they're required if we're to see our land healed and forgiven. Please continue to help me understand Your ways and requirements. Amen.

Luke 3:11–14

"John answered, 'The man with two tunics should share with him who has none, and the one who has food should do the same.'

"Tax collectors also came to be baptized. 'Teacher,' they asked, 'what should we do?'

"'Don't collect any more than you are required to,' he told them.

"Then some soldiers asked him, 'And what should we do?'

"He replied, 'Don't extort money and don't accuse people falsely—be content with your pay.'"

Notes

_____

_____

_____

_____

_____

_____

➡ **Read and think about the Scripture for Meditation in the left margin, and begin the lesson with prayer.**

❖ ❖ ❖

Showing Fruits of Repentance

Repentance is not just saying you're sorry. Repentance is a turning from sinful ways to live in God's ways. During the ministry of John the Baptist, religious leaders came to him to be baptized as a sign of repentance. John's response was, *" 'You brood of vipers! Who warned you to flee from the coming wrath? Produce fruit in keeping with repentance. . . . Every tree that does not produce good fruit will be cut down and thrown into the fire' "* (Luke 3:7–9). The crowd then asked him what they should do.

➡ **1. Read Luke 3:11–14 in the margin below, and underline the things John said would be the fruit (sign) of repentance. We've underlined one.**

➡ **Pause to pray and ask the Lord to reveal what actions He would want you to take to show the signs of repentance toward racism or sectarianism. As He begins to reveal what you should do, write notes in the margin below.**

If we've sinned against others in a way that has hurt them materially or financially, we need to do everything we can to make restitution. If we have taken something wrongly or caused harm in some way, we need to do what we can to restore what was taken or harmed. That's what Zacchaeus did when he offered to pay back anyone he had cheated four times the amount he had taken (Luke 19:8).

Knowing how to make restitution in the area of racism is much more difficult. Many questions are raised when we try to put a monetary value on sins of the past. We suggest that you be careful not to drive wedges or build walls over this matter of restitution. If you're on the side of those who have been sinned against, turn your mind and heart toward God as your provider. One of the "hard-to-follow" statements of Jesus applies to you: *"If anyone takes what belongs to you, do not demand it back. . . . Be merciful, just as your Father is merciful"* (Luke 6:30, 36). You must trust the Holy Spirit to bring conviction to those who should make restitution. Don't try to play the role of the Spirit in this matter. Trust Him, and don't try to force the issue because of unbelief. He can do the convincing effectively. Let Him work with others the way He worked in Zacchaeus' life. Who knows, He may tell the offender to pay back four times! Be sensitive, however, to ways the Holy Spirit may call on you to *"speak the truth in love."*

If you find yourself in the position of the offender, you need to let the Holy Spirit guide you in knowing how to respond. Don't depend on your own reasoning, because it will be biased by selfishness. Ask the Spirit to guide you to know what and how much to do. Then obey Him completely, even if it's costly to you.

➡ **2. Which of the following suggestions on restitution do you sense you need to follow (if any)? Check one or more if they apply.**
   ❑ a. Don't drive wedges or build walls over this matter of restitution.
   ❑ b. Trust the Holy Spirit to bring conviction to those who should make restitution. Speak the truth when the Holy Spirit calls you to.
   ❑ c. Don't try to force the issue because of unbelief.
   ❑ d. Ask the Holy Spirit to guide you to know what and how much to do.
   ❑ e. Obey Him completely, even if it's costly to you.

Sometimes we may not know if or how restitution should be made. We may have difficulty deciding who should be responsible. If the Holy Spirit has not given clear guidance on this matter, you have one more consideration to give.

Choosing to Be a "Good Samaritan"

God's objective is to bring health to the members of the body of Christ. He will use many people to help build up the ruins and restore the broken places—even people who may not be directly responsible for the problems.

➡ **Read the story of the Good Samaritan in Luke 10:25–37 in the margin, and answer the following questions.**

➡ **3. Who sinned against the man who was beaten and robbed? Check one.**
❑ the band of robbers ❑ the priest ❑ the Levite ❑ the Samaritan

➡ **4. Which two decided they had no responsibility to help the beaten man?**
❑ the priest   ❑ the Levite   ❑ the Samaritan

➡ **5. Which of the following best describes the care the Samaritan gave to the man? Check one.**
❑ a. He did the least he could do and still get credit from God for helping.
❑ b. He tried to cut corners every way possible to keep the expenses down.
❑ c. He gave sacrificially and went far beyond what might have been expected to meet the man's needs until his health was restored.
❑ d. He helped just enough to get the man on his feet and then moved quickly to remove himself from further responsibility.

➡ **6. What did Jesus recommend we should do with the example of the Samaritan?**
❑ a. Try to be like the priest or the Levite unless someone is watching.
❑ b. Follow His example by showing mercy to people who need our help.
❑ c. Help only those who are needy because of our personal sin.

The Samaritan didn't cause the man's needs. He could have acted just like the priest and Levite and concluded he wasn't responsible. But instead, the Samaritan showed Godlike love. He did all he could do to see the man restored to health. He wasn't satisfied to cut corners and try to get by in the least-expensive way possible.

God wants us, like the Good Samaritan, to take responsibility to be agents of healing by loving our neighbor as ourselves. Love is a selfless concern that even takes responsibility for the consequences of the sins of others. Love meets needs and reveals our faith. If we don't help meet needs when we have the opportunity and the resources, we show that our faith is *"dead"* (see James 2:15–17).

All of us have benefited by Jesus' taking responsibility for our sin even though He wasn't guilty. Our natural tendency is to deny taking responsibility. Instead of looking for a way to deny responsibility, however, we ought to ask, "Lord, do You want me to assume responsibility even if I'm not guilty?" God may give us the privilege of acting like Christ in such a situation.

➡ **What, if anything, do you sense God has said to you through today's lesson? Write *one* of the most meaningful things He has said below.**

_____

_____

➡ **Conclude today's lesson by praying.**
• Ask if there are specific actions you need to take to show the fruit of repentance.
• Submit yourself to be God's instrument in restoring health to a member or group of members in the body of Christ.

Luke 10:27–37
" '"Love the Lord your God with all your heart and with all your soul and with all your strength and with all your mind"; and, "Love your neighbor as yourself."

" 'You have answered correctly,' Jesus replied. 'Do this and you will live.'

"But he wanted to justify himself, so he asked Jesus, 'And who is my neighbor?'

"In reply Jesus said: 'A man was going down from Jerusalem to Jericho, when he fell into the hands of robbers. They stripped him of his clothes, beat him and went away, leaving him half dead. A priest happened to be going down the same road, and when he saw the man, he passed by on the other side. So too, a Levite, when he came to the place and saw him, passed by on the other side. But a Samaritan, as he traveled, came where the man was; and when he saw him, he took pity on him. He went to him and bandaged his wounds, pouring on oil and wine. Then he put the man on his own donkey, took him to an inn and took care of him. The next day he took out two silver coins and gave them to the innkeeper. "Look after him," he said, "and when I return, I will reimburse you for any extra expense you may have."

" 'Which of these three do you think was a neighbor to the man who fell into the hands of robbers?'

"The expert in the law replied, 'The one who had mercy on him.'

"Jesus told him, 'Go and do likewise.' "

James 2:15–17
"Suppose a brother or sister is without clothes and daily food. If one of you says to him, 'Go, I wish you well; keep warm and well fed,' but does nothing about his physical needs, what good is it? In the same way, faith by itself, if it is not accompanied by action, is dead."

LESSON 5 GODLIKE FORGIVENESS

Scriptures for Meditation
"Bear with each other and forgive whatever grievances you may have against one another. Forgive as the Lord forgave you" (Colossians 3:13).

"He who covers over an offense promotes love" (Proverbs 17:9).

A Beginning Prayer
Father, when I was dead in sins, You forgave me. When it was my sins that Jesus carried to the cross, You forgave me. When I fail or rebel against You, You're willing to forgive me. When I sin over and over again, You call me back like a prodigal son and forgive me. When You ask me to forgive others that way, I know I can't—not by myself. I need the love and mercy of Christ in me to enable me to forgive that way. Please show me all the brothers and sisters I still need to forgive. Then enable me to forgive in the unlimited and unconditional way Jesus forgives. Amen.

➡ **Read and think about the Scriptures for Meditation in the left margin, and begin the lesson with prayer.**

❖ ❖ ❖

We learned in an earlier lesson that God-honoring relationships call for us to accept others as Christ has accepted us. Accepting people who are different may not be nearly as difficult as forgiving those who have hurt or offended us. In today's lesson, we see that God calls us to forgive others the way He has forgiven us.

Forgiven by God
Christians who have placed their faith and trust in Christ and repented of their sin have been forgiven by God. Since we're called to forgive others in the same way, let's take a look at how God has forgiven us.

➡ **Read the Scriptures below, and answer the questions that follow.**

"This is my blood of the covenant, which is poured out for many for the forgiveness of sins" (Matthew 26:28).

"He was delivered over to death for our sins and was raised to life for our justification" (Romans 4:25).

"When you were dead in your sins . . . God made you alive with Christ. He forgave us all our sins" (Colossians 2:13).

"God demonstrates his own love for us in this: While we were still sinners, Christ died for us" (Romans 5:8).

"In him we have redemption through his blood, the forgiveness of sins, in accordance with the riches of God's grace" (Ephesians 1:7).

"All the prophets testify about him that everyone who believes in him receives forgiveness of sins through his name" (Acts 10:43).

➡ **1. What did it cost Jesus to provide for the forgiveness of your sin?**

_____

➡ **2. What did you have to do to be forgiven for your sin?**

_____

Even before you were born, Jesus shed His blood and gave up His life to provide for your forgiveness. That's how God showed His love for you. You *receive* forgiveness by *faith* and *belief* in Him and His provision for your sin.

How Are You to Forgive?
Today's first Scripture for Meditation describes how you're to forgive others: *"Bear with each other and forgive whatever grievances you may have against one another. Forgive as the Lord forgave you"* (Colossians 3:13). You're to forgive others as God in Christ has forgiven you. Jesus gave you a good reason to forgive others:

"If you forgive men when they sin against you, your heavenly Father will

also forgive you. But if you do not forgive men their sins, your Father will not forgive your sins" (Matthew 6:14–15).

➡ **3. According to Jesus, why should you forgive others?**

_____

If you don't forgive others when they sin against you, your heavenly Father won't forgive you. That's serious business! This doesn't have anything to do with the forgiveness you received at salvation—that's settled. But it does have to do with your fellowship and right relationship with God.

> If you don't forgive others when they sin against you, your heavenly Father won't forgive you.

If you're not willing to be reconciled to your brother in Christ, you can't live in a reconciled relationship with God. Notice that Jesus didn't specify that you should just forgive your fellow Christians. He said you must forgive other "men" (women included). Both Christians and non-Christians are included. If we're to experience unity in the body of Christ, we must be reconciled to God and each other. We can't experience that without forgiving others.

> If we're to experience unity in the body of Christ, we must be reconciled to God and each other. We can't experience that without forgiving others.

➡ **4. Look back at activity 5 on pages 149-150. If God evaluated your life right now on the basis of the way you've forgiven others, would He forgive you? Check the truth below.**
   ❏ a. As far as I know, I've forgiven everyone. I hold nothing against anyone. I believe God would forgive me.
   ❏ b. I still haven't forgiven one or more people or groups. According to Jesus' guideline, God would not forgive me.

Is that a tough question or what? There's no in-between. God doesn't issue exceptions. He offers no waivers. He accepts no excuses. If you don't forgive others—all others—God does not forgive you. Therefore:

> *Do not grieve the Holy Spirit of God, with whom you were sealed for the day of redemption. Get rid of all bitterness, rage and anger, brawling and slander, along with every form of malice. Be kind and compassionate to one another, forgiving each other, just as in Christ God forgave you* (Ephesians 4:30–32).

Forgiveness isn't just for the other person, either. It's also for your sake that you forgive. Bitterness will produce terrible fruit in your life. It will sap your strength and spiritual vitality. The lack of forgiveness creates a foothold to bring alienation and bitterness. Unconditional forgiveness breaks this stronghold. So get rid of any bitterness, rage, or anger you may be carrying around toward others.

> Bitterness will produce terrible fruit in your life. It will sap your strength and spiritual vitality.

When a Brother Sins Against You
In Matthew 18:15–17, Jesus gave some instructions about how to deal with a brother who has sinned against you. Here's a summary. If your brother sins against you:
1. *"Go and show him his fault, just between the two of you"* (verse 15).
2. *"If he will not listen, take one or two others along"* (verse 16).
3. *"If he refuses to listen to them, tell it to the church"* (verse 17).
4. *"If he refuses to listen even to the church, treat him as you would a pagan or a tax collector"* (verse 17).

These steps have a clear order to them. You don't start by telling other people what your brother did to you. You don't write an open letter to the newspaper first. You don't begin by spreading the word about the sin to others in the church.

➡ **5. Where do you begin to correct a brother who has sinned against you?**

_____

Then Peter came to Jesus and asked, "Lord, how many times shall I forgive my brother when he sins against me? Up to seven times?"

Jesus answered, "I tell you, not seven times, but seventy-seven times" (Matthew 18:21–22).

Forgive without limit.

When Jesus said *"seventy-seven"* times, He implied: You forgive without limit. In another passage, Jesus instructed:

"If your brother sins, rebuke him, and if he repents, forgive him. If he sins against you seven times in a day, and seven times comes back to you and says, 'I repent,' forgive him" (Luke 17:3–4).

➡ **6. Suppose your Christian brother sinned against you seven times in a single day and each time said "I repent. Please forgive me." How would you respond? Check your *real* answer.**

❏ a. I've heard this before. I don't believe you have any intention of changing. First show me you've changed, and then I'll forgive you.
❏ b. This is it. I forgive you this one last time. Seven times is enough. The next time. I won't forgive.
❏ c. If you really were sorry, you wouldn't keep doing this to me. I'm not going to forgive you this time.
❏ d. Because of the way Jesus forgives me, I forgive you.

Jesus said you need to take a brother at his word every time. If he seeks forgiveness, you should give it. That's not our human way. Most of us would respond with *a, b,* or *c* above.
- But what do you do if someone sins against you and doesn't ask for forgiveness?
- What if he never says he's sorry?
- What if he doesn't even think (or agree) that what he did was wrong?

Jesus' Example

Let's look at the life of Jesus for our model. Jesus was arrested and falsely accused of blasphemy against God and treason against Rome. He was mocked, spit on, slapped, beaten, whipped, and had a crown of thorns placed on His head. He was nailed through His hands and feet to a cross and hung up to die. While He was on the cross, no one asked for forgiveness. None said they were sorry. None of the leaders who led the "lynching" felt they were wrong. Yet here is what Jesus said as He hung on the cross, dying:

> *"Father, forgive them, for they do not know what they are doing"* (Luke 23:34).

Do you realize that your sins helped put Him on that cross? The divine forgiveness Jesus demonstrated goes far beyond any forgiveness man is capable of giving. Stephen—one of the early Christians—was being stoned to death because of his faith in Christ. Because of the new nature Christ had given Stephen, he also was able to forgive those who were unjustly putting him to death (Acts 7:60).

Acts 7:60
"'Lord, do not hold this sin against them.'"

If you wait until others (especially those who aren't Christians) confess their sin and seek forgiveness, you'll likely become a bitter person. Forgiving like Jesus will require you to forgive all offenses against you. When you forgive others without limit, your relationships will honor God and lead to unity that pleases Him. It will also free you from the bad effects of bitterness!

➡ **7. Review the people and/or groups you checked in activity #5 (page 149). Pause for a moment of prayer. Ask God to help you forgive every person or group in just the same way Christ has forgiven you.**

Biblical Instructions

❑ Forgive those who sin against you (Matthew 6:14).

❑ Don't hold grudges over past offenses.

❑ *"If your brother sins, rebuke him, and if he repents, forgive him. If he sins against you seven times in a day, and seven times comes back to you and says, 'I repent,' forgive him"* (Luke 17:3–4).

❑ Forgive as often as your brother asks for forgiveness (Matthew 18:21–22).

❑ Forgive others even when they don't say they're sorry or seek forgiveness (model of Jesus in Luke 23:34 and Stephen in Acts 7:60).

❑ When asked, offer genuine forgiveness by a choice of your will. Don't let your feelings, human reasoning, or someone else's counsel keep you from forgiving.

❑ *"Get rid of all bitterness, rage and anger, brawling and slander, along with every form of malice"* (Ephesians 4:31).

❑ *"When you stand praying, if you hold anything against anyone, forgive him, so that your Father in heaven may forgive you your sins"* (Mark 11:25).

❑ Don't talk to others about the way you've been offended and cause further division (Proverbs 17:9).

➨ 8. Read the list of biblical instructions in the margin. As you read, check the instructions that you believe God wants you to apply in relationships to other believers.

➨ What, if anything, do you sense God has said to you through today's lesson? Write *one* of the most meaningful things He has said below.

_____

_____

➨ For each lesson this week, you've been recording what you sense God has said to you. Review the final activity for each of the previous lessons on pages 148, 150, 152, and 154. What's the major emphasis of what you sense God wants you to do in response to this unit's lessons? Pray and ask Him what He wants you to do. Then write notes below, in the margin, or in a separate notebook. You might use these questions in your prayer:

1. What do You want me to do in my personal relationship to You?
2. What do You want me to do in relationship to other people in my church or denomination?
3. What do You want me to do in relationship to Christians in other denominations or Christian traditions?
4. What do You want me to do in relationship to Christians of other races or ethnic backgrounds?

_____

_____

_____

➨ Conclude today's lesson by:
- confessing any unforgiveness or bitterness you hold toward others.
- asking for the Lord's help in forgiving each one.
- then seeking the Lord's forgiveness for your unforgiving spirit.

UNIT 10 INTERDEPENDENCE

Scripture Memory Verse
"There should be no division in the body, but ... its parts should have equal concern for each other."
—1 Corinthians 12:25

Unit Learning Goal
You will understand your interdependence with the rest of the body of Christ, and you'll demonstrate your willingness to serve others as well as receive from them in the body.

Overview of Unit 10
Lesson 1: Interdependence in the Body
Lesson 2: The Principle of Interdependence
Lesson 3: Caring for All Members of the Body
Lesson 4: Final Course Review
Lesson 5: Seeking God's Assignment

PRINCIPLE 8
Interdependence: As we recognize our differences, we also realize that God has placed us as members in the body of Christ where we need and depend on the contributions of each member.

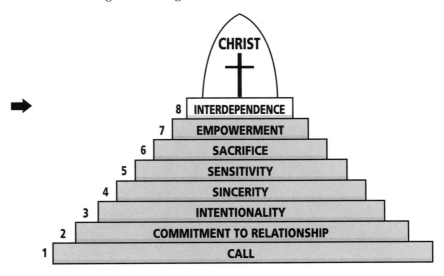

The Body of Christ

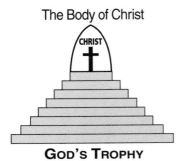

GOD'S TROPHY

Key Summary Statements from Unit 10
- The goal of interdependence in the church (and among churches) is to reflect the unity of the body of Christ in the midst of its diversity.
- He puts the body of Christ on public display as a trophy of His grace accomplished through Christ.
- A healthy body of very different parts shows His power and grace most clearly to a watching world.
- Interdependence says, "You can't do it alone."
- God made us unique. We both bring something to the relationship that's needed.
- The body of Christ functions best when the members are equally valued.
- When God comforts you, that's preparation to be used by God to help others in similar circumstances.

A UNIQUE PARTNERSHIP

By Louis Lee

I'm an American Born Chinese (ABC) who grew up near Detroit, Michigan, with all Anglo friends. My parents made little effort to teach me anything about the Chinese language or culture. I thought of myself as being no different from my Anglo friends.

I attended an Anglo church during my college years and continued to do the same during my first two years at seminary. God used several other ABC seminar students to help me discover and learn about Chinese churches and ministry opportunities. When I graduated from seminary, I began seventeen years of pastoral ministry in several different Chinese churches in northern California.

I began learning about racism among the Chinese and Asian communities. There were many examples of how Asians were the victims of racism. Offenses came in the form of both individual acts as well as corporate acts of the government, such as the internment of Japanese-American citizens during World War II and exclusion acts that grossly limited immigration of Asians compared with other groups of people seeking to enter this "promised land."

However, it became painfully clear to me that racism was also inflicted by Asians toward non-Asians, as well as toward one another! I even learned that there were prejudices among Chinese toward one another because they spoke different dialects of Chinese and came from different parts of the world! But one ugly common denominator I saw was the racist attitude of many Asians toward African Americans.

This is what made my experience over the past four years so amazing and wonderful. In the summer of 1992, I helped start an Asian-American church. The denomination that

helped this new work begin utilized a "host church" system. This host church would provide a meeting place and other resources.

Unfortunately, the Anglo host church that had planned to help us was forced to suddenly withdraw its partnership with us when it experienced serious internal problems. God miraculously provided us with a new host church in less than two weeks! Pastor Ray Jones presented our need to his monthly council meeting at the Fremont Bible Fellowship. With little discussion, the vote was unanimous to provide us with total assistance in beginning this new Asian-American church. What has made this partnership even more unique is the fact that the church is a predominantly African-American church.

I was especially blessed to hear how the decision was made to become our host church. The pastor apparently took just a few moments to state the details of our need. Then he asked his council leaders a simple question before the vote was taken: "What do you think Jesus would want us to do?"

For the past four years, they've provided us with free use of their facilities, as well as of their office equipment. They even support us financially every month! For me personally, one of their greatest contributions was the respect and love I always felt from their congregation and leadership.

I realize there are many factors involved in the problem of racism. But could all of us Christians learn something simple yet profound in this question posed by Pastor Ray Jones? In terms of how we behave, think, and feel toward others, "What would Jesus do, think, and feel?" Jesus, our Lord and Savior, treated all people with the same love and respect. And Jesus died for all the world.

LESSON 1   INTERDEPENDENCE IN THE BODY

Scriptures for Meditation

"There should be no division in the body, but . . . its parts should have equal concern for each other" (1 Corinthians 12:25).

"The eye cannot say to the hand, 'I don't need you!' And the head cannot say to the feet, 'I don't need you!' On the contrary, those parts of the body that seem to be weaker are indispensable. . . . God has combined the members of the body . . . so that there should be no division in the body, but that its parts should have equal concern for each other. If one part suffers, every part suffers with it; if one part is honored, every part rejoices with it" (1 Corinthians 12:21–22, 24–26).

A Beginning Prayer

Father, I do want to be a part of a healthy body of Christ. Teach me today about my own need for a greater sensitivity to the needs of brothers and sisters in Christ. Help me learn how to work together with others so the whole body is healthy and built up into a trophy for Christ. Amen.

PRINCIPLE 8

Interdependence: As we recognize our differences, we also realize that God has placed us as members in the body of Christ where we need and depend on the contributions of each member.

Call
Commitment to Relationship
Empowerment
Intentionality
Interdependence
Sacrifice
Sensitivity
Sincerity

➡ First Corinthians 12:25 in the left margin is your Scripture memory verse for this unit. Remove the perforated card in the back of the book, and begin memorizing it. Read and think about the other Scripture verses for meditation, and start the lesson with prayer.

❖ ❖ ❖

Congratulations, you're in the home stretch! This is the final unit in our study together. We have looked at eight principles during the study. During this unit, we'll look at the last one: interdependence.

➡ **Remove the perforated card for principle 8 from the back of your book. Read the principle two or three times. The same text is in the box in the lower left margin.**

❖ ❖ ❖

➡ **1. Based on the statement of interdependence, how are you related to other members in the body of Christ?**

The goal of interdependence in the church (and among churches) is to reflect the unity of the body of Christ in the midst of its diversity. God has gifted different parts of the body to build up the whole. As the body functions in the way God intends, He uses it to draw alienated, hurting people to the good news of Jesus Christ. This is where we began our study. Jesus prayed, *"I pray . . . that all of them may be one, Father, . . . that the world may believe that you have sent me"* (John 17:20–21).

During our study, we've focused on the healthy body of Christ that God builds through a ministry of reconciliation. As people are first reconciled to God, they are also reconciled to one another and placed in the body. Then God reveals His wisdom to powers in heavenly places. He puts the body of Christ on public display as a trophy of His grace accomplished through Christ.

➡ **2. In the diagram below, see if you can place the principles in the proper order from 1 to 8. The names of the principles are in the margin in alphabetical order. Write one principle on each line in the diagram. Then look back to page 159 to check your work.**

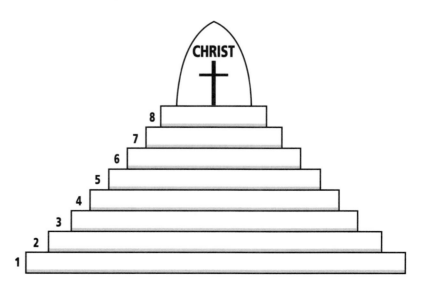

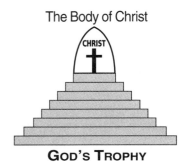

The Body of Christ

GOD'S TROPHY

1 Corinthians 12:4–5, 7, 12–20

⁴*"There are different kinds of gifts.
. . . ⁵There are different kinds of service. . . .*

⁷*"Now to each one the manifestation of the Spirit is given for the common good. . . .*

¹²*"The body is a unit, though it is made up of many parts; and though all its parts are many, they form one body. So it is with Christ.* ¹³*For we were all baptized by one Spirit into one body. . . .*

¹⁴*"Now the body is not made up of one part but of many.* ¹⁵*If the foot should say, 'Because I am not a hand, I do not belong to the body,' it would not for that reason cease to be part of the body.* ¹⁶*And if the ear should say, 'Because I am not an eye, I do not belong to the body,' it would not for that reason cease to be part of the body.* ¹⁷*If the whole body were an eye, where would the sense of hearing be? If the whole body were an ear, where would the sense of smell be?* ¹⁸*But in fact God has arranged the parts in the body, every one of them, just as he wanted them to be.* ¹⁹*If they were all one part, where would the body be?* ²⁰*As it is, there are many parts, but one body."*

All the first seven principles are moving toward a healthy body of Christ. When repentance and forgiveness provide cleansing for the body, it is empowered to function as God intended. He intended the body to be interdependent—every member needing every other member. When that happens in a local church and in the larger body of Christ, God has a trophy for Christ!

➥ 3. Read 1 Corinthians 12:4–5, 7, 12–20 in the margin to see how the different parts of the body of Christ are to be related. Then answer the following questions.

➥ **4. For whose "good" does the Spirit manifest Himself through spiritual gifts? (verse 7)**

_____

➥ **5. Which is better for the body: sameness (uniformity) or difference (diversity)? Circle one.**

➥ **6. Which of the following statements is true about the relationship of the members of the body of Christ? Check one.**
   ❏ a. Members don't really need each other. As long as they're connected to Christ, they can make it just fine on their own.
   ❏ b. Members really do need each other. Life without the other members will be far less than God intended. He put the body together so that members would need each other.

God put the body together in such a way that members need each other. Each has a contribution to make to the whole. The Spirit works through each member for the common good. Sameness and uniformity were never God's intention for the body. What He's interested in is unity in the midst of diversity. A healthy body of very different parts shows His power and grace most clearly to a watching world. As diverse members of the body of Christ, we need each other.

In tomorrow's lesson, we'll look at the principle of interdependence more closely.

➥ **What, if anything, do you sense God has said to you through today's lesson? Write *one* of the most meaningful things He has said below.**

_____

_____

➥ **Conclude today's lesson by praying.**
   • Thank the Lord for your experiences of interdependence in the body of Christ.
   • Ask the Lord to help you give as well as receive as a member of the body of Christ.

LESSON 2

THE PRINCIPLE OF INTERDEPENDENCE

Scripture for Meditation

"Just as each of us has one body with many members, and these members do not all have the same function, so in Christ we who are many form one body, and each member belongs to all the others" (Romans 12:4–5).

A Beginning Prayer

Father, thank You for the great variety You have built into the body of Christ. I confess that it's beautiful. At times it also is painful when we don't know how to benefit from our differences. Teach me, my church, and all in the body of Christ to "belong to each other" in a way that would help us all grow into Christlikeness. Amen.

PRINCIPLE 8

Interdependence: As we recognize our differences, we also realize that God has placed us as members in the body of Christ where we need and depend on the contributions of each member.

➡ **Read and think about the Scripture for Meditation in the left margin, and begin the lesson with prayer.**

❖ ❖ ❖

➡ **Review the statement of the principle of interdependence in the lower left margin.**

❖ ❖ ❖

Interdependence is a level that most relationships never achieve. This principle, however, will determine whether reconciliation becomes reality or not. This is especially true in a society that so emphasizes independence. Society says, "You can do it by yourself; go for it." Interdependence says, "You can't do it alone."

➡ **1. Which of the following has been most true of your life prior to taking this course? Check one.**

❑ a. I've been more independent. I've tried to make it on my own in nearly every area of my life.

❑ b. I've learned interdependence. My life is enriched as I contribute ministry to others and receive ministry from them.

Followers of Christ usually recognize their dependence on God. Like Paul we say, *"I can do everything through him who gives me strength"* (Philippians 4:13). Without God, even the best we have to offer is as "filthy rags" (Isaiah 64:6). But have you ever wondered at the fact that God made Himself a partner with us? God's plan for world redemption—His plan to reconcile the world to Himself—was made known to a small band of disciples who were charged to spread the word. Jesus ascended to heaven, but He left His followers in a spiritual body to carry on His work of reconciliation. Disciples equipped and empowered by the Holy Spirit became God's holy plan. Though God is complete and sufficient in Himself, He voluntarily chose to link His plan to our response. The amazing part is that God chose us to spread the Good News.

Interdependence says that we need each other. Just as God chose to use us, we must choose to partner with the person God would have us reconcile with. While on the surface this might seem logical, in practice it's difficult.

➡ **2. Try to define interdependence in your own words.**

_____

_____

To be interdependent is to say, "God made us unique. We both bring something to the relationship that's needed." This is the kind of equality God is talking about in 2 Corinthians 8:12–13:

> *For if the willingness is there, the gift is acceptable according to what one has, not according to what he does not have.*
> *Our desire is not that others might be relieved while you are hard pressed, but that there might be equality.*

➡ **3. When you think about Christians of other races, social standings, or denominations, do you have a tendency to think they're better (or worse) and more valuable (or less valuable) than you are to God's kingdom?** ❑ yes ❑ no

➡ **4. Can you think of an experience where you felt superior or inferior to**

163

The body of Christ functions best when the members are equally valued.

other believers? If so, briefly describe a time in the margin.

The body of Christ functions best when the members are equally valued. The perception of (or presence of) racism or alienation is a major stumbling block in cross-cultural relationships. Historical racism was built on a rationale of racial superiority. Society and the church reinforced that through laws and norms and even doctrinal teaching from the pulpit. The white community must participate in frank sharing (sincerity). It must purposefully seek to gain understanding (sensitivity) of how deeply minorities feel the oppression of racial superiority that seems constantly to be expressed. Ambassadors of reconciliation will seek to overcome this by first understanding and then acting.

Paternalism
Unless we understand the pain of racism, we'll suffer from paternalism. Paternalism has plagued cross-cultural missions for decades because we haven't understood interdependence. Efforts to reach out to others who are different is often motivated by compassion. Yet compassion without interdependence in relationships is paternalism. Whenever an adult is patronized, he is devalued, and true unity is harmed.

A large and well-known church sought to use an upcoming Promise Keepers conference as a reconciliation opportunity. When the tickets went on sale, the people bought hundreds in a block purchase. They then went about putting together a plan to distribute the tickets. Next they contacted an inner-city black church with an invitation to participate. The white church made the tickets available for free, but the black church needed to follow the white church's guidelines.

As the distribution plan was carried out, the black men felt more and more patronized. The white church asked them to do things to qualify for tickets that seemed strange, demeaning, and devoid of trust. "What made them [whites] think that we all wanted a free ride? We could and should have had the opportunity to pay for the tickets," one black leader responded. What began as a sincere effort to reach out in reconciliation deteriorated into racial struggle. When best-laid plans go astray in the racial arena, it leaves people wounded and confused.

Whites responded, "We were trying to do something positive, only to be shot down because we made a few small mistakes." The problem? The white church didn't understand the principle of interdependence.

➡ **5. What do you think the white church could have done differently to avoid making the black men feel demeaned or patronized?**

Understanding interdependence, the white pastor would have called the black pastor as the idea was conceived. "Hey, we know the conference is going to sell out, and we know that many guys in the black community don't even know about Promise Keepers. How can we combine our efforts and get men from both our churches there together? Let's sit down and figure this out."

That approach would have acknowledged that both parties bring something to the table, and a partnership could have developed, resulting in the best approach. The old baggage of "We want to help you people" would have been avoided. However, not all is lost from such an experience. If both parties could get together and talk through the experience in a spirit of sincerity and sensitivity, next year could be great.

➡ **6. If you've ever felt patronized, describe an experience in the margin. You don't have to write in sentences; just write some notes.**

➭ What, if anything, do you sense God has said to you through today's lesson? Write *one* of the most meaningful things He has said below.

_____

_____

➭ Conclude today's lesson by praying. Ask the Lord to continue teaching you the value of your brothers in Christ.

LESSON 3 CARING FOR ALL MEMBERS OF THE BODY

Scripture for Meditation

3 *"Praise be to the God and Father of our Lord Jesus Christ, the Father of compassion and the God of all comfort, ⁴who comforts us in all our troubles, so that we can comfort those in any trouble with the comfort we ourselves have received from God. ⁵For just as the sufferings of Christ flow over into our lives, so also through Christ our comfort overflows. ⁶If we are distressed, it is for your comfort and salvation; if we are comforted, it is for your comfort, which produces in you patient endurance of the same sufferings we suffer"* (2 Corinthians 1:3–6).

A Beginning Prayer

Father, I have faced troubles, and I don't know how I could have survived without You. You have been my rock and my salvation. You've been my comforter and encourager. Show me how my experiences of Your comfort have prepared me to minister to others in need. Teach me also how to receive the ministry of others as You use them to comfort me in my own troubles. Amen.

➭ Read and think about the Scripture for Meditation in the left margin, and begin the lesson with prayer.

❖ ❖ ❖

➭ Read 2 Corinthians 1:3–6 (Scripture for Meditation) again, and circle the words *comfort, comforts*, and *comforted* each time one of them occurs. Then answer the following questions.

❖ ❖ ❖

➭ 1. What names of God do you find in this passage? Fill in the blanks.

God and Father of _____

the Father of _____ the God of all _____

➭ 2. When does God comfort us? (verse 4)

in all our _____

➭ 3. What can we do for others after we've received comfort from God? (verse 4)

_____

➭ 4. When suffering flows into our lives, what should flow out? (verse 5)

_____

God is the Father of all compassion and the God of all comfort. He comforts us in our troubles, trials, and times of suffering. When we've received comfort from God, we're equipped to be used by God to comfort others who may be going through the same trouble. When the sufferings of Christ flow into our lives, God works in such a way that comfort can overflow to others.

Receiving and Giving Comfort

During a conference in New Mexico, a man from Texas requested prayer. His father had just died. He asked if someone who had experienced the death of a father would come and pray with him.

The man sitting beside him had prayed as he entered the room, "Lord, where do You want me to sit?" He had felt led to sit beside this young man. Now he knew God was up to something. His father had died not that long ago, and God had comforted him during that time of grief. He knew how to pray for this brother who was grieving the loss of his dad.

165

Matthew 5:4

"Blessed are those who mourn, for they will be comforted."

2 Corinthians 7:6

"God, who comforts the downcast, comforted us."

Psalm 23:4

"Even though I walk through the valley of the shadow of death, I will fear no evil, for you are with me; your rod and your staff, they comfort me."

Psalm 119:50, 52

"My comfort in my suffering is this: Your promise preserves my life.... I remember your ancient laws, O LORD, and I find comfort in them."

1 Corinthians 12:24–26

"God has combined the members of the body and has given greater honor to the parts that lacked it, so that there should be no division in the body, but that its parts should have equal concern for each other. If one part suffers, every part suffers with it; if one part is honored, every part rejoices with it."

After prayer, he learned that the man from Texas lived in the same town as his widowed mother. The man requesting prayer now realized God was inviting him to become a comforter to the mother of the man who just prayed for him. The one comforted now had the opportunity to go home and become a comforter.

➡ **5. Read the verses in the margin, and underline the words describing times or ways God comforts people.**

God comforts those who mourn, those who are downcast, those who are facing death, and those who suffer. His presence and guidance comfort people. His promises and "ancient laws" (His Word) comfort people. God places members in the body of Christ to show concern for other members. When one needs comfort, God uses other members to provide it.

➡ **6. Think about your experiences of God's comfort. What are some times or ways God has comforted you? Use the list on the left below to help you remember times or circumstances when God provided comfort to you. Write notes to the right about your own experiences of God's comfort.**

Possible Circumstances	Your Experiences of God's Comfort
• abandonment	_____
• business failure	_____
• death of a loved one	_____
• discrimination	_____
• disability	_____
• financial crisis	_____
• homelessness	_____
• hunger	_____
• illness of a family member	_____
• invalid parent or family member	_____
• loss of a job	_____
• personal illness	_____
• physical, mental, sexual abuse	_____
• sexual or racial harassment	_____
• victim of a crime	_____
• victim of natural disaster	_____
• victim of slander or gossip	_____
• wayward or rebellious child	_____

➡ **7. Suppose you had been comforted by God as you faced a circumstance in the column on the left below. Match it with the kind of person God might use you to comfort in the column on the right. Write a letter beside each number.**

You Were Comforted by God When:	God May Use You to Comfort:
___ 1. spouse died	a. coworker who was laid off job
___ 2. child had cancer	b. church member who filed for bankruptcy
___ 3. teen ran away	c. man whose wife died
___ 4. lost your job	d. family whose child has leukemia
___ 5. rejected because of race	e. lonely person in a nursing home
___ 6. were lonely	f. young black man who feels rejected by society
___ 7. needed financial help	g. parents whose child has disappeared

When God comforts you, that's preparation to be used by God to help others in similar circumstances. (Answers: 1-c; 2-d; 3-g; 4-a; 5-f; 6-e; 7-b)

When God comforts you, that's preparation to be used by God to help others in similar circumstances.

➡ **8. Based on the ways God has comforted you (#6 above), what are some of the kinds of people God may use you to comfort? Describe some of the kinds of people on the next page.**

_____

_____

➡ **9. Are you going through a trial, time of trouble, or suffering right now where you sense that you need to be comforted?** ❏ yes ❏ no

➡ **10. If yes, briefly describe the trouble or trial you're experiencing.**

_____

_____

➡ **What, if anything, do you sense God has said to you through today's lesson? Write _one_ of the most meaningful things He has said below.**

_____

_____

➡ **Conclude today's lesson by praying.**
- Ask God to reveal to you specific people He wants you to minister to by giving comfort.
- If you need to be comforted yourself, ask the God of all comfort to comfort you through His presence, His Word, and His people.
- Ask Him to help you be willing to receive the comfort from whatever source He may choose to provide it.

LESSON 4 FINAL COURSE REVIEW

Scripture for Meditation
"As iron sharpens iron, so one man sharpens another" (Proverbs 27:17).

A Beginning Prayer
Father, I've been sharpened by the small-group process with other men. Thank You for using them in my life. I pray You will continue to guide me in the ministry of reconciliation for Your glory. Amen.

➡ **Read and think about the Scripture for Meditation in the left margin, and begin the lesson with prayer.**

❖ ❖ ❖

Our study is winding down. Now let's review what we've been studying.

➡ **1. Why did Jesus pray that His followers would have complete unity?**

So that the world would believe _____

_____

➡ **2. What's the basis for our unity?**

_____

➡ **3. What's the primary root sin of racism and sectarianism?**

_____

➡ **4. Name _two or more_ biblical illustrations of our unity as God's people.**

_____   _____

_____   _____

➡ 5. See if you can list the eight principles of reconciliation and unity. Then see if you can number them in the proper order. Write the number for each principle in the box. Check your work on page 159.

Principle ☐ _____

Principle ☐ _____

Principle ☐ _____

Principle ☐ _____

Principle ☐ _____

Principle ☐ _____

Principle ☐ _____

Principle ☐ _____

➡ 6. See if you can quote your Scripture memory verses from memory. If you have trouble, use your memory cards, and keep reviewing them regularly.
- John 17:23: "I in them . . ."
- Ephesians 2:14: "He himself . . ."
- 2 Corinthians 5:19: "God was . . ."
- John 13:34: "A new . . ."
- Ephesians 4:3: "Make every . . ."
- Ephesians 4:15: "Speaking . . ."
- Matthew 7:12: "In everything . . ."
- Philippians 2:3–4: "Do nothing . . ."
- Colossians 3:13: "Bear with . . ."
- 1 Corinthians 12:25: "There should . . ."

➡ Conclude the lesson with prayer. Reflect on what God has said to you during the course, and talk to Him about the matters that concern you most.

LESSON 5   SEEKING GOD'S ASSIGNMENT

Scripture for Meditation

"Conduct yourselves in a manner worthy of the gospel of Christ. . . . Stand firm in one spirit, contending as one man for the faith of the gospel without being frightened in any way by those who oppose you" (Philippians 1:27–28).

A Beginning Prayer

Father, Thank You for all You have said and done in my life during this study. I pray that You will enable me to stand firm and do all You call me to do in unity with my brothers to see Christ exalted in our community and nation. Amen.

_____

_____

_____

_____

_____

_____

_____

_____

_____

_____

_____

_____

➡ **Read and think about the Scripture for Meditation in the left margin, and begin the lesson with prayer.**

❖ ❖ ❖

During this lesson, we want you to talk to the Lord about what He wants you to do next related to unity and reconciliation.

➡ **Ask the Lord to guide you as you review what He has been saying to you during this study. Ask Him what He wants you to do next.**

➡ **1. Flip back through the previous nine units, and review the end of each lesson to see what you sensed God was saying to you. See if you can get a sense of the major theme or focus of what He's been saying. After you've done this review, summarize the thoughts that seem to come through the most clearly.**

_____

_____

_____

➡ **2. How has your relationship with other members of the body of Christ been affected most during this course?**

_____

_____

➡ **3. Which of the following best describes what you've experienced during this study so far? Or write your own statement.**
- ❑ a. I already had a close and interdependent relationship with other believers.
- ❑ b. I'm beginning to grow toward interdependence, but I'm still a long way off.
- ❑ c. I've been growing and experiencing wonderful aspects of interdependence. I know the best is yet to come.

- ❑ d. Other: _____

➡ **4. Turn to page 187 in the appendixes, and read the "Intentionality Project Ideas." As you read through them, ask the Lord if you or your group need to take on any one of these or something similar. Let the Lord speak to you about anything specific He may want you to do next to see biblical reconciliation and unity experienced more broadly in your church and community. If you do sense God is giving you clear direction, write down what He's leading you to do in the margin.**

➡ **Conclude the course by praying. Share your heart with your heavenly Father about what you've learned and experienced. Talk with Him about the things you sense He's leading you to do. Ask Him to reveal anything He may want you to discuss with your group this week.**

Thank you for joining us in this work of reconciliation. May the Lord richly bless you!

HOW TO BE RECONCILED TO GOD[1]

A man's relationship with his father is basic. The benefit of a strong, affirming bond with Dad is powerful. On the other hand, the pain of a lost or nonexistent relationship with a father can last a lifetime. Insecurity and crippled relationships with others are often traced back to what wasn't gained from a loving, accepting father.

God Loves His Sons
"God so loved the world that he gave his one and only Son" (John 3:16). God's love is strong, fatherly, and complete. Men from all over the world are beginning to understand this relationship for the first time. Many of us, some for years, have been trying to gain God's approval by performance—doing good things. But it is impossible to live like God's sons before we're in a relationship with Him. A wall of separation has come between God and man. Instead of a relationship, we find a barrier. But there's good news!

Reconciliation Is Through Christ
Do you need to be reconciled? The wall that separated us from our Father God has been broken down. Reconciliation is now possible. If you're not in a family relationship with God as a son to his Father, this is your primary need. Here are some questions you may have:
• If God made me, why would I need to be reconciled?
• What happened to the original relationship?
• If I choose to stay the way I am, what are the consequences?

If you're distanced from God and His acceptance, keep reading to learn more about the relationship that's available.

What We Lost: A Relationship
Adam, the father of the human race, made a terrible choice. We, his sons, live in the aftermath of his failure. It started with an act of disobedience. He willingly joined his wife in doubting their Father's word and ignoring His instructions. Their response was not according to the design of God.

The result? Man's relationship with God was broken. In the process, he failed his wife. From then on, there were times of contention in their relationship. And as if that wasn't bad enough, the man lost his job and was kicked off the family farm. He found some temporary jobs until he could get back with his Father. But this work was cursed from the start and resulted in pain and difficulty. His family rela-tionships went from bad to worse. One of his sons even killed another! (You can read about this in Genesis 2–4.)

We've inherited a diseased spiritual DNA. It's no wonder we find failure and sin in our lives today. And by our choices we continue to exist outside a relationship with God.

This leaves us without the bonds of communion with our Father that all of us are meant to have. The ties have been cut. This alienation is described in the New Testament as being *"separate from Christ . . . without hope and without God in the world"* (Ephesians 2:12).

Most men understand accountability and consequences! If we die still alienated from God, we'll experience the horrible reality of God's judgment that man's rebel spirit has merited—eternal separation from God.

What We Need: A Restored Relationship
Jesus Christ is the only one able to restore the relationship we lost by giving us life. Because we're dead and God is alive, we must be made alive to be able to have a relationship with Him.

There's another obstacle to becoming a son of God. Men tend to be fix-it-myself people. We admit we're weak in establishing relationships. We admit we're far from perfect. We are, in fact, sinners! The problem is that our theme song is "I did it my way."

When we do it our way, we remain isolated by our own sins. We separate ourselves not only from God, but also from right relationships with our families and others. In our relationship with God, we can't be do-it-yourselfers. We can't fix what's wrong by our own efforts.

How Can the Relationship Be Restored?
Why do we need Jesus? God in human form took our place of judgment for sin to put us in His place as a son of God. On His cross, Jesus broke down the walls of isolation that sin had built.

Now we know why we can't just do a little better ourselves: *"For it is by grace you have been saved, through faith—and this not from yourselves, it is the gift of God—not by works, so that no one can boast"* (Ephesians 2:8–9).

This is what a lot of men miss! A relationship with God is a gift. We can't earn it. We can't buy it. We can't boast or feel a sense of accomplishment about achieving it. It's given out of love.

But a gift must be received: *"To all who received him, to those who believed in his name, he gave the right to become children of God"* (John 1:12). Don't be too proud to admit you need God's new life within you. This is God's way—through Jesus, the gift!

If you would like to accept this gift—eternal life in relationship with God—Jesus Christ has secured it for you. You can simply tell God. It's not the exact words but the attitude of your heart that matters.

Pray to Accept or Reaffirm Your Acceptance of Christ:

Father, I've come home. Please make me Your son. I turn from my sin. I accept Your forgiveness made possible through Jesus Christ by His death and resurrection. I place my faith and trust in Jesus Christ alone. I receive Him as my Savior and Lord. I want to follow and serve You. Let today be the beginning of my new journey as Your son and a member of Your family. You've always kept Your promises. Help me to keep my promises, too. In Jesus' name. Amen.

[1]Adapted from "Promise Keepers Evangelism Plan" (Denver: Promise Keepers, 1996).

The Expectations of My Relationship with God

As you begin to live with integrity as God's son, the dynamic reality of this new relationship will be known by you . . .
- in your confidence of eternal life (1 John 5:13);
- in open communication through prayer (1 John 3:21–23);
- in closeness to God through His Spirit (Romans 8:16–17);
- in having the Holy Spirit within (2 Corinthians 1:21–22)

and by others around you . . .
- through your changed life (2 Corinthians 5:17);
- through your focus on God and others (Mark 12:30–31);
- through your promise keeping (Ephesians 4:25).

Steps for Follow-Through:

1. Read your Bible each day.
2. Talk to God in prayer each day.
3. Go to a church that believes and teaches the Bible, and tell the pastor of your commitment to Jesus.
4. Share your decision with a close friend (your wife if you're married).
5. Find a small group of Christian men to help you grow in your faith.
6. Drop a note to Promise Keepers to let us know. Write to Promise Keepers, P. O. Box 101651, Denver, CO 80250-1651.

KEY STATEMENTS OF PROMISE KEEPERS

PURPOSE STATEMENT

Promise Keepers is a Christ-centered ministry dedicated to uniting men through vital relationships to become godly influences in their world.

PROMISE KEEPERS STATEMENT OF FAITH

1. We believe that there is one God eternally existing in three persons: the Father, the Son, and the Holy Spirit.

2. We believe that the Bible is God's written revelation to man and that it is verbally inspired, authoritative, and without error in the original manuscripts.

3. We believe in the deity of Jesus Christ, His virgin birth, sinless life, miracles, death on the cross to provide for our redemption, bodily resurrection and ascension into heaven, present ministry of intercession for us, and His return to earth in power and glory.

4. We believe in the personality and deity of the Holy Spirit, that He performs the miracle of new birth in an unbeliever and indwells believers, enabling them to live a godly life.

5. We believe that man was created in the image of God, but because of sin, was alienated from God. Only through faith, trusting in Christ alone for salvation which was made possible by His death and resurrection, can that alienation be removed.

SEVEN PROMISES OF A PROMISE KEEPER

1. A Promise Keeper is committed to honor Jesus Christ through worship, prayer, and obedience to His Word in the power of the Holy Spirit.

2. A Promise Keeper is committed to pursue vital relationships with a few other men, understanding that he needs brothers to help him keep his promises.

3. A Promise Keeper is committed to practice spiritual, moral, ethical, and sexual purity.

4. A Promise Keeper is committed to build strong marriages and families through love, protection, and biblical values.

5. A Promise Keeper is committed to support the mission of his church by honoring and praying for his pastor and by actively giving his time and resources.

6. A Promise Keeper is committed to reach beyond any racial and denominational barriers to demonstrate the power of biblical unity.

7. A Promise Keeper is committed to influence his world, being obedient to the Great Commandment (Mark 12:30–31) and the Great Commission (Matthew 28:19–20).

The Great Commandment

" 'Love the Lord your God with all your heart and with all your soul and with all your mind and with all your strength.' The second is this: 'Love your neighbor as yourself.' There is no commandment greater than these" (Mark 12:30–31).

The Great Commission

"Go and make disciples of all nations, baptizing them in the name of the Father and of the Son and of the Holy Spirit, and teaching them to obey everything I have commanded you. And surely I am with you always, to the very end of the age" (Matthew 28:19–20).

BIBLICAL UNITY AND BIBLICAL TRUTH
A Necessary Tension

"For he himself is our peace, who has made the two one and has destroyed the barrier, the dividing wall of hostility" (Ephesians 2:14).

Unity—a beautiful word, a powerful ideal, a biblical concept. Regrettably, through the years. confusion has developed in the church over it, and what was meant to be a glorious reality has become an elusive, fleeting, and divisive dream. On one extreme stand those determined to achieve unity at any cost; on the other, those who claim that any pursuit of unity comes at the expense of truth. Truth and unity have come to be viewed by many as antithetical—you can align with one or the other, but not with both. Promise Keepers believes Scripture teaches that this is a false dichotomy and that the Word of God commands us, and the love of God compels us, to pursue both.[1]

While regional splits have always existed within the church, from its founding and for the first one thousand years, there was but one recognized church. When errors of teaching were discovered, they were addressed, and various church councils were called to deal with doctrinal disputes over important issues such as the nature of God and the deity of Christ. The first major division took place in A.D. 1054, resulting in the Eastern Orthodox and the Roman Catholic Churches. A little more than 500 years later, another fracture occurred, leading to the creation of the Protestant church. Protestantism, in turn, has experienced the formation of a myriad of denominations and sects, each intending in its own way to maintain the purity of the gospel and to uphold biblical Christianity.

Since its inception, with varying degrees of intensity, the issue of unity has been an ongoing matter of discussion within the church. In the late 1800s and early 1900s, the controversy began to focus on what has been called the Ecumenical Movement. Intending a broad-based reunification, the movement was plagued by one major difficulty: the idea that church unity should be achieved "at any cost" — to the extent of sacrificing the essential truths of the Word of God. Opposition arose from individuals, churches, and denominations committed to the defense and proclamation of the truth, generally dividing the church into what have come to be known as "liberal" and "conservative" camps. This division persists in our day, with those on one side of the issue perceived as willing to pursue love apart from truth, compromising the integrity of the gospel message, and those on the other side viewed as defending the truth of God's Word at the expense of love, often leading to coldness, arrogance, and pride.

In view of this history, and in spite of the difficulties involved, Promise Keepers believes the Lord is calling Christian men to denominational reconciliation in our day. The ministry has, therefore, sought to find a common ground upon which all Christians can unite—one it believes to be entirely biblical and consistent with the will of Christ for His church. Simply stated, Promise Keepers believes: *We must be committed to truth, and we must also be committed to unity.*

Theologians call it an antinomy—two truths which at times seem to be in conflict, but which nonetheless are equally true. In obedience to God and His Word, we do not believe one should be sacrificed for the other. Each is vital to accomplishing God's purposes. We believe He calls us to pursue *both*. Therefore, while Promise Keepers desires to call men of all Christian denominations together in biblical unity, that unity must be based on the historically essential truths of Christianity.

Doctrine, right belief—it is the core and essence of Promise Keepers. Everything we do is guided and informed by biblical doctrine. Realizing that any doctrinal stand has the potential to divide, the ministry nonetheless believes that such a stand is not inconsistent with the love of Christ. Indeed, Promise Keepers seeks to reflect Christ as He embodies the truth and love of God. While recognizing that our ultimate unity has been accomplished by our Lord through His death on the cross, we believe the sectarianism that characterizes the church is hurting the cause of Christ. We feel compelled, therefore, to call believers together according to our highest common denominators—faith in Christ and the truth of God's Word. Our pursuit of unity, then, is based on a core theology of historic doctrines of the church, which is represented by our statement of faith.

At a time when surveys indicate that up to 42 percent of those who call themselves evangelical Christians believe that there is no such thing as absolute truth,[2] Promise Keepers takes the stand that the Bible is the inspired, inerrant, infallible Word of God (2 Timothy 3:16). Although some are troubled by the subject of inerrancy, we believe that everything hinges upon it. If God, who is without error, is not able to reveal Himself through the written Word in an inerrant fashion, how can we trust His revelation through His Living Word, Jesus Christ? If we believe the Bible has errors, we place ourselves above it, determining for ourselves what is and is not truth. But if the Bible is the infallible revelation of Almighty God, then we must place ourselves under it, even though our understanding may be incomplete.

Nor do we believe that it is enough just to call men to worship God. The Word of God says we are to worship Him in spirit *and* in truth (John 4:24). We do not want men to have their emotions merely stirred by Christian music or to worship the experience of worship. Our desire is for the men who attend Promise Keepers conferences to worship the true and living God of the universe, the one who created all things and is sovereign over all. Our question for every man is, are you worshipping some vague idea of God or the God revealed in the Bible who eternally exists in three persons—the

NOTES

STATEMENT ON DENOMINATIONAL RECONCILIATION

Father, Son, and Holy Spirit? *This* is the God we believe in and the one we want men to meet.

Some just want to lift up Jesus, believing that in so doing, all men will be drawn to Him. But this will only happen if the *authentic, biblical* Jesus is exalted (Galatians 1:6–9). Only a clear understanding of God's Word will lead men to exalt the Jesus who is God of very God; the Jesus who took on human flesh, was born of a virgin, lived a sinless life, and died on the cross, making atonement for our sins; the Jesus who was buried, rose again on the third day, was seen by many witnesses, has ascended on high, sits at the right hand of God the Father, and intercedes for us; the Jesus who is going to return in power and great glory to judge the world. *This* is the Jesus we are exalting and teaching.

Men need to understand the person and work of the Holy Spirit. He has birthed us anew in Christ and has come to fill us with power to live a godly life (Acts 1:8). He is not simply some impersonal "force" that men can call upon to fulfill every whim, but He is the third Person of the Trinity who indwells believers, enabling them to walk in obedience and holiness, and in the Word and will of the Father (John 16:13). *This* is the Holy Spirit we want men to understand and experience.

An alarming percentage of those who claim to be born again believe they can get to heaven by good works. However, the Bible tells us that salvation is not by works, but by faith in Jesus Christ *alone*: *"For it is by grace you have been saved, through faith— and this not from yourselves, it is the gift of God—not of works, so that no one can boast"* (Ephesians 2:8–9). Salvation is by grace alone, through faith alone, in Christ alone. When we stand before Almighty God and He says, "Why should I let you into My perfect heaven?" the only answer is, "Because I have trusted in Your Son, Jesus Christ, who paid the penalty for my sin on the cross at Calvary."

The above five tenets form the core beliefs in our statement of faith. We believe they provide a firm biblical foundation upon which Christians can join together and live out the unity called for in John 17:22–23, where Jesus prayed to the Father, *"I have given them the glory that you gave me, that they may be one as we are one. . . . May they be brought to complete unity to let the world know that you sent me and have loved them even as you have loved me."*

With the apostle Paul, we implore all men who share a common faith in the biblical Jesus to *"live a life worthy of the calling you have received. Be completely humble and gentle; be patient, bearing with one another in love. Make every effort to keep the unity of the Spirit through the bond of peace"* (Ephesians 4:1–3). For too long now, the church has allowed its differences to divide it, preventing it from ministering effectively and from displaying the

BIBLICAL UNITY AND BIBLICAL TRUTH

glory God intended for it. As a consequence, the church has lost its "saltiness."

Is it not terrible to realize that by overemphasizing our differences, we have actually served to hinder the Father's answer to our Lord's prayer for oneness in the church, as well as our witness to the lost? If, after all, Christians can't love and embrace one another, expressing the oneness that is already ours in Christ, the world will rightfully question the validity—and the value—of our faith. *"By this all men will know that you are my disciples, if you love one another,"* Jesus proclaimed (John 13:35). Furthermore, as Jesus' prayer in John 17 indicates, while division and divisiveness are "natural" in this life, there's something *supernatural* about unity that even the ungodly can recognize. When Christians merely display the love of Christ to each other, the world knows that God sent Jesus, and He receives the glory due His name. Biblical unity, then, is one of the most powerful testimonies that exists to the reality of God.

"How good and pleasant it is when brothers live together in unity!" (Psalm 133:1). At Promise Keepers, we are not preoccupied with a man's denominational label, nor do we wish to see all church distinctives disappear. Rather, we are committed to calling Christian men to reach beyond labels and to enter into vital relationship with each other based on our common faith in Jesus Christ. Through loving relationship, we can demonstrate to a hopelessly divisive world that, by God's grace, men can live peacefully together in spite of their differences. This way, we can also know if a man holds to the core doctrines of God's Word. If he does, we are brothers in Christ. If not, we may be used by God to lead him to the knowledge of the truth. As it has been said, "In essentials, unity. In nonessentials, liberty. In all things, charity."

Many are grateful for and committed to their denominational affiliation and heritage—and rightfully so. But while it is vital to fight for truth, the day has come when we must not allow ourselves to be separated by sectarian labels and secondary issues. At a time when only approximately 10 percent of the world's 5 billion people are professing Christians, and when Christianity is under attack on virtually every side, it is imperative for us to reach out to one another in love and unity. While respecting our differences, we must come together in relationship, ensuring that each man is trusting in the finished work of Christ for his salvation, thereby receiving God's gift of eternal life and becoming a fellow member of God's family. To continue down the road (or roads) we have been traveling is to court further divisiveness, disunity, loss of witness, and disaster.

Finally, it is truth—the truth of Christ—to which we call all men, and it is in this truth that we can find biblical unity—unity in truth. When we stand before Jesus in the Judgment Day, we believe those who strive for this ideal will hear the words, *"Well done, good and faithful servant.*" For our Savior's sake, for His glory, and that the world will know that God sent Him, we can do no less.

As fellow members of His church, we need each other,

> "*. . . so that the body of Christ may be built up until we all reach unity in the faith and in the knowledge of the Son of God and become mature, attaining to the whole measure of the fullness of Christ*" (Ephesians 4:12–13).

NOTES

---

[1](Ps. 119:9,160; Ps. 133; Jn. 4:24; 10:16; 17:17–23; Acts 2:1,42; 20:29–31; Rom. 12:4–5; 15:4–7; 1 Cor. 1:10; 12:12–13; 2 Cor. 13:11; Gal. 3:26–28; Eph. 2:14–18; 4:1–16; Phil, 1:27; 2:1–5; 2 Tim. 2:15; 3:16; 1 Pet. 3:8; 1 Jn. 4)

[2]George Barna, *Virtual America: The Barna Report 1994-95* (Ventura, Cal.: Regal Books, 1994). Used by permission.

SENSITIVITY BUILDERS

A HISPANIC PERSPECTIVE
by Jesse Miranda

(Jesse Miranda is associate dean of urban/multi-cultural affairs at Azusa Pacific University and serves on the board of directors for Promise Keepers.)

Hispanic Diversity

Being culturally relevant to historical distinctives and cultural traits of Hispanics will help you as you begin building relationships. First, you need to understand some terms used for this group. Some use the term *Hispanic*, while others use the term *Latino*. The majority of the Hispanic community is from Latin America—especially Mexico. *Latino* refers to immigrants from Latin America. This term tends to exclude those from the Caribbean and from Spain. The term *Hispanic* is more inclusive, since all these people trace their roots to Spain.

It's also important to know Hispanics in terms of how long they've been in this country. There are the recent arrivals; some are resident and others are not. Then there are the assimilating Hispanics who have one or two generations of residency. And finally, many Hispanics have totally assimilated into mainstream America and have little in common with the recent arrivals. The important point here is to understand that there is great diversity even within the Hispanic population.

Another aspect of diversity among Hispanics is the national origin of their ancestors. Hispanics from Cuba are culturally different from Hispanics from Mexico or Puerto Rico. Hispanics from a South American country are different from those from Spain.

One way of better understanding Hispanics is to make some contrasts with those of the mainstream population. Although these are generalizations, they offer some insight into Hispanic life.

Task vs. Relationship

Anglo Americans think and talk in terms of "doing." Most Hispanics think in terms of "being." Anglos focus more on tasks, while Hispanics focus more on relationships. Take, for example, a conversation between people who have never met. An Anglo might introduce himself by saying, "Hi, I'm John Doe. I'm a lawyer from Beverly Hills." He sees his identity related to what he does (he's a lawyer) and has achieved (he lives in Beverly Hills).

A Hispanic might introduce himself by saying, "Hola, I am Juan, the son of Don Jose from the town of Morelos." He sees his identity related to who he is in relationship to others. He's a son (of Don Jose), and he comes from a community of people (the town of Morelos). His sense of identity comes from his roots.

Cultural Differences

Hispanic culture normally values functions differently from the mainstream culture in America. This chart points to some of the differences.

Anglo Culture	Hispanic Culture
1. Truth	1. Honor (acceptance)
2. Accuracy	2. Relationship
3. Individualism	3. Community (family)
4. Precision	4. Courtesy, gallantry
5. Blame	5. Compromise
6. Repayment	6. Resentment

The fact that something is of cultural value does not make it right, but it helps develop understanding and respect for one another. Any effort toward reconciliation must include some knowledge of the other person's cultural values.

Methods of Communication

Suppose Jim, Amed, and Jose get together in an accountability group. They enjoy open discussions about their goals in life and confess their shortcomings to one another. Jim and Amed wonder, however, why Jose is reluctant to participate openly in the discussions. Jim, who is white, and Amed, an African American, don't understand that Jose's family circle is where he discusses his personal matters, and he's less experienced in open discussion with people outside his family.

Or suppose John (white) is planning a meeting, and he invites Juan (Hispanic) to attend.

John: "We have a meeting coming up at the end of the month. Are you coming?"
Juan: "Yes, I'll be there."

At the end of the month, Juan does not show up and John is disappointed and does not understand. John places high value on accuracy and truth, and he took Juan's words at face value.

Juan's values are placed on the relationship. He may or may not have intended to attend the meeting, but he wants to maintain John as a friend. Because he values the friendship, Juan gave John the "Hispanic polite yes." He didn't want to embarrass John or hurt his feelings by saying he wouldn't attend. The way to assure that Juan comes to the meeting would be to follow up and even perhaps pick him up for the meeting. These actions would emphasize the importance of the relationship.

These illustrations show the way different values and cultural emphases may affect relationships. If you don't know the differences, you will experience confusion that can cause misunderstanding. Here's a simple contrast between Hispanic and Anglo communication styles.

Anglo Communication
1. Direct (active voice)
2. Confrontational
3. First person
4. Straightforward
5. Logical

Hispanic Communication
1. Indirect (passive voice)
2. Accommodating
3. Third person (indefinite)
4. Relational
5. Harmonious

Anglo Americans prefer direct forms of communication. But this method comes across as blunt, rude, and brash to those cultures who prefer the indirect method of communication. Anglos seek to correct a mistake or set the record straight, whereas Hispanics may use an indirect method such as silence to react to a situation or preserve honor. Their response, however, may be interpreted as deceitful or dishonest by others.

Hispanics see a continuity between the person and an idea communicated. While the freedom to criticize ideas and behavior is acceptable in directness, Hispanics believe that to criticize the idea and/or behavior is to criticize the person. No distinction exists between the person and the idea.

AN AFRICAN-AMERICAN PERSPECTIVE
by Rodney L. Cooper

(Rodney Cooper is national director of education for Promise Keepers. He has served as associate professor at Denver Seminary and has written two books: *We Stand Together* and *Double Bind*. The following text is adapted from *We Stand Together* by Rodney L. Cooper. Copyright 1995, Rodney L. Cooper. Moody Press. Used by Permission. 47-59.)

A few years ago, a researcher performed an experiment using carp and a glass plate. Several carp swam in a tank of clear water, with a large plate of glass dividing the aquarium's middle. The experiment consisted of some food being placed on the other side of the glass plate—food that was very desirable to the carp.

Every time the carp tried to reach the food, they didn't see the glass and so swam full speed into it, only to be stopped by the solid but invisible object. This went on for several days, with the carp finally "wising up"; they saw the food but stopped trying to reach it. After about a week, the glass plate was removed from the tank so that the food would now be accessible to the fish. An interesting phenomenon happened. Every time the carp would head for the food, they would stop just short of it and not get it. Although they were hungry and the glass plate had been removed, they still operated as if the glass were there. Their past experiences kept them from attaining what was now readily available.

The Power of the Past
If a child grows up in a closed family system—a system marked by a pervading sense of unacceptability—he or she will be influenced in a notably negative way. Consider the likely outcomes in social relations, status, and security:

Social Relations
1. The world is seen as a hostile, unsociable, closed place.
2. Most people are considered unfriendly and uninterested in personal relationships.
3. The child begins to dislike and avoid close companionship with certain others.

Status
1. The world is seen as a competitive place full of prejudice and discrimination, with little opportunity.
2. Most people are perceived to be treated with unequal fairness and respect, and their strengths and personal worth go unnoticed by others.
3. The child feels little worth, and his strengths are unrecognized by others.

Security
1. The world is viewed as a harmful place that's unpredictable and full of worry and incertitude.
2. Most people are thought to be untrustworthy.
3. The child mistrusts the motives of others.

In American society, dominated by the Euro-American, white majority, most members of minority races feel and often have been treated as though they have been raised in a closed family system. They believe the world is hostile and unsociable, a competitive place full of prejudice and discrimination. They believe that most people can't be trusted. And they act according to this closed-system viewpoint. In addition, many minority men have grown up in families dominated by a closed system. Thus, both society and their families of origin have given them a restricted and negative view of their world.

A Sense of Shame

As a counselor and psychologist, I have found that anybody, regardless of race, who comes from a closed system will have a profound sense of insecurity and inferiority—in essence, a sense of shame. If the family is in disarray, the schools are poor, and the neighborhood is unsafe, then everywhere the individual looks, he will see reasons to not trust or not feel trustworthy. In contrast, if his childhood environment is stable and positive, the family whole and loving, the schools good, and the community stable and safe, he will believe in himself and have confidence.

I'm not saying that one cannot overcome a difficult childhood, but a mind-set is established in childhood about whether we can approach the world with confidence—a strong self-image—or with shame and doubt—a poor self-image.

Every man has an innate capacity for insecurity. But our experiences can expand and deepen that tendency to feel insecure. The experiences of black people as a whole—indeed, of most minorities—have ingrained a deepened sense of doubt, shame, and inferiority upon their minds. We feel shame for what we are. People feel guilt because they did something wrong, but people feel shame because they *are* something wrong.

Among black people, social shame has existed for a long time, tracing all the way back to the slave days in the early 1800s. Social shame is when one group is despised and rejected by another. Most minorities endure the stigma of skin color, an easy way for the majority culture to label the minority. And skin color is perhaps most obvious within the black race, since all minorities are being compared against the white-skin majority. The condition of being black in America means that one is likely to endure more wounds to one's self-esteem than others, and that the capacity for shame and doubt born of these wounds will be compounded and expanded by the black race's reputation for inferiority based upon past experiences.

Abandoning the Stereotypes

If you are a nonblack, your past family experiences have influenced your attitudes toward blacks. In many cases, nonblacks have not had direct contact with African Americans. If that's your case, you probably have picked up stereotypes from your family, friends, television, movies, and newspapers. The stereotypes help you classify a group of men you don't know. They also let you lump together people who are unique.

The solution to this unfair generalizing is to get to know African Americans by spending time with them in different settings. Research has shown that attitudes about other races do not change by legislation but by relationships. Only through the context of relationships will we be able to overcome the stereotypes that have kept us apart.

Generally speaking, this is a process and will take time. We must recognize that our cultural experiences are a part of who we are—not all of who we are. Every man shares common human experiences and feelings. We must also realize we are relating to an individual—not the total race—whose personal experiences make him one of a kind. Thus, we should treat each person as unique.

For reconciliation to occur between black men and white men, I offer the following dos and don'ts for nonblacks, especially my white brothers as they cross over to the black man's turf.

Dos

1. Do assume blacks are human, with individual feelings, aspirations, and attitudes. Sometimes there's a tendency on the part of whites to make generalizations or to say, "Well, you're an exception." No, I am me.
2. Do assume blacks have a heritage of which they are proud. Even though the history books don't record many of the accomplishments of blacks, there are actually many to celebrate. Recognize them and celebrate them.
3. Do assume blacks are angry. Everyday experiences remind the black man that he is not acceptable. Anger is an ever-present emotion in a black man.
4. Whiteness/blackness is a real difference, but not the basis on which to determine behavior. It's true, people are different in skin color, but that's where we must stop. All people have the same needs and desires to live a good life. We must not look at a person's behavior as indicative of an entire race but of that person only.
5. Do assume most blacks can handle whites' authentic behavior and feelings. Blacks value openness and authenticity. Do not try to "identify" by taking on mannerisms of the black person, but be yourself and be open to learn. Be authentic.
6. Do assume blacks want reconciliation. Blacks want harmony to exist in the body of Christ. Reconciliation means we value each other equally. Blacks desire this greatly.
7. Do assume that you may be part of the problem. Take time for self-reflection, and see if there are any negative attitudes or unhealthy stereotypes that could keep reconciliation from happening.

Don'ts

1. Don't assume color is unimportant in interpersonal relationships. Color has distinguished the

black man as the scapegoat in our society. Just because it has not been an impediment to you does not mean it's not an issue.

2. Don't assume blacks will always welcome and appreciate inclusion in white society. Expect to be met with suspicion when you approach a black man. In years past, blacks have been included because of guilt and not on their terms. Sometimes blacks have felt included as an afterthought. So there may be resistance.

3. Don't assume white society is superior to black society. Instead, the two are different. For instance, many blacks are event-oriented rather than time-oriented. Event-oriented individuals usually go somewhere with the attitude "When we get started we start—and we end when we end." In contrast, a time-oriented individual begins and ends with time as the issue. Neither perspective is right or wrong; they're just different. However, if a black man is "late," he is seen as undependable by the majority culture. Instead of judgment, we need acceptance of differences as simply being that—difference in cultural behavior.

4. Don't assume blacks are oversensitive. Instead, blacks strongly support what they believe. That's how it should be—every man a strong advocate for his position. I have taught in a seminary where most of my students are white. I remember presenting a position on an issue with passion. I was not committed to the position, but I presented it with zeal to stimulate class discussion. No one asked a question for fear they would be shot down. I explained to the class that most blacks come across as advocates for their position. This gets things out on the table to discuss.

AN ASIAN-AMERICAN PERSPECTIVE
by Bruce Fong

(Bruce Fong is a professor at Multnomah Bible Seminary and is author of *Racial Equality in the Church* [Lanham, MD: University Press of America, 1996].)

My first memory scar of racism happened while I was just a youngster in California. On a hot Sacramento summer day, my parents dropped off my brothers and me at a public pool. We stayed until closing time. In the shower rooms, most people had already left. As my brothers and I were putting our gear together, three much older white teens confronted us. The taunts, the mockery, the derision, and the name-calling had an awful effect on me. I was frozen in place. My knees turned to jelly. And I couldn't understand the reason for such verbal abuse. I thought we were in for the beating of our lives. Then, there was a change. The

boys abruptly stopped their vicious barrage and melted away out of the locker room. A presence behind me made me turn. There an adult white male had his eyes fixed on the exit where those boys had disappeared. Without addressing us, he sternly declared, "Trash! They are just trash." As our champion picked up his bag and left, my two brothers and I followed close behind him.

I learned two things that day. The world is populated by two kinds of people: racists and champions. Racists take every opportunity to live a life of hatred and abuse. They attempt to dominate others through intimidation. Champions use the very same opportunities and issues to help others. They use their position and values in life to aid those who are victims of racial hatred.

The Value of Asian-American Friendships
The Asian-American experience includes its share of mistreatment. History records those difficult episodes. But it is not as volatile or painful as the history of African and Native Americans. Yet, as with other ethnic minorities, seeing America through Asian eyes may be a big step in the right direction for further reconciliation on a personal level.

Asian-American friendships can provide a helpful transition in the arena of racial reconciliation. If you are white or black, you may find that a friendship with an Asian American can be a valuable first step in cross-cultural relationships, a bridge to more difficult areas of reconciliation.

As you consider a friendship with an Asian American, keep in mind that programs and official functions or events will be limited in their effect. Something longer lasting requires not a single meeting or the creation of a new position, but a commitment to building a meaningful relationship. Friendships are a vital part of the Asian-American identity, though a depth of intimacy may be slow to develop in the early stages of these friendships.

Be sensitive to the cost to an Asian-American friend. Blacks who engage in reconciliation endeavors with whites are called "Oreos." Asian Americans are called "bananas"—yellow on the outside and white on the inside. Asians who are closer to their cultural roots call fellow Asians involved with reconciliation "Jooksing." It is loosely translated as "bamboo." The derision is in the fact that bamboo is hollow on the inside. It has end caps but nothing in between—no culture, no traditions, no history. Those willing to pay the cost of being your friend will be friends of great value.

Differences in Generations
When I left the West Coast and moved to Texas to attend

seminary, I was warned by several fellow Asian Americans about life in the South. I went to an early new-student reception and met many new people. One couple and I struck up a friendly conversation. After a number of pleasant topics, I was faced with an inquiry. With a distinctly southern drawl and innocent spirit, this fellow student's wife asked me, "Now, Bruce, tell me, what part of China are you from?"

I took advantage of the situation to inject a little humor mixed with some new information. I responded, "I'm from one of the far eastern provinces called California. And I was born in a village called Sacramento."

"Oh, Bruce, I am so embarrassed!" she said as we laughed together.

Asian Americans define their ethnic identity within the tension of two elements. One factor is their closeness to their cultural roots. The other is the inevitability of assimilation of the surrounding culture. The influence of these factors varies during life and according to individual experiences.

The closer an Asian American is to the generation of his forebears who immigrated to the United States, the more closely tied he is to his cultural roots. The further he is from those original immigrants, the more he will reflect American culture in speech, choices, and values. Thus, intentionally building a relationship with an Asian American should begin by understanding what generation he belongs to.

Most Asians find it awkward to be asked, "What are you?" or "Where do you come from?" It is more beneficial to be asked, "What generation are you?" This kind of intentional inquiry shows an understanding of the great tension experienced by Asians in this country. Expectations, stereotypes, and limitations by the majority white society are still common. In starting a relationship with an Asian American, you might ask questions like:
- What country did your ancestors emigrate from? When did they immigrate?
- What generation are you from the first immigrants to this country?

The generational issues among Asians can perhaps be best understood by looking at their use of language. Those of the immigration generation are usually tied to their culture and Asian identity through their speech. Their mother tongue is their primary expression. Those of the second generation—that is, the first generation born in America—grow up bilingual. They speak their mother tongue at home, largely at the insistence of their parents. But they speak English at school, in the shops, with their friends, and at work. The third and subsequent generations use English as their primary language. Except for a few phrases, the mother tongue is not a daily practice. This is inevitable. It has little or nothing to do with one's loyalty to one's culture. Those outside the Asian realm who understand this phenomenon will be far more successful in building relationships with Asian Americans.

The Pain of Racism
Every ethnic minority group in America has experienced the pain and scars of racism. Many continue to receive fresh wounds today. The hurt from racism is more than an inconvenience in the day's schedule. It's more than a thoughtless or even a naively spoken word. Rather, it is a deep hurt that humiliates and strips a person of his human dignity. Every Asian group that has come to America has experienced the pain of rejection and isolation. Those experiences taint the context of trust and intimate relationships. An ethnic minority is either prepared for racial tension or suspicious that it is lurking behind a new face. Most of us have been hit too hard too many times to be caught unawares.

Sensitivity to an Asian American will require that you understand he has real hurts due to racial injustices and prejudices that have occurred in his life. Ignoring those or joking about them will keep you from a meaningful relationship. Take time to build trust and accept feelings as real and important.

Valued for Their Contribution, Not Quotas
I desire to be valued as a contributing team member. A relationship is not gratifying if I am perceived as a token minority; but I can thrive as a contributing member of an organization, company, or ministry team. In the heart of every Asian American is the same passion that drives any person. It's a desire to be valued for his genuine contribution.

Tokenism compounds the problem of racial tension. If impersonal quotas become the basis of a relationship, reconciled relationships will seldom be achieved. Minorities are well versed in patronizing attitudes that feel safe once quotas are reached.

If you choose to build a friendship with an Asian American, do it because you anticipate he will make a valuable contribution to your life. Let him assume a position of influence in your life and there will be mutual benefit.

American-born Asians are often gifted individuals. But they can be overlooked in churches that haven't taken the time to know, relate to, and value individual members of the body. Because of a humble spirit, many Asian Americans will not assert themselves. Without the rest of the body's encouragement, they may remain quietly on the sidelines when they could make significant contributions.

In the local church and in Christian organizations, actively discover Asian Americans who have the gifts and capabilities to serve in meaningful ways. This is not an advocacy for affirmative action, where quotas are the driving force, but a recognition of how God has gifted individuals by His Spirit to benefit the body of Christ as a whole. Find value in their service, and cheer them on to continued ministry.

A NATIVE-AMERICAN PERSPECTIVE
by Huron Claus

(Huron Claus is North American Director for C.H.I.E.F. Ministries in Phoenix, Arizona.)

In the early 1970s, a book was published titled *Bury My Heart at Wounded Knee.* The words of the writer ripped out the hearts of readers as he unfolded the picture of the history of the Native American people during the Indian Wars with the U. S. Government in the 1800s. Stories were told of many Indian tribes and the intentional efforts to diminish and even exterminate them and take their land. It was a book that stirred the soul of America.

A fire of anger toward the past was ignited in the hearts of our native youth in the early 1970s. Almost 100 years after these injustices and atrocities took place, a strong, militant voice known as A.I.M.—the American Indian Movement—trumpeted through our land. Today there is a burning that still resides in the innermost parts of our people. If you look deep in the eyes of our Native American people, you will see much pain, anger, bitterness, unforgiveness, and an unsettledness.

Looking Back at Our Legacy
It has been estimated that before Columbus came to this land, there were approximately 9 to 12 million indigenous peoples who lived here. Today there are about 1.9 million Native Americans from 515 federally recognized tribes and about 200 not yet officially recognized.

Native Americans inhabited the land from the east to the west and the north to the south. There were no land boundaries to the Native American people. They understood it wasn't their possession to keep. In the minds of our people, we were given the stewardship by the Creator God to be the keepers of the earth. That was precisely what God called Adam to do in Genesis.

At the beginning of the nineteenth century, the native population plummeted below 250,000 due to diseases and the Indian Wars. What was once the home of the Native-American people was being possessed in the name of "Manifest Destiny," until today only 4 percent of all our country belongs to the various tribes.

As I read and hear about the history of my people, my heart is broken, and tears well up inside me. I remember traveling through the Denver International Airport on my way to speak at a native men's meeting in Mission, South Dakota. I had just finished reading the chapter of *Bury My Heart at Wounded Knee* telling of the "Long Walk" of the Navajo people, and I began to cry uncontrollably. It was a journey forced by the U. S. government that starved and killed thousands of Navajo people. I have a Navajo friend who tells a story, passed down through his family, about that unforgettable walk. When the Navajos began the walk in the bitterly cold winter, they were given government-issued blankets. It was later discovered that those blankets were infested with smallpox and cholera. Thousands of Navajos died as a result. My dear friend has a beautiful Indian blanket that has been passed down as a memorial of what his people went through.

My heart breaks because I know that many of our people carry the weight of the past on themselves, and it has almost crushed them beyond hope. Only at the foot of the cross of Calvary have I found peace and rest regarding the past deeds done to my people. There I have seen Christ as our supreme example of someone crushed and rejected, bruised and despised. He cried out to the Father to forgive His tormentors through the love and power of God. There I have learned to bury my heart at Calvary.

The Road of Reconciliation
The theme of reconciliation has permeated the lifestyle and culture of the Native American people. The word that is often used in place of *reconciliation* is *unity*. There is a great desire to be in unity, or right relationship, with everything about them. Each of the 515 federally recognized Native American tribes in the U. S. is as different in its ways of life as the Germans are from the Chinese. Language is different. Styles of worship can have varying implications. Customs are different. We are not all the same, yet there's a thread of similarity that runs throughout all tribes. One point of similarity is the importance of relationships.

Relationship with Mankind
The horizontal relationship of mankind is valued by the Native American. He sees himself as part of the

whole picture rather than focusing on the individual. With this type of mind-set, our people can be easily misunderstood. I have heard it said at times that we lack initiative or are lazy. In reality, because of our communal social structure, it would be unheard of to promote oneself above others. Even in discussion, our people contemplate first before giving their opinion. Often they offer their thoughts only after being asked. When talking with a Native American brother, he may not look you directly in your eyes. This is a sign of respect, considering the relationship with others more important than oneself. Relationship to others is essential to our people.

Relationship of the Family/Tribe

The family has a high priority among our people. Each family member plays a vital role in the function of our society. You most likely are familiar with the role of the chief or tribal chairman. In some tribes, the clan's mother plays just as important a responsibility in tribal decisions as the chief. And elders are highly revered in honor of their wisdom and experience in life. To reach out to Native-American families and nations, the key is the elders. History has proved that when a Native-American elder chooses to enter relationships with outsiders, families often follow.

The tribe is also important. When you meet a Native-American brother, begin your conversation by asking him, "What tribe do you come from?" You have just communicated to him not only your interest in him ethnically as a Native American, but you also are giving him opportunity to honor his heritage by telling about his tribe. Our people are proud of their tribal heritage. Each tribe has special leaders and chiefs. Each contributes in his unique way. It's important to know your tribe within native society. It reminds me of a time when a well-intentioned lady came to me and was excited to meet a Native American. She was telling me of her interest in our people since she was a youth. She went on to say that she had Native American ancestry in her family line that she believed was from the "Chihuahua" tribe. I thought that very interesting!

As you develop a friendship with a Native American, you might begin by sincerely asking questions about the importance of relationships among his people. Share with him similar insights about your own relationships. Ask about his tribe and the history of his people. Listen to his pain, and share

with him a painful time in your life that God brought you through. Describe what you have learned by it, and ask to pray with him in his pain. Prayer is a vital part of the Native-American culture.

Building Trust

Dr. Ralph Winter once said, "The Native American people are one of the hardest people groups in the world to reach with the gospel of Jesus Christ." I believe he's right and that it is largely due to broken relationships and promises in the past. When sharing Christ with my own people, I often hear them say, "Christianity, that's the white man's gospel, the white man's religion. We have our own way of worship. We have the Native-American way." When I hear that kind of response, I understand the hurt they feel. I can even accept the hostility they demonstrate to me regarding the past. As a Christian Native American, I find the greatest challenge in my life is to be intentional in demonstrating to our people that Jesus Christ, God's Son, came to reconcile with *all* the people of the world—the Native-American people included.

Historically, more than 300 treaties were made by the U. S. government with the Native-American tribes, and few were kept. When you begin to build a relationship with our people, build it on the "potential" or on the outcome of the relationship, not on the "plight" of the people. Stay away from the stereotypes of Native Americans. Acknowledge your ignorance about native peoples, but show a desire to understand them more. When you approach your friendship with that openness and sincerity, it encourages your Native-American brother to be open in return. Understand that relationships, actions, and time are much more important than words. Allow time for trust to be developed for greater levels of brotherhood.

There's an increasing willingness of white Christians to come to Native Americans and confess the sins of the past and ask for forgiveness. Confession and repentance from the white man and forgiveness from the Native American have great potential for healing. But remember that words have proved to be shallow. Don't stop at words of confession just to ease a sense of guilt. Go on to relationships and actions. Show by your love and actions that the repentance is genuine. Value your Native-American brother and the contributions he may make to your life and faith. Move into a relationship where you both can live out reconciliation and unity in Christ.

A WHITE PERSPECTIVE
by Glen Kehrein

For people of color, race is a significant issue. But for the whites in the majority community, it's not. We think about it only when there's a problem. Even then, most whites don't understand what the big deal is. Much of today's racial insensitivity comes from ignorance rather than overt hostility. In brief, white folks just don't know—we don't understand.

As is the case in any country, most folks of the dominant culture interact little with the minority cultures. Even though legal segregation is past, racial and class separation is a reality. Many whites live in racial isolation and don't have much experience or knowledge of people of color. When racial issues become public, we may be sincerely shocked. But when such things "blow over," life returns to normal, and little thought is given to racial issues until the next incident.

God Is Moving
Today, there's a significant change in this pattern. Many white men are beginning to leave their comfort zone and reach out for reconciliation. Why? God is moving their hearts. God seeks to bring an end to racism between brothers in Christ. He has already made it possible through Christ's death on the cross. Will men of color look beyond their pain, anger, and distrust and reach out too? If you will, we can all join God in this vital work.

White guys, for the most part, don't see the depth of the issue. They don't relate to the pain of a minority, but some are trying. The response from the minority community is cool and cautious. I understand the reaction: "Here we go again. The white guy wants to do it, and I'm supposed to jump." But what if God is doing it? What if God is moving in men's hearts to reach out? I ask you to meet us halfway and lead us toward understanding.

Perhaps you've been at a Promise Keepers conference and have seen white men respond by the thousands to the call for reconciliation. Most have little understanding of what that means and know less about what to do back home. They live in suburbs and small towns, which have become isolated, homogeneous communities. But God is opening up their hearts. How many are genuine? Only God knows, but I'm sure that many are genuinely seeking to obey God and seek reconciliation. One thing is for sure: God has brought reconciliation to the front burner.

Our Way with Questions
When white people reach out to establish relationships, we do that by asking questions—Where do you work? Where do you live? What did your father do? How long have you been married? What are your hobbies? Often, people of color bristle, "Man, they are nosy!" or "What do they want to know all that for?" Or if distrust is running deep, "What are they going to do to me with this information?" As a person who crosses subcultures often, I've seen this common dynamic. White men ask questions to get to know others. Men of color shy away. But guess what? If I go to a party with a group of strangers who are white, I get the same questions. It's our ordinary way of social interaction and how we get to know each other. White folks don't have a clue that they are perceived as prying.

Superiority and Inferiority
A great issue that exists between the races in this country is superiority and inferiority. This has deep historic roots. Using the rationale of superiority, the white culture enslaved and dominated Africans and American Indians. We used it to take land from indigenous peoples, both Mexican and Indian. It is deep in the fabric of this thing called racism. But today we find only radical groups standing for and espousing this philosophy. Nevertheless, it exists just below the surface in many whites, including Christians. I believe that whites are insensitive and minorities are hypersensitive to the existence of the superiority/inferiority dynamic.

Many whites have a strong, self-confident, and take-charge manner. They have found it's the fastest way to get a job done. When they bring that take-charge spirit to cross-cultural experiences, they usually do not stop to think about how domineering it appears to men of color. They also may have a sincere heart to help meet needs. With a spirit of generosity, they may give to meet a need without stopping to think about the feelings of the receivers. They may not be sensitive to respect, dignity, and interdependence issues. We can wind up hurting men of color through our ignorance and insensitivity.

These kinds of mistakes will happen. But reconciliation demands that we work through difficulties with commitment. When we open ourselves with sincerity, we can build sensitivity and break the back of racial alienation and division. When confronted with such experiences, people of color often do one of two things: 1. Confront the whites and condemn their racism, or 2. Bury their feelings and say nothing.

The first response leaves whites bewildered and frustrated. It can eventually lead to anger: "No matter what I do, it's never enough!" The second response leaves a false sense of relationship and creates a distance that's not understood.

For bridge-building to work, people of color must be willing to "speak the truth in love." Truth without love can be brutal, but love without truth is hypocrisy. Because whites are often "clueless" about how their actions are perceived by others, reconciliation demands sincere and loving honesty. Truthful and loving interaction produces understanding, clarifies misperceptions on both parts, and builds trust.

Race Fatigue

Failed attempts at cross-racial relationships produce a kind of race fatigue. Well-meaning white folks get quickly burned out because we're not appreciated and affirmed. We don't understand how deep the issues are. We know little about the history of minority groups and don't understand how it affects them today. Our heritage often is not too significant. We conclude that our identity is "American." With that, we don't even think that our ancestors came by choice, seeking and getting a better way of life. When minority groups express that the "land of opportunity" and the "American dream" have not been their experiences, whites can't conceive of why not. It's not with hatred or racist—it's just our perception of reality. Most of us determine "truth" through the grid of personal experience. Until our experiences teach us otherwise, we'll hold on to our perceptions as facts.

Many minority people say to me, "I get tired of educating white folks, especially when they don't want to be educated." I understand that. But I believe God is doing a new thing. Christian men's hearts are opening. We have much to teach each other, but it will take commitment with perseverance from both sides. The majority and minority Christian communities all could be justified to just quit and leave things the way they are. But God is calling us all to the table of brotherhood in Christ in unity and reconciliation. Will we respond to His call? Will we be faithful and pay the price? Will you men of color stay with us until we can get our education and sensitivity about people of color and start responding in new and meaningful ways? We pray that you will. We need your help.

INTENTIONALITY PROJECT IDEAS

God is calling members of the body of Christ to live out unity in reconciled relationships with one another. Intentionality needs to be God-centered and God-directed. Pray as you read through the following list, and ask the Lord to guide you to be intentional in reconciliation and unity. Keep in mind that He may give you a totally different direction from anything listed here. He is a God of great creativity and diversity. Perhaps He may use some of these ideas to stimulate your thinking in other directions.

Individual and Family Projects

- Build a close personal relationship with a Christian brother who is different racially or denominationally. Commit to having breakfast or lunch with that person once every week or two. What's the purpose behind these meetings? Just to talk to one another. Do this for six months with no other agenda. Be open and transparent. If the person asks you why, say, "Hey, I believe God wants me to get to know and understand people different from myself." But it takes intentionality. If things click and the relationship develops, joint ministry will grow out of it.
- Invite a church member, neighbor, coworker, or international student who is racially different to dinner in your home, adjusting however necessary to make the person comfortable.
- Work with a brother to take a family outing with both families. You may prefer limiting the trip to wives only. Plan a picnic, dinner out, trip to a museum or local place of interest, etc.
- While on vacation, special occasions, or at planned times, visit a culturally different church or a church of a different denomination.
- Watch a sensitivity-building video together with your family, and discuss feelings and perceptions afterward.
- Attend a conference together with a Christian brother who is different. Travel together, eat together, and room together to get better acquainted.
- Attend funerals and weddings related to your new Christian friends who are different.
- Open your home to a foreign exchange student. Seek to know and understand his culture while sharing your own.
- Look for opportunities to interact at work or in other settings. Take the first step to initiate dialogue and relationships.
- When an individual or family from a different ethnic or denominational background visits your church, invite them to lunch, and get acquainted.
- Watch for opportunities at social events to show interest and acknowledge the presence of people who are different.
- Get to know your neighbors who are from a different cultural background.
- Look for opportunities to learn from others.
- Participate in foster care, and accept children of other races.
- Volunteer your services and time to an inner-city ministry or in a cross-cultural mission project.

Church Projects

- Partner with a church that is different to conduct more mixed small-group studies of this workbook. Use your existing group members as co-leaders for future studies. Select one co-leader from each church/group so you have the strength of interdependence as they work together.
- If your church is in a homogeneous (one-race) neighborhood, establish a "sister church" relationship with a congregation of a different race. In a sister church arrangement, the pastors/leaders develop relationships with one another and provide opportunities for their congregations to fellowship, worship, work, and minister together.
- If your neighborhood is changing or already diverse, recruit and develop ethnic leadership rather than moving the church to a "better" place.
- Multi-ethnic and interdenominational pastors' groups can coordinate joint worship services, pulpit exchanges, and project partnerships.
- Join with congregations of other races to plant new churches in areas where there's a need. Planting a new cross-cultural church is sometimes easier than trying to convert an existing church to a multi-cultural church. Keep in mind, however, that God can do both effectively.
- If your congregation is multi-cultural, hold Fudge Ripple Sundaes (or Banana Split Sundaes, etc.) to facilitate dialogue about and between the cultures as a growing and also a preventive measure. See page 105 or the fuller story in *Breaking Down Walls* (see resources on page 189).
- To gain understanding of other denominations, work with your pastor to invite a visiting pastor, priest, minister, or elder to speak to your congregation about his denomination's history, common and unique doctrines, worship practices, and so forth. Provide a question-and-answer period. These will be most effective when your pastor has already developed a relationship with the potential guest.
- Change worship and music to include several cultural styles. Invite guest worship leaders to a teaching time (panel discussion) about their distinctive worship styles.

Community-Wide Projects

- Join with other Christian groups for regular prayer meetings or "concerts of prayer."
- Participate in community worship services at Easter, Thanksgiving, and Christmas.
- Participate together in community-wide events like the March for Jesus, Promise Keepers conferences, Christian music concerts, or evangelistic crusades.
- Hold a citywide "Break Down the Walls" workshop, and begin networking men and churches together for small-group studies of this workbook.
- Join with other Christian churches in ministry projects to your city during disasters, special festivals, or in places of great need. In one city, Christians provide free car washes and the like and then offer to provide a home with a copy of the *Jesus* film as an evangelistic outreach.
- Work together with other Christians and churches in meeting human needs in the name of Christ. Demonstrate Christian love for the hungry, prisoner, naked, sick, oppressed, orphan, stranger, and others whom God has said in His Word that He loves.
- Participate in "prayer walking" through sections of your city, praying over the people in every house, church, school, business, and ministry.
- Conduct citywide sacred assemblies once a year or at times of crisis, God's discipline, or recognition of gross immorality.
- Pull the Christian community together and provide a high-quality, low-cost (or free) Christian school in the inner city or other places where minorities would not otherwise have access to it. Call out the best Christian teachers as missionaries to help kids come to know the Lord and get the best education possible. Jointly underwrite the cost so that tuition is low. Provide a way for churches and individuals to give scholarships so that no child is turned away because of financial need. Let God put on public display what He can do to change a community through changed lives.
- Sponsor citywide discipleship-training events for families, couples, and individuals.

RESOURCES FOR FURTHER STUDY

Special Note: The resources marked with an asterisk (*) below have been written or developed from a secular perspective. We couldn't possibly endorse all that you may read or view in them. Some may contain statements or language that will be offensive to the Christian reader or may challenge the Christian faith. Nevertheless, we (the authors) believe they are valuable tools in developing sensitivity and understanding of the cultural experiences of other ethnic groups. Read or view these resources with caution to seek knowledge and understanding. You may want to consider securing one of these resources from your library, a bookstore, a video rental store, or from the sources listed with some of the resources.

RECONCILIATION AND UNITY

Cooper, Rodney L. *We Stand Together: Reconciling Men of Different Color.* Chicago: Moody Press, 1995. Cooper and four other experts from different races offer personal experiences and research findings to help men understand each other.

Evans, Tony. *Let's Get to Know Each Other.* Nashville: Thomas Nelson Publishers, 1995. Evans provides insights about myths that have kept blacks and whites separated and brings understanding of the black church experience in America.

Perkins, John and Thomas A. Tarrants III, with David Wimbish. *He's My Brother.* Grand Rapids: Chosen Books, 1994. Perkins and Tarrants tell their personal experiences of racism and testify to the power of the gospel to change lives. They offer a workable strategy for building bridges between the races.

Perkins, Spencer and Chris Rice. *More than Equals: Racial Healing for the Sake of the Gospel.* Downers Grove, Ill.: InterVarsity Press, 1993. Perkins and Rice describe the difficulties faced and offer biblical and practical insights in building cross-cultural relationships.

Porter, Phillip. *Let the Walls Fall Down.* Lake Mary, Fla.: Creation House, 1996. Porter shows how to prevent prejudice from separating you from other believers and calls you to do your part to be one with God and with other believers.

Reconcilers. Jackson, Miss.: Reconcilers Fellowship. This quarterly magazine is dedicated to racial healing and community rebuilding. Available free by contacting Reconcilers Fellowship, P.O. Box 32, Jackson, Miss. 39205; Phone: 601-354-1563.

Washington, Raleigh and Glen Kehrein. *Breaking Down Walls: A Model for Reconciliation in an Age of Racial Strife.* Chicago: Moody Press, 1993. Washington and Kehrein tell the stories and give a variety of illustrations to show how the principles of reconciliation and unity have affected their own lives as they've experienced reconciliation in the middle of a world of strife.

This is not a duplication of this workbook but gives much additional insight to application of the principles in real life.

DEVELOPING ETHNIC SENSITIVITY

Asian Americans

Lin, Tom. *Losing Face & Finding Grace.* Downers Grove, Ill.: InterVarsity Press, 1996. Lin guides Asian Americans to better understand their cultural influences on their faith. This small-group Bible study would provide "outsiders" with helpful insights into Asian American culture.

*Sandmeyer, Elmer Clarence. *The Anti-Chinese Movement in California.* Champaign, Ill.: University of Illinois Press, 1991. This secular and technical work describes the culture of Chinese immigrants and the struggles they have faced early in their American experience.

African Americans

Eyes on the Prize: America's Civil Rights Years 1954-1965. Boston, Mass.: Blackside Inc., 1992. Available from PBS Home Video at 1-800-538-5856. This Public Broadcasting System video series is a documentary tracing the Civil Rights Movement that has changed the course of American history. A companion book by the same title by Juan Williams is also available. New York, N. Y.: Penguin, 1987.

Hispanics

Chicano. (Available from National Latino Communication Center at 1-800-722-9982). This secular video presentation highlights the Hispanic struggles for civil rights and identifies the hurdles, issues, and victories—primarily from a Mexican perspective. Also available in longer three-part series *Yo Soy Chicano.*

Native Americans

*Moses, L. G. and Raymond Wilson. *Indian Lives.* University of New Mexico. 1985, 1993. These essays provide insights and current perspectives from Native American leaders.

*Brown, Dee. *Bury My Heart at Wounded Knee.* New York, New York: Henry Holt and Company, 1990. This book provides insight into the anger and bitterness of Native Americans toward white people and the United States Government due to broken treaties, massacres, cruel atrocities, and injustices.

How the West Was Lost Collector's Edition Vols. 1-3. Discovery Channel, 1993. This video series from a Native American perspective provides a historical overview of the destruction of the nation's first people. Available at 1-800-633-1116.

SMALL-GROUP LEADER'S GUIDE

GENERAL INSTRUCTIONS

Break Down the Walls has been designed for use in small groups. Each small group will need a leader or facilitator to guide the group sessions. If you've been selected to lead a small-group study, the following suggestions should help you understand your role and how to lead the group to experience biblical reconciliation and unity. Before you read the following suggestions, you should review "Before You Begin This Course" on pages 8-14.

➡ **Check here when you have read pages 8-14: ❏**

In that introduction, we suggested that you discuss this study with your pastor. This is a sensitive topic, and he needs to be aware of the study. He also will have helpful insights about what group of men you should start with in this study.

➡ **If you haven't contacted your pastor, do that before you go too far in preparing for the course. Check here when you've discussed the study with him: ❏**

Your Role as a Small-Group Facilitator

Each small group should select a leader or facilitator for the discussion time. This normally should be the same person for the entire study to provide continuity. Since you're reading this section, we'll assume you are that person. You don't have to be an expert on reconciliation and unity. Neither do you have to master the material and deliver a lecture on the weekly topics. Your role is to guide discussion and prayer related to the content that members will have studied during the week. The Holy Spirit will be the primary teacher, and this book will be a tool He uses to help members study the Scriptures. In a sense, you're a player-coach for the small group, and you follow the leadership of the Holy Spirit.

Following these general instructions, you'll find suggestions for twelve small-group sessions. These include one introductory session, ten sessions related to the content units, and one midterm get-together that doesn't require additional homework. These suggestions should provide more than enough help for a session of ninety minutes to two hours. You should feel free to adapt the suggestions and questions for discussion to meet the specific needs of your group. One of your primary roles is to guide the group to seek the Lord and His counsel regarding building relationships across racial, ethnic, social, and denominational lines.

Preparing for the Study

This workbook has been designed for self-paced, interactive learning. That means an individual can study the course at his own speed. The content is designed to interact with the student. Thus, a segment of content will be presented. Then a learning activity will call the student to respond. Where correct answers can be identified, the content following a learning activity will help the student review his answers. The individual study, however, is not complete without a small-group session to process the learning and help with application. This small-group process will take at least twelve weeks. The relationships developed during the small-group sessions will probably be the most significant outcome of this study. Our prayer is that reconciled relationships, unity, and a healthy body of Christ will result from your study of this course.

Forming a Group

The ideal group for this study will be *Christian men* who are different—racially, ethnically, socially, or denominationally. Your group may include:
- Coworkers from the same workplace
- Denominational diversity
- Economic diversity
- Educational diversity
- Fellow church members
- Fellow Promise Keepers
- Friends and acquaintances
- Inner-city and suburban men
- Political diversity
- Racial/ethnic diversity
- Regional diversity (natives from different parts of the country)
- Theological diversity (liberal, conservative, fundamental, etc.)
- Workplace diversity (labor/management)

The first group may be composed of potential leaders who will lead groups of their own after the first round. Someone, perhaps you or another church leader, should take the lead in forming a group. We'll look at some suggestions for enlistment in a moment. First, let's look at the size and type of group.

If your first group is composed primarily of individuals who are alike (not different racially, socioeconomically, or denominationally), you should plan to go through the study a second or third time with men who are different. Interacting with brothers in Christ who are different is the setting in which men are most likely to *experience* reconciliation and unity. Until your group has experienced those, it hasn't really completed the course.

Size of Group for Effective Learning
The discussion and prayer that will take place in the small-group sessions needs to be personal and in-depth. If a group is too large, some people will feel left out or frustrated by not getting to participate adequately. Because of the topics, some sessions may last longer because of the intimate sharing that will begin to take place. For these reasons, we suggest that you form groups for every *four to six people.* Eight should be a maximum number in a group. If you have more than eight interested people, form groups for every four to six. If you have several groups meeting in the same location (e.g., a church) and at the same time, you may want to schedule a couple of joint sessions so that people can describe what God is teaching them. Your pastor may even want some of the members to offer a testimony in a worship service or prayer meeting.

Enlist Participants
Prayer is the place to begin enlisting participants. Ask the Lord to guide you to the people He would want in your group. Trust that He will be working with the right men. Don't get discouraged if someone turns you down. Trust the Lord to guide the response of the men who need to be in your group. Keep in mind, however, that this course is designed for Christian men. Unbelievers will harm the unity that the Spirit can produce among brothers.

Use the checklist (pp. 11-12) of men God may be leading you to consider. You may want to discuss the course with fellow Christians and see if they express an interest in participating. You may already have a group in place that may choose to use this study to facilitate discussion. Keep in mind, too, that because homework is involved, a participant needs to be committed to the process.

Order Resources
You'll need one copy of *Break Down the Walls* for each group member. You may order these through your local Christian bookstore or through Promise Keepers at 1-800-456-7594. If you decide to use "The Reconciliation Song" (page 7) as a theme song, you may want to order the "Break Down the Walls" cassette tape or compact disk so the group can sing along.

One other *recommended but optional* resource for small-group sessions is the *Break Down the Walls* video training tape. On this tape, each of the eight principles is taught briefly with testimonies and vignettes of men from a variety of ethnic backgrounds. These tapes will make an excellent supplementary teaching tool. We recommend that you use the teaching for each principle (approximately 10 minutes each) during the session that focuses on that given principle. If you use the video clips we recommend you use, add that time to the minimum ninety-minute session. This video is also available from Promise Keepers at 1-800-456-7594.

Collect Book Fees
Churches that coordinate the small groups may want to cover some or all of the cost of books. However, in most cases, members will be expected to buy their own books. You'll want to announce the cost of the book as you enlist participants so they will be prepared to pay at the introductory session. Watch for people who may need financial assistance. In those cases, you may want to subsidize the cost of the book or provide one on a "scholarship" basis. You may find that a man has a friend he wants to invite to be a part of the group, and he may want to provide the book for his friend. You may even have a person who would want to provide books for all the group members. Be sensitive to how the Lord would have you do this to allow maximum participation.

Develop a Time Schedule
You need to allow for a ninety-minute to two-hour session. Sunday evening may be a good time for many in your group. However, be careful that you don't have such a tight schedule before a worship service that you can't adjust if the discussion gets intense toward the end of the session. Another evening will work as well as long as you hold to a reasonable quitting time. Let the group members help you determine the optimum time for your meeting.

Help Members Memorize Scripture
Some members may not have memorized Scripture before. Use the suggestions on page 18 to introduce the discipline to them. Show members how to use the memory cards in the back of the book. Check up on memory work each week to hold men accountable to memorize Scripture for the Lord's glory.

Conducting an Introductory Session
Because members will need to complete the first week's lessons prior to your first small-group session, plan to conduct an introductory session prior to your first official session. The introductory session may be offered to all interested men based on an open invitation. Once people at this session make a commitment to participate, you can divide them into small groups. If you need more leaders, enlist some from those who have agreed to participate. Suggestions for the introductory session begin on page 198.

Conducting Small-Group Sessions
The small-group sessions are designed so that you'll

need to make only minimal advance preparation. Each session will include the following five elements:
1. Opening prayer
2. Content review (fifteen minutes)
3. Discussion questions (fifteen to thirty minutes)
4. Building brotherhood (thirty to forty-five minutes)
5. Praying for one another (fifteen minutes)

Each segment of the session has suggested time allotments. These add up to roughly a ninety-minute session. You may want to adjust these to best meet the needs of your group. You may shorten discussion to fifteen minutes one week in order to allow for forty-five minutes of building brotherhood. If your group is willing to spend two hours together, add the additional thirty minutes to brotherhood building and praying for one another.

Suggestions for weekly small-group sessions begin on page 199. You'll notice the suggestions are broken down into two sections. One section focuses on "Building Brotherhood." Because this process will vary from group to group, we've included the entire process for the course in a separate section. During preparation for each session, you'll want to evaluate where your group is in this relationship-building process. You'll be guided to select the next step for the members to take in discussing their personal experiences. In this way, every group can customize its discussions to best meet the needs of the members.

The second section includes suggestions for opening prayer, content review, discussion questions, praying for one another, and other helps for the session. These suggestions will be far more than you can cover. You'll need to read the content review and discussion questions before the session. Select the ones that will be most helpful for your group.

WARNING: You may be tempted to cover all these questions and wind up missing time for building brotherhood. Resist that temptation! Ask members to help you guard the discussion and closing prayer time. You may want to set a timer or clock to go off after 90 minutes so everyone will know it's time to draw things to a close. You may even decide to *start* some sessions with brotherhood building just to guarantee you have adequate time for it.

Mid-Term Get-Together

After the first five units of study, we recommend you take a break for a mid-term get-together. One reason is to provide men an opportunity to catch up on homework if they're behind in their lessons. The second reason is to allow for a special time of getting better acquainted. You may want to keep this time light and informal, or you may decide to continue using the "Building Brotherhood" activities to go deeper in your relationships with one another.

Feel free to plan an event or activity that will facilitate deeper relationships. You may want to involve group members in deciding on an agenda. Make your plans early enough so men can get the date on their calendars and make the necessary preparations. The following are merely suggestions to get you thinking.

- Use your regular meeting time to continue building brotherhood. You may be working on second or even third base by this time. Use the entire session for discussing life experiences.
- Plan for a shared meal with no set agenda. Just get together at a time convenient for all the group members and eat a leisurely meal.
- Plan for an outdoor trip if weather permits. This could be a camping trip or a hunting or fishing outing if all group members share a common interest or are willing to go along for the fun anyway.
- Attend a sporting event together. If the event is out of town, try to arrange to travel together in a van. Use travel and meal times for sharing life experiences. You may even want to use some of the suggestions for building brotherhood during these times.
- Plan a family picnic or covered-dish meal, and invite families to attend. Wear name tags, and take time at the beginning to introduce families. Keep in mind that spouses and children probably won't have the benefit of having built relationships prior to this time. You may want to plan some fun entertainment or do some group icebreakers to get better acquainted. Pick a cross-cultural or non-denominational team of two to plan the activities.
- If members come from different churches, you might consider attending worship at one of the churches and going out to lunch together following the service. Make sure members plan for substitutes at their home churches if they have responsibilities there.
- If your group is multi-denominational, consider asking pastors from the different churches to come and give a brief historical background of their denomination or tradition and an overview of distinctive teachings or practices. Encourage them to promote understanding, not "conversion." Allow time for questions and answers.

This is not an exhaustive list. Let these ideas spark your own. The key is to plan time to get together with brothers in a setting where sharing and relationship building can take place.

A Further Word About Confidentiality

Confidentiality is vital to the small-group process if men are to feel free to speak openly.
➥ **Read again the ground rule about confidentiality on page 13.**

As a leader, you need to keep in mind that there are a few exceptions to that rule. You, too, should maintain confidentiality unless there's a compelling reason to do otherwise. Here are three difficult but compelling reasons. In each case, you should privately discuss with the member involved the reasons that you must break confidentiality. You may also want to get counsel from your pastor or a professional counselor.

1. Suicidal. If a member says things that indicate he is considering (or has recently considered) killing himself, you need to step in to help. Unless you're a trained counselor, you're probably not prepared to give the help this person needs. If this happens during the session, make an appointment at that moment to meet with the individual afterward. In that meeting, talk further about his feelings and thoughts. Be directive in suggesting (even requiring) that he talk with a trained counselor who can help—your pastor may be the first choice. Help him make the appointment, and if possible, take him for the first meeting. Ask for his permission to discuss this with his spouse or other close family member.

2. Child Abuse. Most states have laws that require reporting physical and sexual child abuse to proper authorities. If a member should describe actions that require you to report, prayerfully approach the member privately. Explain your need to report his actions, and discuss his need for help. Offer to walk with him through the process. Ideally, you would want to get him to go with you to confess his actions and seek help. If he's unwilling, seek your pastor's help as you fulfill your duty. You also need to be sure that a spouse or close family member knows of the situation in case that person needs to take action to prevent future abuse.

3. Serious Criminal Action. If you have a member confess to a previously unknown criminal act, your state laws may require that you report it. Murder would be one such serious act. If you have questions about whether reporting a specific act is required, you should *anonymously* contact a criminal attorney or other legal officials in your city or state.

Prayer Preparation
Spend time in prayer for yourself and your group as you prepare so you'll be ready spiritually for the session. Pray regularly for your group members. You may even want to enlist some "prayer warriors" who aren't in the group to be praying for you and the group members. May the Lord guide you and use you in a special way during these coming weeks!

CHECKLIST FOR THE SMALL GROUP LEADER

The following checklist will help you make sure you're ready for the introductory session. Check off items after you've completed them.

❏ I have prayed about this course and sense that God wants me involved.

❏ I talked with my pastor and have his approval for this study. We have discussed leadership and composition of the group.

If you haven't gone through these two steps, do so before going further.

❖ ❖ ❖

❏ I believe God wants our study group to include: (check those that apply, and begin keeping a separate list of names of individuals that come to mind)
   ❏ Leaders in my own church.
   ❏ Men in my own church.
   ❏ Men from sister churches of the same denomination as ours.
   ❏ Men of different colors.
   ❏ Men of different denominations or Christian traditions.
   ❏ Men from different socioeconomic groups (rich, poor, middle-class).

❏ Other: _____

❏ Date, time, and place set for the introductory session:

_____

❏ Day, time, and place set for regular meetings:

_____

❏ Frequency of meetings and pace of the study (check one)
   ❏ Weekly meeting, one unit per week.
   ❏ Weekly meeting, half unit per week (two or three lessons).
   ❏ Bi-weekly meeting (every two weeks), one unit per meeting.
   ❏ Monthly meeting, one unit per meeting.
❏ Other: _____

❏ I have read the general instructions for leaders beginning on page 190.
❏ I have invited/enlisted the potential group members for the introductory session.
❏ I have secured enough books for each potential member.
❏ Optional: I have secured the cassette tape or compact disk for "The Reconciliation Song."
❏ Optional: I have secured the course videotapes.
❏ Now I'm ready to prepare for the introductory session on page 198.

BUILDING BROTHERHOOD

The following text briefly describes the way your group members' relationships will progress toward Christlikeness. This has been adapted from *Brothers! Calling Men Into Vital Relationships,* by Geoff Gorsuch and Dan Schaffer, (Colorado Springs, Colo.: NavPress, 1994). If you need extra help in small-group leadership skills and understanding, this book may prove to be a good companion. One chapter that may be especially helpful is chapter 8, "The Equipment Closet: Troubleshooting." It gives how-to suggestions for difficulties that may arise during the group process.

During the coming weeks or months, your group members will develop close relationships with one another. You'll be the player-coach as you help them help each other become more Christlike. The relational diamond described below will serve as a structure for the building brotherhood section we have already described.

BROTHERS
By Geoff Gorsuch and Dan Schaffer

Being a man has never been easy. But the Bible teaches that there are spiritual resources available to help men face the challenge. God has given His Spirit, His Word, and one another so we don't have to do the job alone. We have brothers!

Why Brothers?
The cross is more than the end of a search. It's the beginning of an adventure! To come into relationship with God through the cross of Jesus Christ is the great introduction to all that men were intended to be. As one of the early church leaders said, we were called *"to be conformed to the likeness of his Son . . . the firstborn among many brothers"* (Romans 8:29). God's purpose is to make us Christlike! We all *"are being transformed into his likeness"* (2 Corinthians 3:18).

Our response to this call begins as a disciple. A disciple is a learner! He's an apprentice who follows his master by faith. However, as we progress through the New Testament, the word *disciple* is replaced by another word: *brother.* And it is as brothers that the full intent of Christ's life and mission to the world is to be lived out.

What Is a Brother?
Brothers are the sons of a common Father. They're heirs of a common spiritual inheritance, so brothers should be there for one another. Brothers should stand together and take care of one another.

Christ never wanted His disciples to live out their Christian lives alone. When the brothers are accepting, encouraging, and exhorting one another to full maturity in Christ, His command to "love one another" is being obeyed. People all over the world are looking for this kind of relationship. United as brothers, therefore, we become laborers bringing real hope to the world!

You Need Not Be Alone!
In spite of the clear biblical mandate to *"love one another,"* most Christian men struggle profoundly with their relationships. Many would like to have friends on whom they could really count. Brothers! Yet, in spite of these desires, most adult males are relatively friendless.

To show you how to overcome this distance between us, consider the following model you're already familiar with—the game of baseball. Because male relationships develop slowly, to reach home plate we'll need to have time and some good coaching. But most of all, we'll need courage to round the bases.

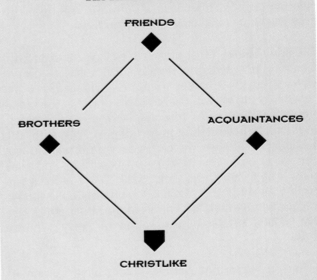

The Relational Diamond

The Bases
As you can see, each base on our relational diamond corresponds to a biblical command relating to the "one anothers" of the New Testament. At first base, we are learning to *"accept one another"* and exploring the potential of the relationship. At second base, we develop our friendship as we "encourage one another." At third base, after much time and coaching, we should feel free to *"exhort one another"* as we face life together. As you round the bases, you should allow adequate time. But the goal of Christlikeness is worth the investment!

Each phase is good and serves its purpose to get us to home plate. However, all our acquaintances and friends do not have to become brothers. If we'll keep "stepping up to the plate" and take some risks, we can become the brothers of a few. So, "let's play ball!"

Heading for First

Men seem to need activities to get to know one another better and to begin the task of trust-building. These activities may vary, but their goal is always the same—to help the men "accept one another." Though light, cliché-level conversation will characterize this phase, what the men want to do as a group, and why, should be settled as they move on to second.

Sliding into Second

Sliding implies friction! There will be a need to adjust expectations as the conversation passes from the cliché level to the level of ideas and opinions. This will require skill in resolving conflicts. Where the men are encouraged to fully express themselves, however, there will be bonding. This dealing with conflict produces the mutual respect necessary to move on. When conflict arises, use the following guidelines:
1. Focus on the problem, not many problems.
2. Focus on the problem, not the person.
3. Focus on specifics, not generalities.
4. Focus on "I" statements, not "you" statements.
5. Focus on understanding, not winning.

Rounding Third

Too many groups get to third base and turn right! That is, they never get to exhortation. They never get to covenants and accountability. They never enter into the struggle for moral excellence together. When they do, a team is built that can take on some of the challenges and succeed.

Heading for Home

As every man is helped around the bases by his brothers, the momentum builds. The dream each man had as he "stepped up to the plate" will be within reach. As brothers, they can help each other become men of genuine integrity: Christlike!

Safe!

That's what the umpire will cry as we cross home plate, for this game is safe when it's played by God's rule book. And that's exactly what men need to know: They will be safe! They need to know that after they've shared their lives, they will not be betrayed. Better yet, they will have bonded in Christ's love. They'll know what it means to be brothers!

SMALL-GROUP LEARNING ACTIVITIES FOR BUILDING BROTHERHOOD

(You may want to photocopy these pages of building brotherhood activities so you can have them visible together with the plans for each session. You have permission to copy these three pages.)

During each small-group session, you'll devote thirty to forty-five minutes to building relationships between members of the group. This relationship building will progress at different speeds for different groups. The more alike members are, the quicker the process will flow. However, a group that is very different may face a crisis situation together through sharing or experience that will bond them together quickly and deeply.

Since we can't determine beforehand how quickly your group will round the bases, we have separated this section of suggestions. Before each session, you'll want to review where your group is in the process. Ask the Lord to help you determine which questions to use for stimulating discussion. Pray about how long to stay at one stage before moving to the next. You'll want to take the process slowly enough that all the members can move together around the bases. This is a subjective and flexible approach. If you find you're moving a little too fast, you can always back up and spend more time at the previous base.

First Base: Acquaintances

"Accept one another, then, just as Christ accepted you" (Romans 15:7).
On the way to first, focus on:
• developing listening skills
• setting purpose and parameters
• accepting one another
• committing to confidentiality

Much of this ground will be covered *during the introductory and first sessions*. Your emphasis will be more on getting acquainted. The purpose and parameters for the group time will be established early. For building brotherhood on this first level, consider some of the following:
1. Try to get men to communicate as if they're sitting around the campfire on a hunting trip.
2. Agree on confidentiality.
3. Discuss dealing with conflict before it surfaces.
   • The goal is to understand, not to correct.
   • You're not here to debate issues but to gain understanding.
4. Get acquainted by sharing some of the following:
   • What is something interesting or unusual about you that most of us wouldn't know?
   • What is one of your favorite childhood memories?
   • What is one of your dreams for the future?
   • What is your greatest desire for your children or family?
   • Describe your journey in coming to know and follow Christ.
   • What is your greatest challenge in living for Christ in your workplace?
   • What is one of your greatest struggles in following Christ?
   • What is your greatest desire (or dream) concerning

your relationship to the Lord or to the church?

Second Base: Friends

"Encourage one another and build each other up" (1 Thessalonians 5:11).
On the way to second, focus on:
- subjects for men (related to reconciliation and unity)
- developing discussion skills
- developing skills at conflict resolution

You'll probably begin moving toward second even during your first session. You probably will want to work on *second base during sessions 2–5.* Stay flexible, though. Since the members will have been studying content in their homework, they will have material to begin discussing. The suggestions for content review and discussion questions in the session plans will guide that aspect of moving toward second. To move men toward being friends in the building brotherhood segment, consider some of the following:

1. Be prepared to pray for and minister to one another. Wounded brothers in the body of Christ need healing. You can pray with spiritual weapons to demolish strongholds of the past (see 2 Corinthians 10:3–5).
2. Watch for physical signs of someone who may be hesitant to speak but is attentive. Invite that person to participate, but don't push too much.
3. Encourage members to accept feelings at face value. If a person says he feels a certain way, believe it's true even if it doesn't make sense. Then seek understanding.
4. Invite volunteers to reveal their greatest fear (for example: job loss, family instability, poor health, etc.)
5. Invite volunteers to share a time of personal pain or brokenness related to one of the following:
   - divorce
   - death of a family member
   - job loss
   - personal rejection by family or friends
   - failure: moral, family, business, school
   - problems with a wayward child
   - loss of health
   - experience of crime or disaster
6. As volunteers describe their pain or fears, watch for ways to use these as follow-up questions:
   - How did that make you feel? What did you think?
   - How did you respond? How did others respond?
   - What does that cause you to want to do?
7. Ask volunteers to answer: What kind of relationship or lack of relationship did you have with your father? How did that make you feel? How does that influence you today?

Third Base: Brothers

"Teach and admonish one another" (Colossians 3:16).

On the way to third, focus on:
- worship
- team building and forming covenants
- developing accountability to one another

By the time you begin unit 6, members may be ready to head for third base. These activities will be good for use during *sessions 6–8.* As the members begin talking deeply about their pains and struggles regarding prejudice, racism, and/or sectarianism, they will have opportunity to "teach and admonish" based on a growing relationship of trust and interdependence. Because love for brothers is growing stronger by this time, members will be able to talk with sincerity and sensitivity to one another. They will be able to challenge insensitivity and correct prejudices without offending or being offended. As members move toward third in building brotherhood, consider some of the following:

1. Help members develop sensitivity toward people who are different. Encourage members to share:
   - some of the uniquenesses they see "their group" (ethnic or denominational) contribute to the body of Christ
   - myths or stereotypes that are commonly thought, said, or taught about their people
   - hurt feelings that are commonly felt by people in their group
   - common ways other people are insensitive to feelings, beliefs, or practices
   - experiences that are common to members of your ethnic (or denominational) group but may not be common for others
2. Master the use of the statement: "Help me understand . . ." throughout your discussion times.
3. Encourage members to watch for ways they can help, serve, minister to, give to, comfort, and pray for other members. If appropriate, guide the group to discuss ways they can help tangibly. Ask: What part can we play in helping you respond to this situation?
4. Invite volunteers to share pain from racial and/or sectarian prejudice using requests or questions like:
   - Have you ever experienced prejudice because of your skin color? When, who, and how? How did you feel? How did you respond?
   - Would someone of color share a hurt or pain you have experienced because of your skin color? What was it like for you growing up? What is it like today? (Note: If you don't have someone of color in the group, ask: Do you personally know of a person who has had a painful experience because of his race? How does that make you feel?)
   - Have you ever been rejected as an unbeliever or a heretic (one who believes and practices false doctrines) by someone because you didn't attend the "right" church? How did that make you feel? How did you respond?
5. Encourage members to "speak the truth in love" as a

way to instruct or admonish a person so he can correct thoughts, words, or actions that may be inappropriate or insensitive.

Home: Christlike
"May they be brought to complete unity to let the world know that you sent me" (John 17:23).
As members move toward home, focus on teamwork and interdependence.

As members study the principle of empowerment (unit 9) through repentance and forgiveness, they will begin to experience interdependence with each other. As they start to both give and receive from each other in a spirit of oneness, they will reflect Christ in their unity. *The goal of this course is to be moving in this direction by the end of the twelve small-group sessions.* The intentionality project ideas may stimulate your group to think of working as a team beyond the initial small-group study in order to live out Christlikeness in the community or world. As members move toward home in building brotherhood, consider some of the following:
1. Give members opportunity to confess personal sins of racism or sectarianism. These can include the root sins like pride but should also be open to specific actions that were wrong.
2. When appropriate, guide the group or members in the group to offer forgiveness for sins confessed.
3. Encourage the group to help each other struggle with the issues of restitution and the fruits of repentance. Ask: What would love look like in this situation?
4. Begin to pray about and ask, What should I (we) do to see our church, community, nation, or world change for the better?
5. During the final session, guide a sharing of responses to the activities on page 169 (lesson 5).
6. If your group is composed of people primarily alike, discuss plans for mixing with a group that's different and forming two mixed groups for a second round of studying *Break Down the Walls*.

SMALL-GROUP SESSION PLANS
On the following pages, you'll find the specific suggestions for the ten small-group sessions related to the ten units of content in this workbook. They also include the introductory session. In each of the session plans, the page references and activity numbers are given for your quick reference. When appropriate, you may ask members to turn to those pages for review. Specific answers are listed in parentheses for your use as the leader.

Allow volunteers to respond to the questions or activities. In some cases, you may want to break up into smaller groups for discussion of responses to activities

RULES FOR THE GAME
(Thanks to Dan Schaffer for these suggestions.) The following suggestions may be helpful to give members as informal rules for the discussion times you have in the coming weeks. Refer to them periodically to make sure your group is sensitive to one another in the group sessions. If necessary, read through the list at the beginning of a session just as a reminder.

1. Give others a chance to talk.
2. Listen when others are talking. Don't interrupt. Pay attention to what is being said.
3. Look at the person but don't stare him down.
4. Don't distract attention by doing something else while listening.
5. Accept one another as equals (peers).
6. Suspend judgment on actions and beliefs. Try to understand where the person is coming from.
7. Show interest in what the other person is saying, and smile when appropriate to show acceptance.
8. Give others the benefit of the doubt. Trust that they are speaking the truth.
9. Be slow to shoot down another person's ideas.
10. Don't jump to conclusions.
11. Don't rush into arguments.
12. Focus on what is being said now instead of thinking about what you will say later.
13. Don't inject humor when a person is trying to be serious.
14. Don't be a clock watcher.

in the unit's lessons. Watch for those members who may be shy, and try to encourage their participation without putting them on the spot. Remember that you won't be able to use all the activities. Choose those that you sense will be best for your group.

Before the Introductory Session
❑ Review the content of "Before You Begin This Course" (pp. 8-14) and general instructions in "Small Group Leader's Guide" (pp. 190-193).
❑ Secure copies of *Break Down the Walls* for each potential member.
❑ Select a room that is large enough to feel comfortable but small enough to keep you close together. Set up the chairs in a semicircle.
❑ Review the suggestions under "First Base: Acquaintances," #4 (p. 195). Select two or three options for use in the session. Plan to give men a choice of information they can state about themselves in the get-acquainted time. You may want to write these options on a poster or marker board.
❑ Read through the following activities, and prepare to guide the group through an overview of the course.

INTRODUCTORY SESSION

Arrival Activities
As prospective members arrive, greet them and give them the following instructions:
1. Fill out a name tag, and place it on your clothing.
2. Write your name, home address, and phone numbers (home and work) on an index card provided.
3. Take a copy of *Break Down the Walls,* and begin working through the activities under "A Quick Tour" on page 21. Work through numbers 1-4.

If members are paying for their books, collect the book fees at this time.

Opening Prayer
Begin the session with prayer.
- Thank the Lord for these men who have come together.
- Ask the Holy Spirit to guide each one as he makes a decision about participating in the study.
- Ask the Lord to begin breaking down walls that separate Christians so that the body of Christ in your community and in our nation will become a trophy of God's grace.

Getting Acquainted
1. Ask each participant to introduce himself. Ask him to include in his introduction the following:
   - name and information about his immediate family
   - why he is interested in considering this study
   - his church
2. Divide into groups of about four men each. Explain two or three options for talking about themselves from building brotherhood—First Base (#4, p. 195). You may write them here:

_____

_____

_____

3. Ask each man to give a response to one or more of these activities as time permits. Allow about ten or fifteen minutes for the men to get better acquainted.

Content Overview
1. Ask men to turn to page 12. Briefly explain the ground rules: preparation, attendance, participation, confidentiality, and prayer. Explain that group members need to be willing to commit to these expectations if they plan to participate in the study.
2. Tell the members how many lessons in a unit they will be studying between sessions. Explain that

you're going to help them get a head start by studying part of one lesson now.
3. Ask members to turn to page 21 and share their responses to #1 and #2.
4. Ask members to turn the page and complete activity #6. Show them how to check their answers in the paragraph that follows the activity.
5. Ask: Which of these five instructions for godly relationships do you think is the most needed among Christians in the church today? Allow several members to offer responses.
6. Ask members to complete activity #8. Point out that memory cards in the back of the book include the text for these eight principles.
7. Point out the Scripture memory verse cards also. Encourage members to memorize the verse for each week.
8. Offer to answer any questions they may have about the process of study you will use.

Overview Session Plans
1. Explain the reasons for the type of people in the group based on your prior decisions. If the men are diverse racially, culturally, denominationally, or all of these, explain the reasons for wanting a diverse group. If the group members are alike, explain why and point out that the members may want to begin planning for a time to go through the study again with a diverse group.
2. Explain that new members can be added during the next week or two, but that because of the process, no new members will be added after the second session.
3. Discuss plans for the weekly session time, place, and meeting length. Remind men of the importance of attendance and participation.
4. Ask the men who want to participate in the small-group study to turn in their index cards with name, address, and phone numbers before leaving.
5. If you have more people than one group can accommodate, explain options for dividing into two or more groups.
6. Determine the number and membership of each group. If necessary, this can be done following the session, and group leaders can call members during the week to inform them of their group assignments.
7. Answer questions that members may have about the session plans.

Closing Prayer
Close the session with a prayer that God will get glory through this study and that each member will truly live out biblical reconciliation and unity with other members of Christ's body during the study.

SESSION 1: UNITY IN CHRIST

Opening Prayer

Open the session with prayer. Welcome the Holy Spirit as your teacher, and ask the Lord to begin building strong relationships between the members of the group.

Content Review (15 minutes)

During the time allotted, use some or all of the following questions to review the content of this unit.

1. Scripture memory verse: Lead members to recite John 17:23. Repeat for those who have memorized it in the King James Version.
2. Ask: What are two descriptions of the church from Revelation that say what we will be in eternity? (p. 19: bride [Revelation 19:7–9], multiethnic multitude [Revelation 7:9–10]) If that's what we're becoming, what do you sense God would want to be doing in the church to move us toward that reality?
3. Turn to page 21. Ask members to give their responses to activities 1, 2, 4, and 5.
4. According to the Scriptures, what is the basis for our unity? (p. 27) Ask a few members to read their statement in #5 on page 28.

Discussion Questions (15-30 minutes)

Select some of the following questions for group discussion. You probably will not have time for all of these, so pick those that will be most helpful. Watch your time so you'll have time for building brotherhood.

1. (p. 23) Ask: Which of the eight principles for reconciliation and unity do you think will be the most practical or helpful to you, and why?
2. How important to God is unity among believers and why?
3. (pp. 24-28) Why did Jesus pray for unity?.
4. (#1, p. 27) Where do most people, churches, and/or denominations look to attain unity?
5. (#1, p. 29) Ask: How did you evaluate the unity you see among believers in your local church? your denomination? Christian churches in our town? in our nation? worldwide?

6. (#2, p. 29) Ask: How do you think Jesus feels about these evidences of disunity? Why? (Ask about each of the ten items separately.)
7. (#3, p. 30) In your opinion, what sins are the major causes of division and broken relationships between Christians? Why?
8. (pp. 30-31) How does the root sin of pride cause problems in relationships between people of different races, denominations, or social classes?
9. In unit 1, what one statement, Scripture, illustration, or idea has been most meaningful or helpful? What do you sense God has said to you this week, if anything?
10. Turn to page 197. Read through and briefly discuss "Rules for the Game."

Building Brotherhood (30-45 minutes)

Review "Small-Group Learning Activities for Building Brotherhood" on pages 195-197. You may want to photocopy those pages so you can keep them in front of you during the session. In this first session, you probably should limit discussion to questions and activities under "First Base: Acquaintances." If your group already is well acquainted, you may want to move on to second base. Write a #1 (for session 1) beside those questions or activities you want to use during this session. Make sure you conclude discussion in time to allow for the following prayer time.

Praying for One Another (15 minutes)

Close the session by inviting members to state one way the rest of the group can pray for them this next week. Invite volunteers to pray brief or sentence prayers for each other. Invite them to include any prayers about unity among believers that may be prompted by this unit of study.

SESSION 2: A HEALTHY BODY OF CHRIST

This should be the last session in which you permit new members to join your small group. Relationships are already building, and new people will disrupt that process. If others want to join after this session, ask them to wait for the next group to start. If there are two or more, encourage them to start their own group.

Opening Prayer
Open the session with prayer. Ask the Lord to work in your group to help you contribute to the body of Christ—becoming a beautiful trophy for Him.

Content Review (15 minutes)
During the time allotted, use some or all of the following questions to review the content of this unit.
1. Scripture memory verse: Lead members to recite Ephesians 2:14 in the NIV and/or KJV.
2. (p. 36) How did the dividing wall between Jews and Gentiles come down? What similarities do you see between their wall and the walls of separation, prejudice, and hostility between races, classes, cultures, or denominations today?
3. Describe four biblical illustrations of unity of believers. (Holy nation, God's family, holy temple, and body of Christ) What do these illustrations tell us about what our unity would look like today?
4. (#8, p. 37) What are some of the attitudes or character traits that can help maintain the unity of the Spirit?
5. What are some of the attitudes and character traits that may break or destroy unity? (arrogance, haughtiness, harshness, impatience, intolerance, hate, prejudice, judgmental spirit, etc.)
6. (Lesson 4, pp. 44–46) What did Paul have to say to the Corinthian church about divisions?
7. (#7, p. 46) What actions can cause divisions in the body of Christ?
8. (#4, p. 48) What will renewed people of God do to ruined cities and devastated places?

Discussion Questions (15-30 minutes)
Select some of the following questions for group discussion. You probably won't have time for all of these, so pick those that will be most helpful. Watch your time so you'll have time for building brotherhood.
1. (#3, p. 39) What are some ways you have seen or experienced God's people demonstrating a spirit of unity and oneness? How did those experiences make you feel about being part of the body of Christ?
2. What's one of the greatest ways God reveals His glory in the body of Christ? ("When He brings together those of great diversity and causes them to function in unity." [p. 40]) How does this reveal His glory?

3. Turn to page 40. Ask: What are some of the important facts you learned about the body of Christ?
4. Ask members to discuss their responses to #3, page 41.
5. Why is Christ's opinion the only one that's important to the body of Christ? What do you think would cause a person to think his human opinion was important? (pride, selfish ambition)
6. (pp. 42-43) How should members of Christ's body live in relationship to other members? How does this foster unity?
7. (#10, p. 43) Which two or three instructions from Romans 12 do you need to work on the most and why?
8. How will the instructions from Romans 12 (p. 43) help to maintain the unity the Spirit has produced?
9. (#3, p. 45) How do you think God would rate your church regarding its experience and practice of unity? Why? (Note: If unity is lacking, pause to pray for each needy church and its leaders.)
10. Turn to page 48. Discuss your responses to #5.
11. In unit 2, what one statement, Scripture, illustration, or idea has been most meaningful or helpful? What do you sense God has said to you this week, if anything?

Building Brotherhood (30-45 minutes)
Review "Small-Group Learning Activities for Building Brotherhood" on pages 195-197. During this session, you may be ready to move to second base: friends. You'll probably stay on second base for at least the next three or four sessions, so you don't have to hurry. Take time as men relate their experiences, fears, and common pains. You may find that only a few of your group will be able to speak in the time allotted. You can start where you leave off in the next session. That's okay. Write a #2 (for session 2) beside those questions or activities that you want to use during this session.

Be sensitive to what's said and how emotional the person is who speaks. Don't hesitate to stop and pray for an individual after he speaks. You can use your time for praying for one another and spread it out during this sharing time. Praying for one another will be vital as men express themselves. Take time throughout the session *or* allow ample time at the end of the session for prayer.

Praying for One Another (15 minutes)
Close the session by asking men to pray for one another, their families, and their needs that may have surfaced during the session. Close the prayer time by asking the Lord to mold and shape you into a beautiful trophy for His glory.

SESSION 3: CALLED TO RECONCILIATION

Opening Prayer
Open the session with prayer. Call for a volunteer to open with a prayer of thanksgiving for God's reconciliation.

Content Review (15 minutes)
During the time allotted, use some or all of the following questions to review the content of this unit.
1. Scripture memory verse: Lead members to recite 2 Corinthians 5:19 in the NIV and/or KJV.
2. In your own words, how would you describe the principle of call?
3. (pp. 54-55) What does it mean to be reconciled to God? How did God provide for reconciliation?
4. (pp. 53-54) How does what God did to the walls of Jericho encourage or instruct you in breaking down walls of racism and sectarianism?
5. (pp. 53-54) How important is faith in bringing down walls? Why?
6. (p. 56) Based on 2 Corinthians 5:18–21, what is the ministry and message of reconciliation God has given us?
7. (#4, p. 57) What is the first and primary assignment you've been given in the ministry of reconciliation?
8. (#3, p. 60) How did you summarize the two greatest commandments?
9. Turn to page 63. How does our relationship with our brothers reveal the nature of our relationship with God? How did you answer #5 on page 63?
10. (#7, pp. 67-68) If God calls a person to a special assignment in a cross-cultural relationship (or across other barriers), what does He have in mind to do?

Optional Video Segment for Principle 1 (Add 10 minutes)

Discussion Questions (15-30 minutes)
Select some of the following questions for group discussion. You probably won't have time for all of these, so pick those that will be most helpful. Watch your time so you'll have time for building brotherhood.
1. (pp. 57-59) What did you learn from Jesus' example of being a reconciler with the woman at the well?
2. What barriers did Jesus cross over to talk with the Samaritan woman? How did He do it?
3. If Jesus were to call your church to a harvest in your neighborhood, to whom would He call you?

4. When people are reconciled to God, how does that affect their relationships with brothers and sisters in Christ?
5. (p. 62) What does Matthew 5:23–24 have to say about reconciliation to your brother and worship? How well do you think most Christians practice this command to be reconciled? Why?
6. (#2, p. 62) Did you find that you needed to be reconciled with someone? If so, how did you respond?
7. If a person does not receive a special assignment like Peter or Paul to be a trailblazer, why and how must he still be involved in a ministry of reconciliation across human barriers?
8. In unit 3, what one statement, Scripture, illustration, or idea has been most meaningful or helpful? What do you sense God has said to you this week, if anything?

Building Brotherhood (30-45 minutes)
Review "Small-Group Learning Activities for Building Brotherhood" on pages 195-197. During this session, you should be using activities from "Second Base: Friends." Remember that during this section of the session, building relationships is far more important than covering content. Don't try to rush the process. Take time for people to talk. Write a #3 (for session 3) beside those questions or activities you want to use during this session.

The following two activities can be used during the building brotherhood time to process responses to learning activities in the homework:
1. Turn to page 66. In groups of three or four, give your responses to #3 and #4. Explain your responses.
2. Do any of you sense that God has been or is calling you to a trailblazing ministry of reconciliation across racial, cultural, or denominational lines? If so, please tell us what you sense God is saying or doing.

Make sure you conclude discussion in time to allow for at least fifteen minutes of prayer for one another.

Praying for One Another (15 minutes)
Close the session by taking time for members to pray for one another. Encourage them to pray for specific individuals and specific requests. If God seems to be guiding individuals, your group, or a church to some special assignment, take time to pray for those involved.

SESSION 4: COMMITMENT TO RELATIONSHIP

Opening Prayer

Open the session with prayer. Call on a volunteer to pray that the Lord will develop God-honoring relationships within your group for His glory and purposes.

Content Review (15 minutes)

During the time allotted, use some or all of the following questions to review the content of this unit.

1. Scripture memory verse: Lead members to recite John 13:34 in the NIV and/or KJV.
2. In your own words, how would you describe the principle of commitment to relationships?
3. What are some ways God has treated us that model for us what relationships ought to be like? (p. 71; accepted, forgiven, loved, served, comforted)

Optional Video Segment for Principle 2 (Add 10 minutes)

Discussion Questions (15-30 minutes)

Select some of the following questions for group discussion. You probably won't have time for all of these, so pick those that will be most helpful. Watch your time so you'll have time for building brotherhood.

1. (#4, p. 75 and #6, p. 76) What's the best way for you personally to begin overcoming racial or denominational barriers? Why?
2. (#5, p. 76) What's the major danger in separation from our brothers in Christ and why?
3. (Lesson 2, pp. 77-78) What are some characteristics of a committed relationship?
4. Turn to page 80 and review the list in the box for "God's Model for Relationships." Which one of these actions do you think would have the greatest impact on racism and why? on sectarianism and why?
5. Have you ever experienced a wall come down because someone else treated you in one of these godly ways? If so, tell us about it. Why did that make a difference?
6. (pp. 82-83) How has God—Father, Son, and Spirit—accepted us and modeled acceptance for us?
7. (p. 84) How can we apply the instructions from Romans 14:1–22 to be more accepting of our brothers and sisters in Christ?
8. Call on a member to read Mark 9:38–41, and ask the group to discuss what Jesus is teaching us about our need to accept others.
9. Ask a member in advance to read Acts 6:1–7 and 8:1–8. Ask him to prepare to offer some background information about Philip. During the session, ask him to give that information to the group. Now read the story of Philip and the Ethiopian in Acts 8:26–40, and ask the following questions.

A. What were some of the differences between Philip and the Ethiopian?
B. How does this experience provide an example of the ministry of reconciliation?
C. What are some ways Philip could have responded that would have caused him to fail in the ministry of reconciliation?
D. How important do you think this encounter was for the people in Ethiopia?

10. Based on the Scriptures on pages 86-87, what is Christian love to be like? What are things that Christian love will *not* do? Which of these positive and negative expressions of love are most difficult to apply and why?
11. Turn to page 88 and give your responses to #5, explaining your answers.
12. In unit 4, what one statement, Scripture, illustration, or idea has been most meaningful or helpful? What do you sense God has said to you this week, if anything?

Building Brotherhood (30-45 minutes)

Review "Small-Group Learning Activities for Building Brotherhood" on pages 195-197. During this session, you will probably want to continue to operate under the second base activities. However, God may begin moving the discussion to deeper levels. Don't try to hold the group back. Continue your praying as a leader for God's leadership and a spirit of discernment in guiding the session. Write a #4 (for session 4) beside those questions or activities you want to use during this session.

The following two activities can be used during the building brotherhood time to process responses to learning activities in the homework:

1. Have you ever had a committed relationship across racial, cultural, or denominational lines? If so, tell us about one.
2. In groups of three or four, give your responses to activities #1–3 on page 81 and #11 on page 84.

Make sure you conclude discussion in time to allow for at least fifteen minutes of prayer for one another.

Praying for One Another (15 minutes)

Close the session by praying for committed relationships with one another. Invite volunteers to thank the Lord for what He is already doing in your life together. Don't fail to pray for any group members who seem to have a special need. Taking prayer for one another seriously can be one of the best ways to develop deeper committed relationships with each other.

SESSION 5: INTENTIONALITY

Opening Prayer

Open the session with prayer. Ask the Lord to keep you and your group God-centered as you seek ways of breaking down walls intentionally.

Content Review (15 minutes)

During the time allotted, use some or all of the following questions to review the content of this unit.

1. Scripture memory verse: Lead members to recite Ephesians 4:3 in the NIV and/or KJV.
2. In your own words, how would you describe the principle of intentionality?
3. Based on the principle of intentionality, what are three kinds of activities that are required to facilitate reconciliation? (purposeful, positive, planned)
4. (Ephesians 4:1–3, p. 91) What are some ways we're to maintain the unity the Spirit has produced among believers?

Optional Video Segment for Principle 3 (Add 10 minutes)

Discussion Questions (15-30 minutes)

Select some of the following questions for group discussion. You probably won't have time for all of these, so pick those that will be most helpful. Watch your time so you'll have time for building brotherhood.

1. (p. 93) What's the difference between God-centered and human-centered intentionality? Why does it matter whether the intentionality is initiated by God or our own human thinking?
2. (lesson 3, pp. 94-96) Give examples of each of the following: (1) purposeful activities (2) positive activities (3) planned activities.
3. Look at the diagram in the margin on page 97. What did you learn from that illustration and the explanation of it in the text?
4. (#4, p. 98) What's the best approach to take in helping someone else break down his own walls?
5. Review the list in the box on page 98. What do we need to learn and apply from these instructions to be most productive in experiencing reconciled relationships with other brothers in Christ?
6. In unit 5, what one statement, Scripture, illustration, or idea has been most meaningful or helpful? What do you sense God has said to you this week, if anything?

Building Brotherhood (30-45 minutes)

Review "Small-Group Learning Activities for Building Brotherhood" on pages 195-197. Unless the group has already begun to move into third base territory, you may want to continue working on second base. Laying a strong foundation of friendship will help pave the way for going deeper at third. Write a #5 (for session 5) beside those questions or activities you want to use during this session.

Members will be prepared to offer a response to the following learning activity. Be sure to work this activity into your time of discussion. You may want to start the section with this:

1. (#7, pp. 99-100) What intentional activity did you carry out this week? (or have you made plans to carry out in the future?) How did you feel about your experience? What did you learn about your brother that was meaningful or helpful?

Make sure you conclude discussion in time to allow for at least fifteen minutes of prayer for one another.

(NOTE: Remind members that they won't need to complete additional homework before the next session. They should use their study time to catch up on any homework they may have failed to complete. They also should use this as a time for review and prayer about application to life.)

Praying for One Another (15 minutes)

Invite members to pray for one another regarding their intentionality. Encourage them to pray for specific relationships. Close the session by thanking God for the relationships He's building.

MID-TERM GET-TOGETHER

Use the ideas on page 192 to plan a special time together for this session. Focus primarily on relationship building. You may want to keep this time light and informal, or you may decide to continue using the "Small-Group Learning Activities for Building Brotherhood" to go deeper in your relationships with each other.

SESSION 6: SINCERITY AND SENSITIVITY

Opening Prayer
Ask for a volunteer to open the session with prayer, requesting that God would develop sincerity and sensitivity within the group.

Content Review (15 minutes)
During the time allotted, use some or all of the following questions to review the content of this unit.
1. Scripture memory verse: Lead members to recite Ephesians 4:15 in the NIV and/or KJV.
2. In your own words, how would you describe the principles of sincerity and sensitivity?
3. What four things do you share in a committed relationship to show sincerity? (feelings, attitudes, differences, perceptions)
4. (p. 103) What is the "Kehrein-Washington Law of Racial Dynamics," and how would those same dynamics be true of other racial or cultural groups?
5. (p. 112) How did Jesus learn sensitivity to the human condition?
6. (pp. 113-114) What are two ways of developing sensitivity? (read books or view videos; use the request: "Would you help me understand . . .")

Optional Video Segment for Principle 4 (Add 10 minutes)
(Although you studied principles 4 *and* 5 in this unit, use the video segment for principle 5 in your next session.)

Discussion Questions (15-30 minutes)
Select some of the following questions for group discussion. You probably won't have time for all of these, so pick those that will be most helpful. Watch your time so you'll have time for building brotherhood.
1. (lessons 1-2, pp. 103–107) What is sincerity, and why is it important in committed relationships?
2. (#3, #4; p. 106) What's the best time and way to express feelings, attitudes, differences, and perceptions? Would there be times (or ways) when sharing these things might be hurtful to a relationship? Discuss your responses.
3. (See box on p. 107.) What does it mean to practice sincerity in relationships to others? Which of these do you think would be most helpful in building strong relationships?

4. (#8, p. 110) Why should we be concerned about how other Christians are treated? Invite volunteers to say how they responded to #10 on page 111.
5. What are some of the ways you can develop sensitivity about other races, cultures, or denominations? If you've done something this week to develop sensitivity, give us a report.
6. In unit 6, what one statement, Scripture, illustration, or idea has been most meaningful or helpful? What do you sense God has said to you this week, if anything?

Building Brotherhood (30-45 minutes)
Because many of the activities in this unit set the stage for building brotherhood, we recommend that you use some or all of the following activities during this session. Select activities from the following that you sense will be most valuable for your group.
1. Turn to page 104. In groups of three or four, give your responses to items #3–4, and take time to pray for each other.
2. Turn to page 107. How did you respond to #1? As each person responds, ask the other members if they agree.
3. Divide into groups of three or four, and give responses to #3 on page 108. Ask one member from each smaller group to summarize and report to the larger group.
4. Turn to page 110. Ask volunteers to offer responses to activities #5–7.
5. Turn to page 111. Ask volunteers to offer responses to #11 and #12.

Make sure you conclude sharing in time to allow for the following prayer time.

Praying for One Another (15 minutes)
Because of the things being shared during "Building Brotherhood," you should take time during those activities to pray for each other. Space this prayer time out during the building brotherhood time. Ask for a volunteer to lead the group in a closing time of prayer. If time permits, allow for conversational prayer, and encourage members to pray brief prayers as they feel led.

SESSION 7: DEVELOPING SENSITIVITY

Opening Prayer
Open the session with prayer. Ask the Lord to develop your sensitivity toward each other and toward members of the body of Christ who are different.

Content Review (15 minutes)
During the time allotted, use some or all of the following questions to review the content of this unit.
1. Scripture memory verse: Lead members to recite Matthew 7:12 in the NIV and/or KJV.
2. (#5, p. 120) What are some of the things sensitivity tries to remove?

Optional Video Segment for Principle 5 (Add 10 minutes)

Discussion Questions (15-30 minutes)
Select some of the following questions for group discussion. You probably won't have time for all of these, so pick those that will be most helpful. Watch your time so you'll have time for building brotherhood.
1. (#2, p. 118) Why is sensitivity toward others needed? Discuss your answer.
2. What happens when we're insensitive toward others in the things we say or do? How does it affect relationships?
3. What's the best way to develop sensitivity toward a group that's different from you? (personal relationship) Why?
4. (p. 120) If a person has been offended by an insensitive remark or action, what should he do?
5. (p. 120) If a person realizes he has been insensitive toward another person or group, what should he do?
6. Get into groups of two or three and offer your responses to activities #1–3 on page 121.
7. Return to the larger group. What are some of the questions you wrote for activity #5 on page 122?
8. Turn to lesson 3 beginning on page 122. What are the most important or meaningful things you learned about the group you studied? What did you learn that will help you most in building relationships with people of this group?
9. Turn to pages 125-126. How did you respond to #3 and #4?
10. What do you sense is the major strength or contribution of your denomination, Christian tradition, or association to the larger body of Christ?
11. Who are some of the people from your religious group who have made major contributions to the larger body of Christ, and what have they done?
12. Turn to page 126 and give your response to #6.
13. (p. 129) Discuss your response to #4 about the parable of the weeds.
14. How should believers treat other genuine believers who are part of other denominations or Christian traditions?
15. What are some common things Christians do to believers of other faiths that break unity and hurt relationships in the body of Christ?
16. In unit 7, what one statement, Scripture, illustration, or idea has been most meaningful or helpful? What do you sense God has said to you this week, if anything?

Building Brotherhood (30-45 minutes)
Review "Small-Group Learning Activities for Building Brotherhood" on pages 195-197. During this session, you may be moving to activities under "Third Base: Brothers." You'll notice that responses shared during the last session already relate to third base issues. Read through the possible activities, and select those that you think may be most helpful for your group at this stage of their relationships. Write a #7 (for session 7) beside those questions or activities you want to use during this session.

The following two activities can be used during the building brotherhood time to process responses to learning activities in the homework:
1. Have you ever been offended by someone who did or said the wrong thing or who was insensitive? If so, tell us what was said or what happened, and explain why that was offensive. (#6, p. 120)
2. (#2, p. 125) If you haven't already done so, take time for volunteers to give their testimony of how they came to know Jesus Christ as their Lord and Savior.

During the discussion time of building brotherhood, you may have members relate some very painful experiences. Take time throughout this section to minister to one another through prayer. You may ask one or two volunteers to pray for those individuals who seem especially wounded or emotionally and spiritually needy.

Praying for One Another (15 minutes)
You have probably already been using time to pray for one another. Close the session using any remaining time for conversational prayer. Ask members to pray brief prayers about sensitivity building between racial, cultural, and denominational groups.

SESSION 8: SACRIFICE

Opening Prayer

Open the session with prayer. Ask the Holy Spirit to give wisdom and understanding to members as you study together.

Content Review (15 minutes)

During the time allotted, use some or all of the following questions to review the content of this unit.

1. Scripture memory verse: Lead members to recite Philippians 2:3–4 in the NIV and/or KJV.
2. In your own words, how would you describe the principle of sacrifice?
3. What are some of the things we must be willing to give up in order to facilitate reconciling relationships? (status and position)
4. (#2, p. 132) What are some ways Jesus modeled sacrifice?

Optional Video Segment for Principle 6 (Add 10 minutes)

Discussion Questions (15-30 minutes)

Select some of the following questions for group discussion. You probably won't have time for all of these, so pick those that will be most helpful. Watch your time so you'll have time for building brotherhood.

1. What are some of the ways a person could make sacrifices for the sake of racial or denominational reconciliation?
2. Which of the instructions in #4 on page 135 would be most difficult for you to obey and why?
3. Review the responses to #5 on page 135, and discuss why each is an example of the principle of sacrifice.
4. In what ways could the sacrifice of earthly possessions contribute to reconciliation? What human feelings and emotions would make such a sacrifice difficult?
5. Read again the Scriptures about justice on page 137. What are some ways that God's people can stand for justice and demonstrate godliness?
6. (#1, p. 138) What are the primary ways people in the world seek to achieve greatness?
7. (#2, p. 138) How does Jesus say a person can achieve greatness in His kingdom?
8. (#3, p.139) Why do you think Jesus assumed the role of a servant in washing the disciples' feet? What are some ways we can follow the example of Jesus in serving others?

9. Ask volunteers to give their responses to activities #4–6 on page 139.
10. What are some of the costs of getting involved in cross-cultural or interdenominational relationships? (for example: being called "Oreo" or "banana" [white on the inside and black/yellow on the outside], "Uncle Tom," "nigger-lover," losing church members or friends, etc.)
11. (pp. 140-142) Based on the Scriptures you read in lesson 5, what are some specific ways we can serve other believers?
12. Which of the statements in activity #10 on pages 141-142 did you check as the attitudes of servanthood?
13. In unit 8, what one statement, Scripture, illustration, or idea has been most meaningful or helpful? What do you sense God has said to you this week, if anything?

Building Brotherhood (30-45 minutes)

Review "Small-Group Learning Activities for Building Brotherhood" on pages 195-197. During this session, you want to be operating under "Third Base: Brothers" unless, for some reason, your group is hesitating to deal openly with racial and denominational issues. Again, we suggest you be sensitive to the group and not push too hard. Write a #8 (for session 8) beside those questions or activities you want to use during this session.

You may find that responding to homework assignments is easier for the members to process. If you haven't already processed homework activities from previous units/sessions, you can go back to do those during this session. The following activity from unit 8 can be used during the building brotherhood time to process responses to learning activities from this unit's homework:

1. In groups of two or three, discuss your responses to activities #9 and #11 on pages 141-142. Then take time to pray for one another as you seek to be more faithful servants in Christ's kingdom.

Praying for One Another (15 minutes)

The building brotherhood section is probably including some intimate and perhaps painful experiences by now. Take time throughout the discussion time to pray for people who may be hurting. Some may be struggling with obedience. Take time to pray for them as well. Close the session by asking volunteers to pray conversationally as the Spirit leads them.

SESSION 9: EMPOWERMENT

Opening Prayer

Open the session with prayer. Ask the Lord to give wisdom and understanding regarding confession, repentance, and forgiveness. Ask Him to convict of sin and enable members to be reconciled with Him and others in application of the principle of empowerment.

Content Review (15 minutes)

During the time allotted, use some or all of the following questions to review the content of this unit.

1. Scripture memory verse: Lead members to recite Colossians 3:13 in the NIV and/or KJV.
2. In your own words, how would you describe the principle of empowerment?
3. What are the ways described in this principle that we can remove barriers and experience the power of the Holy Spirit in reconciling relationships? (prayer, personal brokenness, repentance, and forgiveness)

Optional Video Segment for Principle 7 (Add 10 minutes)

Discussion Questions (15-30 minutes)

Select some of the following questions for group discussion. You probably won't have time for all of these, so pick those that will be most helpful. Watch your time so you'll have time for building brotherhood.

1. (#2, p. 146) Who needs to experience empowerment: the offender or the offended and why?
2. Read the list of words in #3 on page 146. How do these feelings and experiences create barriers to meaningful relationships? How do these feelings cause weakness rather than empowerment? Which do you think are the greatest barriers to reconciled relationships?
3. (#4, p.147) Why is prayer important to empowerment?
4. (p. 147) What are some ways God may use personal brokenness to prepare a person for effective reconciling relationships?
5. (pp. 148-149) What is repentance? and forgiveness? How are they important to reconciling relationships?
6. Ask a member to read the parable in Matthew 18:23–35. How should we apply the teaching of this parable to relationships we have with brothers in Christ?
7. (p. 151) In Matthew 23:29–36, how were the religious leaders of Jesus' day guilty of the sins of their fathers? Why do you think they didn't recognize their guilt?
8. Why do we need to identify the sins of our fathers and those who have gone before us?
9. (#2, p.152) What are some of the sins (especially the root sins) of our forefathers in the area of racism?
10. (#2, p. 152) What are some of the sins (especially the root sins) of our forefathers in the area of sectarianism?
11. What are some ways we could be guilty of the same

sins, only in different ways? Do you think we declare our innocence too easily? Why or why not?

12. (p. 153) What is "restitution," and when should restitution be made?
13. (#2, p. 153) Who is responsible for convicting a person of the need for restitution? (Holy Spirit) How may the Holy Spirit use us in calling for restitution? What are some guidelines related to the issue of restitution?
14. In the above discussion on restitution, would a person who has been hurt respond to those questions differently from a person who experienced gain or benefit from the offending action? Why?
15. (p. 154) How is the Good Samaritan a good example of one who assumed responsibility for the sins of others? What are some ways we can assume the responsibility for the sins of others in the areas of racism and sectarianism?
16. (p. 157) What can we learn about the way to forgive others from the example of Jesus? of Stephen?
17. (p. 157) What are we commanded to do when a brother sins against us? How often are we to forgive our brother? (without limit)
18. In the list of biblical instructions on page 158, which one do you think you need to practice most? Which one is the most difficult for you to practice?
19. In unit 9, what one statement, Scripture, illustration, or idea has been most meaningful or helpful? What do you sense God has said to you this week, if anything?

Building Brotherhood (30-45 minutes)

Review "Small-Group Learning Activities for Building Brotherhood" on pages 195-197. We hope you're moving toward "Home: Christlike" by this time. Focus attention on the activities under that section unless you sense the group is not ready to move to that stage. Write a #9 (for session 9) beside those questions or activities you want to use during this session. The following two activities can be used during the building brotherhood time to process responses to learning activities in the homework:

1. Ask members to describe experiences of brokenness arising from racism or sectarianism (#6, p. 147).
2. Ask volunteers to give their responses to #5 and #6 on page 150.

Praying for One Another (15 minutes)

Since this session may open up times of confession of sin and offering of forgiveness, praying for one another will need to be integrated into the building brotherhood time. Close the session by joining hands and praying for God to complete in you the process of reconciliation. Ask Him to bind your group members together with a visible spirit of oneness. Don't forget to thank Him for all He's doing already in this direction.

SESSION 10: INTERDEPENDENCE

Opening Prayer

Open the session with prayer. Thank the Lord for all He has done during the course of this study. Ask Him to guide the group to an appropriate conclusion for this study and to make right decisions about what to do next.

Content Review (15 minutes)

During the time allotted, use some or all of the following questions to review the content of this unit.

1. Scripture memory verse: Lead members to recite 1 Corinthians 12:25 in the NIV and/or KJV.
2. In your own words, how would you describe the principle of interdependence?
3. (p. 161) See if members can name the eight principles of reconciliation and unity in proper order.
4. Ask for volunteers to recite one or two verses each from the ten Scripture memory verses. If members have difficulty, coach them or allow them to use their memory cards for help.

Optional Video Segment for Principle 8 (Add 10 minutes)

Discussion Questions (15-30 minutes)

Select some of the following questions for group discussion. You probably won't have time for all of these, so pick those that will be most helpful. Watch your time so you'll have time for building brotherhood.

1. (p. 162) What are some of the characteristics of a healthy body of Christ?
2. How did you respond to #1 on page 163, and how have you changed during this course?
3. (p. 163) What is interdependence, and how do you think it's related to the "trophy of Christ" we have studied in previous lessons?
4. What are some ways we can demonstrate interdependence across racial or cultural lines? What are some ways we can demonstrate interdependence across denominational lines?
5. (p. 164) What is paternalism, and what are some ways to avoid it?
6. (#6–8, p. 166) What are some ways you have experienced God's comfort, and how has that prepared you to minister to others who may need comfort?
7. Who are some of the people God is laying on your heart and mind who would benefit from this same study? What do you sense God wants you to do to help them begin experiencing this study? Is there something God is leading us to do as a group?

8. (#1, p. 169) In unit 10, what one statement, Scripture, illustration, or idea has been most meaningful or helpful? What do you sense God has said to you this week, if anything? How would you summarize what God has said to you throughout this course?
9. Ask members to give their responses to activities #2 and #3 on page 169.
10. Ask members to turn to the intentionality project ideas on page 187.
    A. Which, if any, of these ideas do you sense God may want you to take on as a project?
    B. Do you sense God would have us take on any of these projects as a group? Which one(s)?
    C. Do you sense God would have our church or churches take on any of these projects? Which one(s)?
    D. After discussing responses to the questions above, take time to pray and seek the Lord's directions about the next steps you may need to take for intentional obedience.

Building Brotherhood (30-45 minutes)

Review "Small-Group Learning Activities for Building Brotherhood" on pages 195-197. This is probably your final session together as a group. Unless you have a compelling reason to do otherwise, we recommend that you guide activities from "Home: Christlike."

The following activity can be used during the building brotherhood time to process responses to learning activities in the homework:

1. Ask members to offer their responses to #9–10 on page 167. If a member describes a trial he is currently experiencing, ask one or two people to pray for him before going on to another person or activity.

Praying for One Another (15 minutes)

Close the session by asking volunteers to pray conversationally. Begin the prayer time by asking the Holy Spirit to guide your prayers according to the will of the Father. Pray for one another, and pray for any specific sense of calling to projects or future actions that will facilitate reconciliation on a broader scale.

Unit 3 Scripture Memory Verse

2 Corinthians 5:19, NIV
"God was reconciling the world to himself in Christ, not counting men's sins against them. And he has committed to us the message of reconciliation."

Unit 2 Scripture Memory Verse

Ephesians 2:14, NIV
"He himself is our peace, who has made the two one and has destroyed the barrier, the dividing wall of hostility."

Unit 1 Scripture Memory Verse

John 17:23, NIV
"'I in them and you in me. May they be brought to complete unity to let the world know that you sent me and have loved them even as you have loved me.'"

Unit 6 Scripture Memory Verse

Ephesians 4:15, NIV
"Speaking the truth in love, we will in all things grow up into him who is the Head, that is, Christ."

Unit 5 Scripture Memory Verse

Ephesians 4:3, NIV
"Make every effort to keep the unity of the Spirit through the bond of peace."

Unit 4 Scripture Memory Verse

John 13:34, NIV
"'A new command I give you: Love one another. As I have loved you, so you must love one another.'"

Unit 9 Scripture Memory Verse

Colossians 3:13, NIV
"Bear with each other and forgive whatever grievances you may have against one another. Forgive as the Lord forgave you."

Unit 8 Scripture Memory Verse

Philippians 2:3–4, NIV
"Do nothing out of selfish ambition or vain conceit, but in humility consider others better than yourselves. Each of you should look not only to your own interests, but also to the interests of others."

Unit 7 Scripture Memory Verse

Matthew 7:12, NIV
"'In everything, do to others what you would have them do to you, for this sums up the Law and the Prophets.'"

Unit 10 Scripture Memory Verse

1 Corinthians 12:25, NIV
"There should be no division in the body, but . . . its parts should have equal concern for each other."

Principle 8
INTERDEPENDENCE

As we recognize our differences, we also realize that God has placed us as members in the body of Christ where we need and depend on the contributions of each member.

Principle 7
EMPOWERMENT

Through prayer, personal brokenness, repentance, and forgiveness, we remove barriers and are freed to experience the power of the Holy Spirit in reconciling relationships.

Principle 6
SACRIFICE

We must be willing to give up an established status or position and accept a lesser position in order to facilitate reconciling relationships.

Principle 5
SENSITIVITY

We must seek knowledge about our brothers in order to relate empathetically to people from different denominations, traditions, races, social standings, or cultures.

Principle 4
SINCERITY

We must be willing to be vulnerable and express our feelings, attitudes, differences, and perceptions, with the goal of resolution and building trust.

Principle 3
INTENTIONALITY

Experiencing a committed relationship with my brothers requires purposeful, positive, and planned activities that facilitate reconciliation.

Principle 2
COMMITMENT TO RELATIONSHIP

Loved by God and adopted into His family, we are called to committed love relationships with our brothers.

Principle 1
CALL

We are all called to a ministry of reconciliation, and we are all commanded to be reconciled with our brothers across racial, cultural, and denominational barriers.

Unit 1 Scripture Memory Verse

John 17:23, KJV
"'I in them, and thou in me, that they may be made perfect in one; and that the world may know that thou hast sent me, and hast loved them, as thou hast loved me.'"

Unit 2 Scripture Memory Verse

Ephesians 2:14, KJV
"He is our peace, who hath made both one, and hath broken down the middle wall of partition between us."

Unit 3 Scripture Memory Verse

2 Corinthians 5:19, KJV
"God was in Christ, reconciling the world unto himself, not imputing their trespasses unto them; and hath committed unto us the word of reconciliation."

Unit 4 Scripture Memory Verse

John 13:34, KJV
"'A new commandment I give unto you, that ye love one another; as I have loved you, that ye also love one another.'"

Unit 5 Scripture Memory Verse

Ephesians 4:3, KJV
"Endeavouring to keep the unity of the Spirit in the bond of peace."

Unit 6 Scripture Memory Verse

Ephesians 4:15, KJV
"Speaking the truth in love, [we] may grow up into him in all things, which is the head, even Christ."

Unit 7 Scripture Memory Verse

Matthew 7:12, KJV
"'All things whatsoever ye would that men should do to you, do ye even so to them: for this is the law and the prophets.'"

Unit 8 Scripture Memory Verse

Philippians 2:3–4, KJV
"Let nothing be done through strife or vainglory; but in lowliness of mind let each esteem other better than themselves. Look not every man on his own things, but every man also on the things of others."

Unit 9 Scripture Memory Verse

Colossians 3:13, KJV
"Forbearing one another, and forgiving one another, if any man have a quarrel against any: even as Christ forgave you, so also do ye."

Unit 10 Scripture Memory Verse

1 Corinthians 12:25, KJV
"There should be no schism in the body; but . . . the members should have the same care one for another."